# Inside Culture

# Inside Culture

re-imagining the method of cultural studies

Nick Couldry

SAGE Publications
London • Thousand Oaks • New Delhi

First published 2000

SAGE Publications Ltd
6 Bonhill Street
London EC2A 4PU

SAGE Publications Inc
2455 Teller Road
Thousand Oaks, California 91320

SAGE Publications India Pvt Ltd
32, M-Block Market
Greater Kailash – 1
New Delhi 110 048

**British Library Cataloguing in Publication data**

A catalogue record for this book is
available from the British Library

ISBN 0 7619 6915 2
ISBN 0 7619 6916 0 (pbk)

**Library of Congress catalog card number available**

Typeset by M Rules
Printed in Great Britain by The Cromwell Press Ltd, Trowbridge,
Wiltshire

# Contents

# Figures

*To Louise*

# Acknowledgements

This is a short book that deals with a very large subject. In writing about the methodological issues which underlie cultural studies' practice today, I will have to be selective and will inevitably omit some significant debates. In one sense, then, I should begin with an apology, but in another sense it was precisely a brief, manageable, personal view of a topic for too long left uncharted, or worse obscured, that I found I needed for myself, and therefore hoped that others might also find useful.

My main aim has been to make cultural studies' vast literature of theoretical debate more approachable, but without disguising either the difficulty of the issues, or my personal conviction that it is in the direction of rigorous, wide-ranging empirical research that the future of cultural studies must lie. I have become impatient with cultural studies' writing that uses overelaborate language to evade seemingly simple questions about the empirical accountability of its claims; but I am still less satisfied with 'common sense' attacks on cultural studies' theoretical tradition that dismiss it as a long 'detour' from the supposedly secure terrain of social science. Ironically, it is often cultural studies that has led the way, and traditional social science that has followed, in taking on board important theoretical concerns about the status of researching the cultures and societies in which we live.

Now, however, when its potential as an international, multicentred discipline becomes clear, cultural studies needs some common ground of methodological debate, which can be shared between its practitioners across the world. This book, I hope, is a contribution to establishing that common ground.

I want particularly to thank Julia Hall, my editor at Sage, for her initial encouragement of the idea for the book, and her excellent support throughout its writing and production.

I am grateful to all my colleagues in the Department of Media and Communications, Goldsmiths College, for providing such a supportive environment for this work, particularly Angela McRobbie and Bill Schwarz, who encouraged me when first developing my ideas for a book. Angela

McRobbie also kindly commented on early drafts of some chapters. Thanks to the postgraduate students on the MA Media and Communications, particularly the Methods in Cultural Analysis course, for being stimulating commentators on many of the issues discussed in this book; and thanks to the students I taught on Gareth Stanton's Postcolonial Theory course, an important experience for me. Thanks also to Keith Negus for helpful comments on my original book proposal. Further afield, I have benefited greatly from the exchange between the Goldsmiths' Media and Communications Department and the Department of Journalism, Media and Communications (JMK) at the University of Stockholm. The exchange, over the past five years, has made possible some wonderful discussions which, for me, have been an example of intellectual openness at its very best. I wish to record my thanks to Professor Johan Fornas, the late Kjell Novak and Michael Forsman for their role in making those meetings possible. I also want to acknowledge the 'Researching Culture' conference at the University of North London in September 1999 as a stimulating context for finishing the writing.

I am especially grateful to my friend and ex-colleague Dave Hesmondhalgh (now at the Open University) not only for reading all the chapters and making numerous helpful suggestions and searching criticisms, but also for providing encouragement when my belief in the feasibility of the book was wearing thin. The result, I'm sure, is a better book than I would otherwise have written, even if it leaves unresolved some of the questions he raised.

Finally, I want to thank my parents, Philip and Lilian Couldry, for the love and support they have always given me along my own route to reflexivity and to acknowledge that their history and fortitude has been constantly in my mind while writing this book; and to thank my wife, Louise Edwards, without whose love and insight none of this book could have been written, or even imagined.

Nick Couldry
London, September 1999

# 1 Introduction

Forty years ago, Raymond Williams (1961: 10) wrote that there was no academic subject which allowed him to ask the questions in which he was interested: questions concerning how culture and society, democracy and the individual voice, interrelate. It is cultural studies, we normally assume, that has filled this gap; however, when we look for a consensus about what cultural studies actually involves, we find high levels of uncertainty.

As cultural studies enters a new century, now is a good time to reflect on the space cultural studies occupies and ask in what direction it should be going. I want to map that space, but without the bitterness that has characterized much recent debate.[1] The map is, of course, a personal one; in the contested space of culture, how could it be otherwise?

I shall highlight questions of method. I mean here 'method' in the broadest sense: what types of things should cultural studies be doing? What problems does it face? Those questions necessarily take us through other questions, which we might call 'personal': what is the individual's place within cultural formations? How are those formations involved in forming my voice? The latter questions are not merely for closed introspection: they have a public significance for the cultural life we share. We are forced also to confront issues of pedagogy: what exactly is it that we hope to teach, or study, in cultural studies? All these questions can be brought together in a single underlying methodological question: what is the space from which cultural studies speaks?

My answer, in essence, is that cultural studies is an expanding space for sustained, rigorous and self-reflexive empirical research into the massive, power-laden complexity of contemporary culture.

## Images and principles

To begin with, some images by which to orientate ourselves. First, we can picture cultural studies as the distinctive approach to culture that results when we stop thinking about culture as particular valued texts and think about it as a broader process in which each person has an equal right to be heard, and each person's voice and reflections about culture are valuable. Cultural studies represents that space of equality. That is what Raymond Williams (1961: 321) meant by overcoming the 'long dominative mode' of thinking about culture. This principle is still radical and important today.

We have only to state it, however, to see that culture, as it operates, recognizes those rights of equality very imperfectly. Actual culture involves the concentration, not the dispersal of voices; being represented by others, not speaking directly in our own voice; the commodification of speech and image, not complete openness. That is a basic consequence of the irreversible link between cultural life and the capitalist economy. 'Culture', then, is already a paradoxical term and that paradox is something each of us as an individual may feel. Stuart Hall, while discussing the notion of 'black popular culture', has expressed this well:

> popular culture . . . is not at all, as we sometimes think of it, the arena where we find who we really are, the truth of our experience. It is an area that is profoundly mythic . . . It is there that we discover and play with the identifications of ourselves, where we are imagined, where we are represented. Not only to the audiences out there who do not get the message, but to ourselves for the first time. (S. Hall, 1992a: 22)

This means recognizing the complex and contested nature of culture. As a result, cultural studies thinks of culture in relation to issues of power: the power relations (whether driven by economics, politics or other forms of social discrimination) which affect who is represented and how, who speaks and who is silent, what counts as 'culture' and what does not. The necessary link between studying culture and theorizing *power* is one thing on which most cultural studies writers agree,[2] and it is treated here as fundamental to defining cultural studies as a distinctive area of study.

It is precisely here, however – in thinking about cultural studies as a democratic vision of culture, committed to investigating the links between culture and power – that the self-critique of cultural studies must begin. Applying this vision rigorously, I argue, means revising radically some of our standard assumptions about what 'culture' we study and what researching culture involves.

Cultural studies began with a democratic critique of earlier elitist approaches to culture, recognizing the fundamental importance of 'popular culture': the experiences and pleasures of those outside the cultural elites. This step was absolutely essential in expanding the range of cultural production deemed worthy of academic study. Now, however, our priorities must be formulated in different terms.

There has always been a problem of how cultural studies' academic voice relates to popular culture: academic writing is, by definition, not part of popular culture but analyses it from outside. As Dick Hebdige put it insightfully at the end of his classic study *Subculture*: 'We [the academic analysts] are cast in a marginal role. We are in society but not inside it, producing analyses of popular culture which are themselves anything but popular' (Hebdige, 1979: 139–40). Others have made a similar point (de Certeau, 1984: 41; Chambers, 1986: 216; cf., generally, Ross, 1989). In addition, many have doubted whether something called the 'popular' can be identified which is always subordinated to, or dominated by, another part of culture – 'high' culture. What if this is wrong and it is now popular culture which is dominant?[3] Or, more cautiously, what if the status-map of culture is changing radically, through the overwhelming influence of centralized, popular media such as television? Can cultural studies' relationship to what we call 'popular culture' be unchanged by this?[4]

The problem with the term 'popular culture' is symptomatic of a wider difficulty. If we take seriously the principle that culture is a process in which each person's experience is significant, then surely any limitation on what aspect or 'level' of culture we study – including any bias against or towards the 'popular', the 'marginal', the 'deviant' – is problematic. If we accept this, we must start thinking about culture differently, and radically expand the aspects of culture we study. This means facing up to the exclusions which cultural studies itself has entrenched over the past thirty years. To list a few: the ignoring of the cultural experience of the old; the downplaying of the 'middlebrow' or of any cultural experience which is not 'spectacular' or 'resistant'; the lack of attention to the cultural experience of elites (we cannot assume that the boundaries of elites are unchanging); the limited research (within cultural studies at least) on the cultures of work, business and science; and so on?[5] Indeed if, as Hall points out, popular culture is *not* simply 'what we experience', then we have to study the much larger space suggested by this 'not': the shadows which popular culture casts, as well as the light it projects. This general principle – of opening up much more the range of cultural experience which cultural studies investigates – runs throughout the book.

My original image of cultural studies has a further methodological consequence. If we take seriously the contribution that everyone makes to cultural life, then we have to be sceptical about all attempts to reify culture, that is, to see it as a unified 'object' rather than a mass of open-ended processes. This applies not only to the 'popular'/'high' culture distinction, but also to ideas of national cultures, ethnic cultures, even the idea that an individual's identity can be easily read off from certain cultural or social coordinates. Cultural studies, therefore, should take seriously the full complexity of being 'inside' culture.

This – to anticipate a little – is where method comes in. We should always reject short cuts in cultural description, not because we want complexity for its own sake, but because this is the only way to think culture in a non-dominative way, to recognize it as a space of multiple voices and forces. We need a theory of cultural complexity, but without lapsing into excessively complex language (a fault of some recent cultural studies). We need the tools to think about, and research, cultural complexity in a manageable way.

If we can imagine cultural studies as a democratic space of cultural exchange, we can also imagine it another way. In a cultural situation where we are continually represented within – and assumed to belong to – a cultural 'present', we surely need another space, a space where we reserve the right to refuse those forms of address, or at least question them. We need a space where we can ask: How did those forms of address come to be directed at us, at me? Who, or what, is this 'me' formed by those types of address? Social forces may have helped form our individual voices, but that does not mean our position as individuals within wider cultural formations is unproblematical. This space of questioning and reflexivity is another way of imagining the space of cultural studies itself. Our descriptions and theories of cultural complexity must be brought back to bear upon the individual's experience of culture: the difficult, uncertain questions of belonging and detachment.

In addressing the central issue of cultural studies – the links between culture and power – I shall emphasize these three principles: *openness, complexity* and *reflexivity*.[6] Taken together, they have generated the argument of this book. Chapter 3 looks at the complexities which individual experience generates for broader claims about culture. Chapter 6 then explores in more detail what it means to bring into the work of cultural studies our own voices (whether as researchers, as teachers, or as students) while at the same time maintaining a grasp of the wider forces which shape individual selves. Together, Chapters 3 and 6 explore the significance of reflexivity for the method of cultural studies. Chapters 4 and 5, by contrast, reflect on the complexity of cultural experience from a more general, trans-individual perspective. They look, respectively, at how we should think about texts and about cultural formations. Underlying all these discussions are certain values of cultural democracy which are central to cultural studies; these are developed explicitly in Chapter 2. Chapter 7 connects those values and the book's overall argument with recent thinking about democracy and community.

Taken as a whole, the book brings together two aspects of studying culture which are often kept apart: the 'objective' and the 'subjective' – the scale of social and cultural production, and the scale of individual sense-making and reflection. Yet they are, I argue, two aspects of the same picture: how we speak about others and how we speak personally must be consistent with each other, if our theory is to be fully accountable (see especially Chapter 6). We cannot oversimplify the cultural experiences of others, without caricaturing our own.[7] Cultural studies in this sense involves an ethic of reciprocity, a mutual practice of both speaking and listening, which is inextricably tied to taking seriously the complexity of cultures. It is here that ethics (and politics) converge with method; for it is method that provides the basic tools with which we can empirically research that complexity in a systematic and accountable way. This is the central argument of the book.

## Cultural studies as a discipline?

One measure of the success of cultural studies' central vision has been the wide popularity of the term 'cultural studies'. It has come to be applied to almost any form of theoretically influenced textual study, from literary analysis to art history. I adopt, however, a narrower usage. If we stand by the central vision of cultural studies as the study of culture which addresses its connections with power, then by 'cultural studies' I shall refer only to those areas of research which genuinely have the methodological tools to analyse those connections systematically. Although such tools will include some from literary analysis (inevitably, given cultural studies' ancestry in literary studies), the principal methodological focus is the *sociologically influenced, and fully materialist,* analysis of 'culture', usually traced back to British cultural studies of the late 1950s (especially the work of Raymond Williams). This is an indication of the methodological region in which I see cultural studies as operating; the rest of the book, I hope, justifies this position. I am definitely not claiming that cultural studies 'originated' in Britain, let alone that in such an 'origin' lies its destiny.

Looking in the opposite direction, cultural studies' concern with power and its insistence on certain democratic values at the heart of its method distinguish it sharply from the approaches to culture in traditional social science, or what is formally called 'cultural sociology', which explicitly reject such a 'power-based framework of analysis' (P. Smith, 1998b: 7). Having said that, in recent years the sociology of culture has made various attempts to 'catch up' with cultural studies' work and there are siren calls for cultural studies to be 'reintegrated' into sociology (see generally, Long, 1997). In one way, I am sympathetic to the spirit of those calls, in so far as I am arguing for a cultural studies whose methods are in broad terms 'sociological', but unsympathetic if that means abandoning cultural studies' distinctive values. In fact, the institutional movement can just as easily be read the other way, with (most) sociology of culture representing now a detailed inflection of cultural studies. There are also significant overlaps between cultural studies and contemporary cultural anthropology, now that the latter has extricated itself from its exclusive concern with mapping 'other' cultures.

Later chapters will reflect these connections. However, I am not interested in disciplinary boundary wars. By 'cultural studies' I mean the discipline (see below) that studies the relations between culture and power, using a method the primary orientation of which is very broadly sociological rather than literary (but allowing for borrowings from literary and anthropological analysis and elsewhere). In terms of detailed methods, there is increasingly an interchange between historic disciplines, making absolute boundaries based on method outdated. What remains distinctive, however, about cultural studies and its institutional history is its concern with culture and power, and the values and commitments which flow from that.

Values and commitments lead on directly to the question of the 'politics' of cultural studies' work. As this is a disputed area, I want to make clear where I stand. From time to time I use the term 'politics' or 'political' in relation to cultural studies, particularly as a contrast to, say, positivist cultural sociology. I explore in detail in Chapter 2 what the distinctive values of cultural studies are. I do not, however, naively believe that academic work in itself has automatic political value: that overestimates the significance of academics by some way. Whether cultural studies' work might, in the long term, have real political effects is difficult to judge, and must involve looking closely at how it is taught and in what institutional settings. I broach these issues in various places but they are slightly to one side of the methodological issues which are the central focus of the book. In terms, then, of the actual political effects of cultural studies, I am prepared to be sceptical and cautious. What I do want to insist upon, however, is that the practice of cultural studies is based on certain values and those values, if consistently and effectively applied in the ways we teach and do research, may have long-term implications for the contexts in which we, our students, and maybe others beyond our institutions think about politics. We should not be afraid of acknowledging that the values of cultural studies are those of cultural and political democracy and the progressive undermining of inequalities of power. It is in this, limited, sense that I refer to the 'politics of cultural studies' and cultural studies' potential to empower.

That is enough explanation of the book's overall outlook, but there are a number of other issues which must be broached at this stage, as context for the debates of later chapters.

## Examining ourselves

My emphasis on reflexivity and the personal perspective may seem unusual when the broader aim is to study culture on a large scale. But the paradox is only apparent. To reflect on the individual experience of culture does not mean turning our backs on the social; instead, thinking about the individual story plunges us immediately into the web of relationships out of which we are formed. As the political philosopher Hannah Arendt put it graphically:

> Although everybody started his life by inserting himself into the human world through action and speech, nobody is the author or producer of his own life story. In other words, the stories, the results of action and speech, reveal an agent, but this agent is not an author or producer. Somebody began it, and is its subject in the twofold sense of the word, namely, its actor and sufferer, but nobody is its author. (Arendt, 1958: 184)

An emphasis on the individual perspective might, of course, seem narcissistic, and some of the more unkind attacks on recent cultural studies have suggested this (for example, Moran, 1998: 74). But such attacks completely miss the point of how the individual story works. Ien Ang, discussing her relationship to 'Chineseness' as someone of Chinese origin who does not speak Chinese, has expressed such stories' function in terms of 'a reflexive positioning of oneself in history and culture' (Ang, 1994: 4). Thinking about the individual's relation to culture means thinking about the process of individuation (how we each became 'individuals'). This may be a matter of contested and painful history (Probyn, 1993), and it opens directly onto the social and cultural terrain in which individuals are formed.

The individual perspective is also important in cultural studies for another reason. It is central to thinking about how we *communicate* cultural studies as an academic subject: the question of 'pedagogy', or how and what we teach. Pedagogy has been a neglected issue in cultural studies,[8] which is surprising since, arguably, the subject originated from a pedagogic challenge. As Raymond Williams put it in a much-quoted discussion of the demands for new ways of teaching literature and culture in 1930s and 1940s Britain:

> in adult education, where people who had been deprived of any continuing educational opportunity were nevertheless readers, and wanted to discuss

what they were reading; and even more specifically among women who, blocked from the process of higher education, educated themselves repeatedly through reading . . . both groups wanted to discuss what they'd read, and *to discuss it in a context to which they brought their own situation, their own experience* – a demand which was not to be satisfied, it was soon very clear, by what the universities . . . were prepared to offer. (Williams, 1989a: 152, added emphasis)

This idea of teaching culture so that students can bring 'their own situation' to bear upon it is, as the US educational theorist Henry Giroux (1994: 131–2) has argued, directly relevant to cultural studies today in the context of the multicultural classroom. The link of teaching to experience is, in fact, a general one. As Paulo Freire put it: 'studying is above all thinking about experience, and thinking about experience is the best way to think accurately' (1985: 3).

If cultural studies is to remain true to its democratic vision, it must address the question of experience in all its complexity.[9]

## Method without guilt

More generally, analysing cultural complexity means having the right investigative tools, the tools of method. The word 'method' derives from the Greek words for road (*hodos*) and 'after' or 'about' (*meta*): method is the route down which you go to pursue something. Without some agreement about that route, and the issues which need to be resolved in analysing culture, it is difficult to see how cultural studies can function as a space where people – across many dimensions of difference – exchange and see reflected their experiences of culture. That, I shall argue, means understanding cultural studies as a coherent subject, a discipline with recognizable methods – or at least a recognizable set of methodological debates.[10] Yet defining the methods and disciplinary status of cultural studies is precisely what many writers have resisted doing.

The idea that cultural studies is somehow 'above' disciplinarity has been given credence, partly because it seemed to reflect a consensus over the past two decades that you cannot do serious work in the humanities without drawing on the methods of various disciplines.[11] There is a long line of argument within cultural studies that sees it as essentially inter-disciplinary.[12] And certainly, cultural studies emerged by addressing questions taken from elsewhere – from sociology and literary criticism – in a distinctive way. In that sense, at the level of detailed method cultural studies must remain 'interdisciplinary', inspired by many theoretical perspectives; that is now the situation of most disciplines. But it is quite another matter to argue that cultural studies is not itself a historically distinct discipline.

I want to argue that, in terms of its history, values and overall methodological orientation, cultural studies *is* a distinctive discipline. The arguments for the non-disciplinarity of cultural studies are weak. First, there is the romantic rejection of all disciplinary authority in education.[13] But the power relations inherent in the teaching situation cannot be wished away, since in some form or other they are a precondition of any act of teaching: the attempt to show a way through what is otherwise impenetrable or intractable. Power relations are an inherent part of any critical educational project, including cultural studies (O'Shea, 1998). Second is the idea that what is distinctive about cultural studies is not its methodological stance, but its way of engaging with the cultural and political world. This has been suggested by Lawrence Grossberg in America (1997a, 1997b), and it has sometimes characterized comments by Stuart Hall in the UK (1992b).[14] The Australian cultural theorists John Frow and Meaghan Morris (1996) in an important discussion imply something similar, although they waver on the question of whether cultural studies is a discipline or not. In one way, perhaps, it doesn't matter much: what's in the word 'discipline'? In another, however, it is quite crucial; evasiveness about whether cultural studies is a discipline is an excuse to neglect the fundamental problems of method that contemporary cultural analysis faces.

It is evasiveness on the question of method that has led cultural studies, at the end of the twentieth century, into something of a crisis (cf. Tudor, 1999: 187–94). Without some shared commitment to methodological debate, cultural studies risks being no more than a trail of political interventions by authoritative voices. This is the implication of some of Lawrence Grossberg's statements:

> I would propose that cultural studies, at any particular time and place, is constructed by articulating its practice into particular *projects* and *formations*. Cultural studies always and only exists in contextually specific theoretical and institutional *formations*. Such formations are always a response to a particular political project based on the available theoretical and historical resources. In that sense, in every particular instance, cultural studies has to be made up as it goes along. (Grossberg, 1997b: 252, original emphasis)

In Grossberg's vision, cultural studies risks becoming merely reactive, at the mercy of changing historical and political events. There are two directions in which cultural studies could move to escape that fate: first, by concentrating on making its political interventions in culture more specific, engaging directly with cultural policy (as Tony Bennett has extensively argued: 1992, 1993, 1998a), or second, by focusing more precisely and systematically on the methods of cultural analysis.

I have chosen the second route, not because cultural policy does not matter, but because I consider the problems which face us in understanding what culture *is* to be more fundamental and of greater long-term importance. (That of course leaves open the possibility that cultural studies' research will have detailed implications for policy issues, for example in relation to the democratization of culture.) The most important task, as I see it, for cultural studies in the new century is to open up a terrain of sustained *empirical* research about cultural experience in today's exceptionally complex cultural environments. I shall show how little of its potential field cultural studies has so far explored.

## The aim of this book

Thinking about broad issues of method does not, however, mean imposing a methodological straitjacket. There is, of course, a need for interdisciplinarity at the level of detail and much room for legitimate differences of 'taste' or emphasis. There is no single, ready-made approved method for doing cultural studies! The issues to be analysed are far too complex for that. This book is not, therefore, intended as a 'methods primer' but is an attempt to clear the ground for some consensus on what in cultural studies we should be about; what our priorities for research and study are. Nor, equally, does this book attempt a substantive analysis of, for example, the institutional and economic bases of cultural production and cultural life. I take it for granted that this is necessary and important but, as I see it, it does not raise fundamental methodological difficulties and is, therefore, not a priority here.

My aim, very simply put, is to focus on the sheer difficulty of researching contemporary cultures and the consequences which flow from this. We need not so much a map in the conventional sense, as what the Colombian cultural theorist Jesus Martin-Barbero has called a 'night-time map' (1993: 211–12)[15] – to help us orientate ourselves in very uncertain territory: the space of culture. We need to develop a manageable way of investigating cultural complexity (a method, in other words). One obstacle here is the sheer difficulty of cultural studies texts on these issues and, even more, the difficulty of matching up the different languages and terms which they involve. As a result, each chapter develops its argument by comparing a number of important texts from cultural studies and elsewhere: introducing key authors, explaining their concerns and where necessary their language, and focusing on the key issues where they overlap with or differ from other important texts. This should help to demystify some of the literature. Each of the central chapters concludes with some ideas for further thinking about the debates of the chapter.

Inevitably, however, some of the terrain crossed is difficult. Contemporary cultures are complex, and they pose complex problems of analysis and even description; there is no getting away from that. To assist the reader I have organized the chapters in roughly ascending order of difficulty.

Chapters 2 and 3 are partly historical in focus and they review, from a critical contemporary perspective, material from earlier phases of cultural studies – some of which will be familiar to most readers. Chapter 3 lays the ground for the questions of complexity which the later, more difficult chapters pursue. Chapters 4, 5 and 6 confront directly some central problems for cultural studies' method: the status of the text, rival models of 'culture' and 'cultures', and the importance of self-reflexivity. Because these are difficult issues, it is sometimes best to approach them quite abstractly, in order to get our thinking straight, but any abstract discussions are then worked out in discussions about where specific empirical research either could lead or is already leading. Each of these later chapters ends with a summary of the main argument, as a reference point for readers. By Chapter 6, some of the issues discussed will raise serious issues of a philosophical nature, and potential post-structuralist critiques of the approach taken will need to be addressed; inevitably those discussions are the most difficult, and can safely be omitted by readers less interested in the philosophical background to my approach. Chapter 7 – the concluding chapter – however, summarizes the argument of the whole book in a non-technical way, ending with comments on its broader ethical implications, and returning to the general terrain explored in this chapter and Chapter 2.

## Some theoretical background

The chapters of this book each cover a core methodological question: the nature of cultural studies' values, the nature of 'texts' and 'cultures', the significance of the individual perspective, and so on. While examples are used to illustrate the debates, the overall discussion is deliberately at a more general level, since it is there that the fundamental difficulties lie. The point, however, is throughout to open the way to *empirical* research.[16] There is, of course, some theoretical background to this emphasis on the empirical which needs to be explained.

First, my approach to culture can broadly be described as 'materialist'. I understand cultural production (whether it is a text, a song, a film, an idea or whatever) as the result of what particular people have done at particular times and places, and under particular constraints and limitations. The ultimate origin for this approach is Marx: his rejection in the *German Ideology* of an abstract 'history of ideas' and his insistence on what he called 'the representation of *practical* activity . . . the *practical* process of development of men' (1977a: 165, added emphasis). He put it another way in the *Grundrisse*: 'there is nothing which can escape, by its own elevated nature or self-justifying characteristics, from [the] cycle of social production and exchange' (1977b: 363).

There is, however, enormous room for debate about what precisely count as 'material' conditions. Important here are Raymond Williams's discussions in *Marxism and Literature* (1977) and *Culture* (1981). Williams rejects the position of cruder forms of Marxism which holds that cultural phenomena can and must be reductively explained in terms of material practices at some underlying economic level (the 'base–superstructure' model). Instead, Williams insists that all forms of cultural production are themselves material processes. Quite apart from their directly economic aspects, they involve real material constraints in terms of who speaks and who does not, who is represented and who is not, and so on. In fact, the very separation of 'art' or 'culture' from the rest of social life – which crude base–superstructure models reflected – was itself, Williams argued (1981: ch. 5), a social construct reflecting particular material conditions for the production of art separate from the rest of the economy. There is no getting away from the materiality of culture (for a clear recent statement of this principle, see du Gay et al., 1996).

Secondly, this materialist approach to culture, while clearly involving detailed empirical research, involves an affirmation of the necessity of reflexivity about method: here, again, the difference from (positivist) cultural sociology (P. Smith, 1998a) is plain. Positivist research treats 'facts' or 'data' as unproblematic evidence for an independently existing external world. But an essential part of method in cultural studies is thinking systematically about how specific methods influence the results produced and shape our picture of the world. The sources for the attack on 'positivist' science are multiple (see, for example, Polanyi, 1958; Husserl, 1970; Gadamer, 1975; Bourdieu, 1977, 1990; Harding, 1986), but they matter less than the consensus across much of the social sciences and humanities on the need for reflexivity about method. Cultural studies is part of that wider consensus.[17]

I return to the question of reflexivity in greater detail in Chapter 6, but it is worth mentioning here one specific connection: feminist epistemology (that is, feminist work on how knowledge is produced), the significance of which for cultural studies has until recently been neglected (Skeggs, 1995; Gray, 1997; Pickering, 1997: 89–90). Feminist epistemology (such as the work of the feminist philosopher of science Sandra Harding, 1986, 1993; cf. Haraway, 1991b; Hartsock, 1998) provides a useful entry-point to a question crucial for the rest of the book: namely that a commitment to reflexivity about method and the power relations involved in producing research is perfectly compatible with a commitment to carrying out new empirical research. This is quite different from the 'radical' scepticism about empirical research which has been a feature of some post-structuralist and postmodernist theory.

Harding, for example, makes it very clear that questioning critically the conditions of knowledge production does not make empirical work impossible; on the contrary, it is a resource to make it more objective (1993: 73). As long as those who produce knowledge are from an unrepresentative group (relative to those they write about) – say, they are overwhelmingly men, but writing about women or about 'mankind' generally – then the types of questions they think worth asking will be distorted. So interrogating the power relations which have historically affected who conducts research is a precondition for doing research better. To give two examples: it took *women* researchers (Oakley, 1974; Smith, 1987) to put onto the sociological agenda the domestic work of women and the wider gender inequalities it reflects; and it took a *woman* psychologist (Gilligan, 1982) to raise the possibility that the types of narrative American women tell about themselves and their skills are quite different from those of American men, something which reflects many centuries of gender inequality.

Given this risk of distortion, Harding proposes a form of '*strong* objectivity' in scientific research which involves problematizing not only the 'object of knowledge' (the issue or people to be investigated), but also the 'subject of knowledge' (the situation of researchers themselves): 'a sociology which does not transform those it studies into objects but preserves in its analytic procedures the presence of the subject as actor and experiencer' (Harding, 1986: 155, cf. 1993). More specifically, Harding argues that research questions should be formulated explicitly from the perspective of the marginal and disadvantaged (that is, people at the furthest remove from the social conditions of those who normally produce scientific knowledge); hence the name of this approach: 'standpoint epistemology'. This has something in common with cultural studies' attention to those who are marginalized within culture, but Harding usefully makes it clear that science is not *about* studying the marginal. Instead the 'marginal' standpoint is simply a way of broadening the range of questions which are to be asked, avoiding the trap of reproducing a dominative mode of thinking in reverse into which cultural studies – by focusing exclusively on the 'popular' or the 'marginal' – has sometimes fallen.

Recognizing the individual standpoint is, then, quite consistent with aiming for greater objectivity. The feminist science theorist Donna Haraway has expressed a similar point by arguing for the 'situated' nature of all knowledge claims: 'situated', that is, in the sense of marked by a particular perspective and the limitations of a particular, materially produced position. There is, Haraway argues, no 'view from above, from nowhere' (1991b: 195); from which the conclusion is: not postmodern relativism but rather a continual dialectic, or exchange, between thinking about the 'object' of research (whatever aspect of cultural life is being studied) and thinking about the 'subject' of research (the material processes by which study is conducted and knowledge produced).[18] This is a useful model for cultural studies, which I draw on again in Chapter 6.

The third point about my approach I want to emphasize is a pragmatism in relation to wider theory. Cultural studies should engage with broader theory (not just in sociology and anthropology, but also in linguistics, psychoanalysis and philosophy) not for its own sake, but only if it can open up perspectives for possible empirical work into culture. As Stuart Hall put it, 'the only theory worth having is that which you have to fight off, not that which you speak with profound fluency' (1992b: 280). Cultural studies has no need to adopt, for example, the whole of Freud, Saussure, Derrida, Foucault, Lacan or Deleuze, as if they were 'founding texts'. In deciding what theory can help us understand culture, we should be sceptical rather than reverential.[19] While theoretical work can sometimes transform an area of study (for example Frantz Fanon's work in post-colonial studies), excessive theoretical elaboration can also stand in the way of less 'exciting' but essential empirical work.

I therefore adopt a strategic approach to structuralist and post-structuralist thought, in spite of their great influence and authority in cultural studies. In Chapter 6, for example, I acknowledge the important questions about individual experience which Foucault's late work opens up, but argue that they bring major problems as well and it is better not to be tied to the philosophical complexities of post-structuralist formulations.

We should avoid becoming overwhelmed by the difficult questions which lie unresolved at the broadest level of social and cultural theory: for example, questions about the methodological status of psychoanalysis and its relation to sociological theory. Clearly, these large issues lie beyond the scope of this book, although I should admit my own scepticism (influenced by Foucault) about the centrality of psychoanalysis to social theory and cultural studies. What matters, however, is not whether I am right or wrong on this, but instead to try and formulate the central methodological issues of understanding culture in a way that allows us, so far as possible, to put those deep-seated theoretical uncertainties to one side. Given that we at present lack 'an account of the practices of subjective self-constitution' (Hall, 1996a: 13), there seems to be no other way to move things forward.

In such a situation, the best strategy is greater openness towards a *variety* of theoretical legacies, which might help us think about culture, identity and language, including cognitive psychology and social psychology operating outside a psychoanalytic framework (Potter and Wetherall, 1987; Billig, 1992, 1995; Shotter, 1993; Harre, 1998), cultural anthropology (Miller, 1995; Sperber, 1996), cultural geography (Massey, 1994; Sibley, 1995), and social theory (Maffesoli, 1996). Graham Murdock put the wider issue very well a decade ago:

> Cultural studies' *relative isolation* . . . is one of the penalties of its emergence as a self-sustaining area of academic study with its own selective tradition of canonized texts. To counter this we need to recover the original interdisciplinary impetus and be more adventurous in crossing intellectual check-points. (1997: 88 [1989], added emphasis)[20]

This point continues to apply today.

Finally, if we are to adopt a greater theoretical openness, we need an inclusive rather than an exclusive working definition of what types of detailed research cultural studies might cover.[21] A good approach here is represented by John Frow and Meaghan Morris' wide-ranging collection, *Australian Cultural Studies* (1993). This includes work on art, computer games, media events, music, television series, film landscapes, tourism and the cultural politics of diplomacy. This inclusive approach is preferable to defining cultural studies, effectively, in terms of media studies, as do Graham Turner's early review of British cultural studies (1990), and Barker and Beezer's *Reading into Cultural Studies* (1992), although there was once some historical logic in that approach. A broad working definition is also crucial if we want to think of cultural studies as a global discipline.

To raise the question of the global reach of cultural studies opens up a host of further questions: Can cultural studies be globalized? How can it overcome its original ties to a rather parochial agenda in Britain? Should there be competing 'national' cultural studies? These are questions I cannot resolve here. Nor do I need to, if my underlying assumption is right: that, in spite of inevitable differences in priorities between cultural studies conducted in different parts of the world, there is sufficient common ground to enable shared debate over issues of method. Throughout the book, I make connections between theory and research developed in different parts of the world, and attempt to de-centre the role of British perspectives. Nothing less will do if the democratic vision of cultural studies is to be fulfilled on an international scale.

## Speaking personally

I need to say something of the personal history that brought me to write this book. There are limits and biases built into my position, like any other.

I am British, and am writing from within the trajectory of 'British cultural studies' (but with the crucial qualification that this no longer seems to be a space which determines a particular viewpoint – or even a specific range of questions). Inevitably what I write will be read in the light of that Britishness and the 'authority' which British cultural studies has, rightly or wrongly, acquired. For this reason I emphasize that the whole point of this book is to *undermine* the sense that cultural studies has a necessary trajectory built into it, tied to a particular national origin or source (whether British or otherwise). Cultural studies must operate in an open way without an agenda that appropriates the subject for a particular location. Handel Wright recently posed an important challenge to cultural studies as a subject[22] when he wrote:

> while British cultural studies provides the British intellectual not only with a home but also an authoritative place from which to speak, the absence of Africa in genealogies of cultural studies means that I need to make a case for the very existence and legitimacy of African cultural studies and hence a legitimate speaking position [for myself]. (1998: 39)

As Wright points out, any history of cultural studies should start from the principle of multiple 'origins', perhaps devaluing the notion of 'origins' altogether (cf. Hall, 1996b: 394). Only in that way can it take adequate account of the theoretical and pedagogic practice of, say, Ngugi wa Thiong'o (1986) in contesting the impacts of British colonial 'education' in Kenya in the 1960s, or the origins of cultural studies practice in 1960s Australia (Morris, 1992; Frow and Morris, 1993: xxvi; Stratton and Ang, 1996).[23] This is not just a problem about British hegemony; there is always the danger of forgetting the hegemonic power of 'the West' in the history of all disciplines (Dirks, 1998: xi).

So when I offer this book as a particular way of thinking about cultural studies and its methods, I do not want to close off other possibilities. Inevitably, as I make connections across established lines of difference, yet myself speak from a particular (and in some ways privileged) position, there is a risk of seeming to 'speak for' others, rather than allowing them to speak in their own name (cf. hooks, 1992). But that is the exact opposite of my intention. I am offering just one vision, to take its place among those from other places and perspectives. A central part of that vision is the principle that each person's reflexivity about the vast mass of cultural processes that surround them has significance and must be listened to. Cultural studies (internationally and nationally) must be the space for that mutual openness.

My own stake in imagining cultural studies and its method this way is real, and perhaps ambiguous: the product of two very different educational histories. Although I did not realize it at the time, my initial education matched all too neatly the personal trajectory of many involved in British cultural studies: the 'scholarship boy' who goes to an elite British university (Oxford), as the first to 'make it' from a family of working-class parents, or in my case parents who grew up working-class and then made a difficult and uncompleted journey to middle-class, professional status. But, if that history and my left political leanings fitted me, perhaps, to join the ranks of cultural studies, the match was not made. In the early 1980s I knew nothing of media or cultural studies. The second educational history was much longer: a curious sort of self-education as I tried to read critical thought in my spare time while working in an office by day. New horizons were opened up for me by working as a musician on the edges of the London professional music scene and a chance encounter with media studies at Goldsmiths College in the early 1990s.

I have a personal stake in cultural studies, because this was the space where I began to find a voice and bring a host of dispersed ideas, doubts and anxieties to bear on a single question: how does culture work, and who does it work for? But equally, I have no stake in an exclusive notion of what cultural studies is. The space of cultural studies is, I suspect, far larger and less charted than we have so far imagined; it must be explored from many different directions at once. Cultural studies' strength remains its openness to new voices, and its commitment to an expanding range of empirical research.

It is in that spirit, over the next few chapters, that I want to explore what it means to reflect on our lives 'inside culture'.

## Notes

1  For example, Ferguson and Golding (1997) and Philo and Miller (1997) whose polemical tone has unhelpfully polarized positions between 'political economy' and 'culturalist' approaches.
2  For example, Giroux (1996), Bennett (1997: 51–3; 1998b: 535–8), Grossberg (1997a: 237).
3  Cf. Nowell-Smith (1987), O'Shea and Schwarz (1987), Schwarz (1989: 254).
4  As John Frow points out (1995: 81–4), we need to shift from taking 'the popular' as a taken-for-granted descriptive category to treating it as a normative category,

which needs to be carefully examined and questioned. Cf. also Chapter 3.

5 There are exceptions of course. For example: John Tulloch's (1991) work on the aged audience; Simon Frith's (1986) argument in favour of broadening the range of music that cultural studies covers; the work of audience studies on the 'ordinary' processes of viewing in the home (Morley, 1986; Lindlof, 1987; Silverstone, 1994); various important investigations of the cultures of work (Negus, 1992; du Gay, 1997; McRobbie, 1998). A number of writers have also spoken generally about the validity of cultural studies analysing something other than popular culture (Nelson et al., 1992: 11; Nelson, 1996: 729; Webster, 1996). But the overall pattern of restricting the areas of the cultural field we study remains. For parallel critiques, see Harris (1996) and Miller and McHoul (1998).

6 These principles reflect broader intellectual currents, as I bring out later. Inevitably, therefore, there is overlap with the directions now being taken in other disciplines, for example the current emphasis on complexity in social science (M. Smith, 1998).

7 I am echoing here a famous phrase of Raymond Williams (1958: 306).

8 See especially Henry Giroux (1994, 1996), and cf. McRobbie (1992: 721), and Pickering (1997: 88).

9 Cf. Pickering (1997).

10 Cf. Goodwin and Wolff (1997), Bennett (1998b) and Miller (1998: 43, 48).

11 See, for example: Nelson et al. (1992: 2) and Nelson (1996: 277).

12 C. Hall (1992), Nelson et al. (1992: 4), Murdock (1995), Nelson (1996), Garcia Canclini quoted in Murphy (1997: 80), Grossberg (1997b) and Johnson (1997).

13 For subtle reflections on the issue of pedagogical authority, see Grossberg (1997c: 384–90).

14 Hall's position is, however, rather subtle: 'although cultural studies as a project is open-ended, it can't simply be pluralist . . .Yes, it refuses to be a master discourse or a meta-discourse of any kind . . . But it does have some will to connect; it does have some stake in the choices it makes . . . There is something *at stake* in cultural studies, in a way that I think, and hope, is not exactly true of many other very important intellectual and critical practices. Here one registers the tension between a refusal to close a field, to police it, and, at the same time, a determination to stake out some positions within it and argue for them' (1992b: 278). My underlying argument is that many of those choices must concern issues of method, if cultural studies is to function effectively as a space for engaging with the political dimensions of culture.

15 Cf. de Certeau on culture as an 'oceanic night' (1993: 211 [1974]).

16 On the centrality of empirical research, even in the light of post-structuralism, see McRobbie (1997).

17 Which means, incidentally, that it is no good claiming that cultural studies is *distinguished* by its reflexivity (as, for example, does Grossberg, 1997b: 267–8).

18 An important parallel to feminist epistemology here is the work on sociological and anthropological method by Pierre Bourdieu (1977 [1972], 1990). The necessary dialectic between thinking about the subject and the object of knowledge is condensed neatly into the opening sentence of his *Outline of a Theory of Practice*: 'the practical privilege in which all scientific activity arises never more subtly governs that activity (insofar as science presupposes not only an epistemological break but also a *social* separation) than when, *unrecognised*

*as privilege*, it leads to an implicit theory of practice which is the corollary of neglect of the social conditions in which science is possible' (1977: 1, second emphasis added). See also Chapter 6.

19  From a materialist perspective, it is worth bearing in mind how much, institutionally, is invested in the 'mastery' of these theoretical terrains.

20  Cf. Durant (1997: 205) on cultural studies' 'selective interdisciplinarity which rules out so much interesting thinking'.

21  Cf. hooks (1991: 125) and Ang (1992: 312).

22  The Argentinian Ricardo Kaliman has made a parallel point about how within Latin American cultural studies a theoretical agenda developed under European influences gives insufficient account to 'the consciousness of practitioners of [Latin American] culture' themselves (1998: 263). Cf. also hooks (1992).

23  Cf. Eskola and Vainikkala (1994) on how Scandinavian cultural studies developed independently of British models. As Bill Schwarz has remarked, we need 'an expanded cultural geography of cultural studies' (1994: 389).

# 2 Questions of value – or why do cultural studies?

One can only demand of the teacher that he [sic] have the intellectual integrity to see that it is one thing to state facts, to determine . . . the internal structure of cultural values, while it is another thing to answer questions of the *value* of culture and its individual contents and the question of how one should act in the cultural community and in political associations. These are quite heterogeneous problems. If he asks further why he should not deal with both types of problem in the lecture-room, the answer is: because the prophet and the demagogue do not belong on the academic platform.

Max Weber, 'Science as a vocation' (1991: 146 [1921], original emphasis)

[T]he real problem . . . is that people's questions are not answered by the existing distribution of the educational curriculum.

Raymond Williams, 'The future of cultural studies' (1989a: 160)

You can risk the whole authority of an academic subject on the idea that it transcends questions of value. That was Max Weber's vision of sociology for a world which he saw as riven by irreconcilable conflicts of value; to mix science with values or politics was to fall into 'prophecy' or 'demagoguery'. Given the compromised racial politics of academic life in Germany in the early twentieth century, we cannot dismiss Weber's vision lightly. Alternatively, you can base a subject on the belief that at certain times it is precisely commitments of *value* that academics need to make, clearly and unequivocally. It is this 'political' conception of education and intellectual work that has characterized cultural studies. I defend the second position, not in the abstract but through exploring what, precisely, the underlying values of cultural studies might be. This is perhaps the most fundamental methodological issue for cultural studies.

It is irrelevant, Weber wrote, to the scientific study of culture to answer, and presumably even to ask, questions about 'the value of culture'; that rules out addressing the conflicts of value which underlie the production of what we call 'culture'. On a more personal level, it is irrelevant according to Weber to ask 'how one should act in the cultural community and in political associations' (1991: 146). That would seem to exclude, from the outset, any thought about how culture should contribute to our shared life together. Weber's definition of sociology (which would fit today's sociology of culture) therefore excludes precisely the questions which, for cultural studies, have seemed to matter most: the social conflicts which underlie the apparently innocent surface of 'culture', and the connections between conditions of cultural production and democracy.

In exploring the distinctive values of cultural studies, a useful reference-point remains the vision of Raymond Williams, developed in Britain principally in the 1950s and 1960s. The position is, however, complicated because, in the period since Williams' early writings, all questions of value in intellectual work have undergone a fundamental displacement: a de-centring of the very basis on which intellectual and scientific authority is claimed or assumed. Principles whose foundational importance was taken for granted in the 1950s and 1960s so that they were literally invisible, have not only become visible, but have been subjected to sustained and necessary attack: the cultural and intellectual 'supremacy' of 'the West'; patriarchy (or the naturalized dominance of men over women) and the complex investments of patriarchy in science and other forms of intellectual production; and the cultural and social authority of science itself.

I later attempt to explain some ways in which those displacements have affected the questions and values that Williams articulated. A more general point is, however, obvious: the context and nature of intellectual dialogue has been radically transformed since the early years of cultural studies. What was primarily a British conversation closed within the ambit of 'the West' and a largely unquestioned patriarchal authority, must now be a conversation that is de-centred, non-patriarchal, open-ended, and potentially global. And yet a fundamental principle that Williams articulated *was* dialogue and an interrogation of taken-for-granted investments by power in cultural production and cultural value. So we need, not to jettison Williams' work, but to isolate its key principles and explore how far they can *resonate with* work done in other places and times.

My aim is not to entrench Raymond Williams as a 'founding father' of a globalized cultural studies; that would be absurd. By drawing on aspects of his work and the work of many others, however, the aim is to test how far we can figure out a common space of intellectual and political commitment for cultural studies that works *with* difference and not by *reducing* difference. It is significant that one of the most devastating attacks on the intellectual authority of 'the West' (Edward Said's *Orientalism*) still uses Williams' vision – transcending the 'long dominative mode' of thinking about culture – as a reference point (Said, 1978: 28). This illustrates how, whatever its limitations (on which see below), the question raised by Williams' work remains central: what is the value of studying culture, 'our' culture?

This is a very different question from those posed by two other classic models of cultural analysis: first, Weber's value-free sociology of culture (analysing from a scientific 'distance' how cultures, including one's own, function and operate); and, second, earlier anthropology's attempt to map 'other' cultures from the 'distance' sustained by colonial power. By contrast, cultural studies (wherever we practice it) starts out from the need to study *our* culture: the culture *we* live in and are formed by. Doing that involves developing a critical distance, of course, but not the artificial distance that excludes the fundamental questions that, as a member of a particular culture, I may want to ask: What are the values embedded in, or excluded from, the cultural spaces in which I have been formed? To what extent can I call those embedded values my own, and to what extent should I be critical of them? Is that space a democratic one? If not, why not, and what might make it democratic? These are, by definition, public questions – part of a wider dialogue about the culture I share with others. Putting the questions at the heart of the academic study of culture is the starting point of cultural studies as a discipline. As Raymond Williams put it: 'culture is ordinary: that is the first fact' (1989b: 4). Culture is something that concerns us all.

In the first section, I explore in more detail what Williams meant by the 'ordinariness' of culture and show the parallels between that vision and approaches to culture developed elsewhere: in Kenya (the work of Ngugi wa Thiong'o) and in Colombia (the work of Jesus Martin-Barbero). The second section (Extending the values of cultural studies) notes frankly the limitations of Williams' vision, but goes on, more positively, to explore other approaches to culture which can supplement Williams' work: Donna Haraway's visionary 'A manifesto for cyborgs', written in the context of the cultural politics – particularly gender politics – of the 1980s; Cornel West's and others' visions of cultural politics in contemporary America; and Nestor Garcia Canclini's analysis of the complex hybrid cultures of contemporary Latin America. I also make links with the fundamental re-evaluation of cultural studies in Britain in the 1980s, focused around issues of 'race' and identity.[1] Inevitably, however, in this chapter I can only sample the connections and contrasts relating to 'value' that are possible in the de-centred space of contemporary cultural studies.

An attempt is then made to draw together some principles common to these various writers in spite of all the differences and displacements (Towards common ground?). These principles underlie the methodological explorations in the rest of the book. As values, however, they must be brought back to bear upon the pragmatic question of what it means to teach, and be taught, cultural studies. The final section explores briefly some parallels between Williams' ideas about teaching 'culture' in 1950s Britain and contemporary debates, particularly the work of the American educational and cultural theorist, Henry Giroux. Although separated by three decades, both are practical attempts to build a space for criticism and reflexivity in a dense, and far from democratic, cultural life.

Although this chapter will cover a wide range of authors, a central question runs through it: what are the conditions of a common culture (Williams, 1958: 305) and what values underpin them? I mean here a 'common culture' that stretches across, and does not deny, cultural differences; a vision that is open to the future, yet careful not to squander the continuity of commitment that cultural studies as a discipline represents.

## The ordinariness of culture

### Raymond Williams' vision

The idea that 'culture is ordinary' might suggest that Williams is simply replacing one familiar idea of culture (as great works of art, 'the best that is known and thought in the world': Arnold, 1970: 154) with another, familiar from anthropology: culture as all the practices and distinctions that go to make up a 'way of life' in a particular place. Instead of 'culture' meaning Shakespeare, Beckett or Beethoven, it would refer to the symbolic life of the Azande or the customs of working-class life in the North of England. But this would be to oversimplify Williams' thinking drastically.

Certainly, Williams wanted to go beyond an elitist definition of culture as 'high' culture, and certainly also Williams was well aware of the anthropological definition of culture (1961: 63–4). But it is too simple to say that Williams was replacing the first with the second; a crucial part of Williams' work was to hold on to the idea of analysing works of so-called 'high' culture, but from a new perspective. In fact, the point was to hold *both* notions of culture – as specific works and as ongoing life process – *in tension*.[2]

Instead of seeing the artistic work (the nineteenth-century English novel, for instance) in the abstract, Williams insisted on thinking about it in terms of how it emerged from a much broader range of cultural practice: what

Williams called a 'cultural formation'. Cultural texts should never be seen as isolated entities but always as part of a shared practice of making meanings involving everyone in a particular culture.

These connections are brought out in the following passage from an essay by Williams originally published in 1958:

> Culture is ordinary: that is the first fact. Every human society has its own shape, its own purposes, its own meanings. Every human society expressed these, in institutions, and in arts and learning. The making of a society is the finding of common meanings and directions . . . The growing society is there, yet it is also made and remade in every individual mind . . . A culture has two aspects: the known meanings and directions, which its members are trained to; the new observances and meanings, which are offered and tested. These are the ordinary processes of human societies and human minds, and we see through them the nature of a culture: that it is always both traditional and creative; that it is both the most ordinary common meanings and the finest individual meanings. We use the word culture in these two senses: to mean a whole way of life – the common meanings; to mean the arts and learning – the special processes of discovery and creative effort. *Some writers reserve the word for one or other of these senses; I insist on both, and on the significance of their conjunction.* The questions I ask about our culture are questions about our general and common purposes, yet also questions about deep personal meanings. Culture is ordinary, in every society and in every mind. (1989b: 4[1958], added emphasis)

I have quoted this at length because it shows the direction of Williams' argument, and its originality, very clearly. As the emphasized passage brings out, it is the complex interrrelation of the 'textual' and the 'anthropological' approaches to culture which is important to his thesis.

This had two major advantages. First, it enabled us to ask of a work of art, or literature, or music, a whole set of questions not available in conventional aesthetic theory: How does the work relate to the shared living conditions of its time? What meanings does it have when absorbed into the lives of its audiences? And so on. The second advantage is that those questions apply equally well to *any* work, whether so-called 'high' or 'low' culture; there is no question of 'high' culture being more worth investigating from this point of view. As Williams once put it: 'our real purpose should be to bring all cultural work within the same world of discourse' (1968: 133).

It is easy to take this latter point for granted given four decades of cultural studies practice, so it is worth remembering how different Williams' vision was from conventional analyses of culture at that time. The distinguished American sociologist, Edward Shils, for example, commented in 1961 as if it were plain fact:

> [there are] three levels of culture, which are levels of quality measured by aesthetic,

intellectual and moral standards. These are 'superior' or 'refined' culture, 'mediocre' culture, and 'brutal culture'. (1961: 4, quoted in Tudor, 1995: 88–9)

Can we really deny that a similar division is at work even now in the structuring of higher education and in press attacks (very common in Britain at least) on the status of media and cultural studies? Raymond Williams' point remains a radical one.

It is worth spelling out some further implications. The first is that Williams is not simply arguing that we pay more attention to 'popular' culture at the expense of elite culture. To do that would simply invert the high/low hierarchy without challenging it. As Williams explained in his first major work, *Culture and Society* (1958: 308), categorizing culture in those ways ignores the underlying point that 'cultures' are complex amalgams drawing on *all* social positions: for a start, most cultural production in Britain (although of course not all) draws on the shared resources of the English language, which has a history that crosses social and ethnic divisions.

Instead Williams is arguing for a common culture: a shared culture based on what he calls a 'recognition of practical equality' between its members (ibid.: 305). Putting that into practice means a lot more than just avoiding judgements about cultural production you do not like much. It means positively valuing everyone's common experience in a shared culture, treating everyone's experience of culture as valuable (ibid.: 306). It was this sense of valuing each other that was missing, according to Williams, in 1950s Britain:

> an effective community of experience . . . depends on a recognition of practical equality . . . We lack a genuinely common experience, save in certain rare and dangerous moments of crisis. What we are paying for this lack . . . is now sufficiently evident. We need a common culture, not for the sake of an abstraction, but because we shall not survive without it. (1958: 304)

At the level of understanding how culture works, this meant seeing 'communication' in a much broader way than conventional literary studies allowed. Communication was not just the transmission of some predefined content (which could be read off from the text) but a much more complex process involving the active participation of the readers or viewers of the message. As Williams put it succinctly: 'communication is not only transmission; it is also reception and response' (ibid.: 301).

In *The Long Revolution* (1961) Williams broadened the argument, drawing support from cognitive psychology and other disciplines. Everyone, in the course of making sense of the world and becoming a person, is an active producer of meanings, a creative interpreter (1961: ch. 1). From this he drew an important conclusion:

> If man is essentially a learning, creating, communicating being, the only social organization adequate to his nature is *a participating democracy* in which all of us, as unique individuals, learn, communicate and control. (1961: 118, added emphasis)

But 1950s Britain – and Williams was very clear on this – was *not* a democracy in this sense (ibid.: 339). Reversing this was what Williams meant by 'the long revolution': 'a cultural revolution [which] extend[ed] the active process of learning, with the skills of literary and other advanced communication, to all people rather than to limited groups' (ibid.: 11). Remember that Williams was writing when the hopes generated by the coming of television were still quite fresh. From a contemporary vantage point, we are more likely either to relate Williams' positive vision, perhaps, to computer-mediated communication, or to be pessimistic about the prospects for any such 'revolution' – now or in the future. The question, either way, remains a live one and resonates, for example, in today's USA with its debates about cultural crisis.

To summarize: the concept of 'the ordinariness of culture' is important: first, because it looks at cultural production in terms of the contributions and reflections of all members of a culture; and second, because it stresses the political implications of how culture is organized, its material basis. Culture, in this sense, matters to everyone; it concerns our shared life together.

### Parallel visions: Africa and Latin America

If we apply Williams' own principles, we cannot treat his work as the production of a 'lone genius'. It must be seen in the broader context of social and cultural thought. The important parallel contributions in Britain in the 1950s and 1960s of Richard Hoggart (1958) and Edward Thompson (1961a) are well known, and I will not dwell on them here. Less well known is the long history of adult education in Britain since the late nineteenth century, partly under the auspices of established universities such as Oxford. I come back to the significance of this in the final section, but it is worth noting at this stage the judgement of one historian of the Workers' Educational Association for whom Williams taught from 1946 to 1961:

> We should be sceptical of portraits of Williams in the 1950s as isolated and unassociated with mainstream academic life . . . Put simply, Williams' work in [the 1950s] drew on the adult [education] tradition, especially as it had been developed in Oxford since the late nineteenth century, and may be said to have presented this intellectual lineage and way of understanding society to a large and receptive audience. (Goldman, 1995: 291–2)

The vision of culture as 'ordinary', then, was the result of a sustained social debate and teaching practice in Britain lasting more than half a century.

Rather than dwell on the British context, however, I want to look at some approaches to culture with striking similarities to Williams', developed outside Britain and in very different circumstances. My first reference point is the non-fictional writings of the Kenyan writer, Ngugi wa Thiong'o, particularly his *Decolonising the Mind* (1986). This book develops a rich concept of culture, which itself grew out of debates in Kenya in the 1960s and 1970s about how literature should be taught in the post-colonial era. Just as Williams' work responded to the changing conditions of British cultural life (the condition of an 'expanding culture' – 1958: 12), so too Ngugi's work can be seen as a response to a time of change, even crisis. Ironically, the crisis from which the Kenyan debate resulted arose from the imposition in Kenyan schools after World War II of precisely the English canon of literature whose influence Williams – in a very different way – had been negotiating in Britain a decade or so before. The irony is intensified when we remember that the origins of English literary studies were closely intertwined with the colonial project of governing the peoples of the British Empire, in a history that has only recently been uncovered (Baldick, 1983; Viswanathan, 1990).

Against this background it is, perhaps, not surprising that Ngugi was aware of Raymond Williams' work early on (Ngugi wa Thiong'o, 1986: 90), but tracing 'influences' from Britain is definitely not the point. Ngugi's conception of culture, in contrast, developed precisely as resistance to the imposition of British culture from the outside. Nevertheless there are interesting parallels. Like Williams, Ngugi draws on Marx's analysis in *The German Ideology* (1977a) of how language and culture are formed in the course of the practices of everyday material life.[3] Ngugi develops a rich notion of language as both a direct means of communication and as the carrier of a distinctive culture (1986: 15). Culture is to be seen as part of a complex lived process:

> There is a gradual accumulation of values which in time become almost self-evident truths . . . Over a time this becomes a way of life distinguishable from other ways of life . . . Values are the basis of a people's identity, their sense of particularity as members of the human race. All this is carried by language. Language as culture is the collective memory bank of a people's experience in history. (Ngugi wa Thiong'o, 1986: 14–15)

These values are reflected both in a way of life and in specific works, whether of the oral or written traditions. Ngugi's notion of culture was specifically an attempt to think about his own language and culture (Gikuyu) that the British had set out to destroy by imposing an English-language based education system and literary culture (ibid.: 11–13). This was what Ngugi famously called the 'cultural bomb' which:

> annihilates a people's belief in their names, in their languages, in their environment, in their heritage of struggle, in their unity, in their capacities and ultimately in themselves. It makes them see their past as one wasteland of non-achievement and it makes them want to identify with that which is furthest removed from themselves. (ibid.: 3)

Articulating the grounds of a common culture was, for Ngugi (ibid.: 103) as for Williams, a matter of democracy, but the conditions faced by Ngugi – of conflict with a dominant *outside* culture – were very different from those Williams envisaged.[4]

Another important reference point for the notion of 'ordinary' culture is Latin American work on popular culture, for example that of the Colombian media theorist Jesus Martin-Barbero (1993). Here the context is not, as with Ngugi, the early stages of a post-colonial regime, but rather the long-term consequences of the Spanish Conquest: the complex process of forging national unity in Latin American nations which (as a result of the Conquest) are complex amalgams of indigenous, European, and mixed (*mestizaje*) populations, with enormous variations of literacy and material wealth (Rowe and Schelling, 1990).

Like Ngugi, Martin-Barbero is well aware of the work of British cultural studies along with many other sources for studying the popular (history, anthropology, sociology); but, again, to trace a British 'origin' for his work would be misleading. What matters is that in the Latin American post-colonial context a broad notion of popular culture, parallel to Williams' sense of 'common culture', had to be developed. As Martin-Barbero explains:

> We are not dealing with an increase of information about popular culture in terms of statistics and factual data, but rather with a process that relocates the 'place' of the popular by incorporating it into the constitutive memory of the flow of history . . . [T]his has begun to fragment the once monolithic concept of culture both at the level of the semantic universe and at the pragmatic level. (1993: 62)

Instead of a limited range of texts, culture has to be seen as a mass of social processes operating at many levels.

Martin-Barbero argues, for example, for the importance of studying the cultural life of particular neighbourhoods, such as those of migrants on the margins of large cities (Lima and Buenos Aires), far removed from official politics and from the conditions of life experienced by those who produce the centralized mass media distributed to those neighbourhoods. Culture, in other words, is constituted not by a central collection of texts but by this 'ordinary' local complexity, stretched across a vast social space.

## Extending the values of cultural studies

To evaluate the continued significance of Raymond Williams' work we need, however, to do more than appreciate such parallels. A radical transposition of the terms of his vision is necessary, drawing on a range of recent cultural studies from outside Britain. To set the scene, it is worth outlining some key limitations of Williams' work.

Williams' reference point, whether he is analysing the literary culture of 1840s England or looking forward to the democratic prospects for Britain in the late twentieth century, is always what he calls 'lived' culture. He offers a theory of culture as 'the study of relationships between elements in a whole way of life' (1961: 63), a 'community of process' (ibid.: 61).

A problem, however, is that Williams' whole vision of culture and democracy was anchored in a sense of purely *local* practice; his particular inspiration, as he often made clear, was the Welsh working-class community which he experienced in his youth. This grounding of his theory, in one way, gives it strength and resilience but, in another, shields it from important questions: above all, the question of whether such localized communities are now a relevant, generalizable ideal.

Even if we concentrate on 'community' in the British context, Williams' vision fails to take account of some important factors of conflict and exclusion. Although he wrote in a Britain that after World War II was being changed by significant levels of government-encouraged immigration, Williams' work does not deal with the complexities of 'race' and ethnicity; in fact, he does not deal at all with the cultural implications of Britain's colonial past (Said, 1990: 83). 'Community' is mentioned without any consideration about how cultures are lived amidst conflicts between two or more 'lived' 'traditions'. At the same time, the cultural complexity of Britain itself – and the contribution to Britain's 'common culture' of many different ethnic groups other than the white majority, both during and long before[5] the time of major immigration – is underestimated.

The difficulties with Williams' notion of culture emerge clearly in one of his last books, *Towards 2000* (1983), when he discusses the white racism that has accompanied immigration to Britain. While rejecting racism, of course, Williams tries to insist that the tensions about immigration cannot be dismissed as simply 'racist'. The comfortable liberal view which does so, relies, he suggests, on 'a merely legal definition of what it is to be "British"' (under which immigrants qualify as British) but ignores the conflict with some 'deeper' notion of citizenship:

It is a serious misunderstanding, when *full social relations* are in question, to

suppose that the problems of social identity are resolved by formal definitions. For unevenly and at times precariously, *but always through long
experience substantially*, an effective awareness of social identity depends on
actual and sustained social relationships. To reduce social identity to formal
legal definitions . . . is to collude with the alienated superficialities of 'the
nation' which are the limited functional terms of the modern ruling class.
(Williams, 1983: 195, added emphasis)

While, to be fair to Williams, his suspicions of a Britishness imposed from
the centre derived largely from his own experience as a Welshman living
under Britain's 'internal colonialism',[6] there is a real problem here. As Paul
Gilroy asked: 'how long is long enough to become a genuine Brit?', 'how has
[national identity] come to be expressed in racially exclusive forms?' (Gilroy,
1987: 49–50). If 'full social relations' are to be used as a qualifying hurdle
for cultural existence, then how can we understand the complexities of identity in conditions of migration or cultural mixing, whether in Britain or
elsewhere?[7]

Williams' notion of social identity and community, however, is not completely closed, since at certain points he emphasizes the importance of
openness to others: the need to convert a defensive solidarity into an accep-
tance of 'extending community' (1958: 319). But it is clear that this
extension of community is imagined only in terms of the variable of class,
and that the conflictual terrain of 'race' and ethnicity was not integrated into
his thinking. In any case, even in terms of class and the British case, there is
a strong sense in Williams' early writings that his vision of community – particularly working-class community – was already nostalgic. In *The Long
Revolution* Williams writes of the withering of 'our very idea of society'
under the pressures of capitalism and market forces (1961: 325) and, we
might add, the mass media. Williams was aware of the difficulties resulting
from his reliance on the term 'community' in his early work (1979: 139) and
in some respects moved away from that idea.[8]

There are other major difficulties too. As Williams later admitted (1979:
148–9), his notion of community and of culture did not recognize gender
inequalities and how these are structured into the very organization of cultural production. In addition, the strength and clarity of Williams' vision
derives in part from a closure: a closure around a particular historical ideal
of community. This leaves, on the face of it, very little room for questioning
more fundamentally the value of cultural 'closure' itself. In the transformed
context of the late twentieth century, there are powerful arguments in
favour of avoiding closure – whether around a notion of culture that is ethnically or geographically exclusive, or around forms of intellectual authority
that rely on hidden exclusions (the centuries-long association of the intellectual voice with the male voice), or even around a notion of 'humanity'

(which may now need to be re-evaluated in the light of our relationships with machines).

## Haraway and committed partiality

An important statement of the need to avoid closure has been made by the feminist historian of science, Donna Haraway, in her celebrated article 'A manifesto for cyborgs' (1991a), originally published in 1985. This is an unusually complex and wide-ranging piece of writing to which it is impossible to do full justice here, but I want to explore how far, in spite of the major differences between her work and Williams', there is important common ground between their visions of culture and democracy.

At a broad level, both Haraway and Williams respond to a crisis in culture and politics. Raymond Williams' early writings responded principally to the expansion of cultural exchange in the early years of television. For Haraway, the issue is the crisis arising from 'the social relations of science and technology' (1991a: 205): a complex set of technological changes, summed up in her phrase 'the informatics of domination'. By this Haraway means a number of things (1991a: 203–15: cf. 1997), including:

(a) the increasingly complex interaction between humans and machines (especially computers);
(b) the increasing range and complexity of technological coordination and control over work and leisure, using massively enhanced communications and computing capabilities that connect spaces that were previously unconnected;
(c) scientific developments in biology, cybernetics, and so on, which have enhanced humans' ability to alter the course of nature, including the genetic development of the human species itself;
(d) the impact of communications and computerization in disrupting, or at least complicating, the boundaries between home and work and the previously segregated work roles of men and women;
(e) the new myths of progress and technological futures associated with each of these developments.

The crucial point here is not the details of these changes (important though they are), but the way that Haraway (like Williams) uses a widespread sense of change in the underlying conditions of communication as a springboard for articulating a new vision of our place inside culture.

The fundamental point is political. In a note to the 1991 edition, Haraway explained that 'A manifesto for cyborgs' was written 'as a response to a call for political thinking about the 1980s from socialist-feminist points of view, in hopes of deepening our political and cultural debates in order to renew commitments to fundamental social change in the face of the Reagan years' (1991a: 190). The challenge, in part, is to broaden debates around our shared culture so that they take into account the cultures of science. Haraway shows convincingly here and in later work (1997) that scientific discourse is a part of our culture which we ignore at our peril (compare for example, Penley and Ross, 1991; Martin, 1993; and Kember, 1998).

This is, partly, a question of developing 'literacy': expanding people's knowledge about the cultural claims made on behalf of science (Haraway, 1997: 94–5). Once again there is a striking parallel with Williams, who at the end of the 1950s called for full literacy and full participation in cultural production if we are to respond to changing times (1961: 11). For both, cultural studies is a crucial tool in avoiding a two-tier society where cultural participation is unevenly distributed (cf. Haraway, 1991a: 211).

In spite of these broad similarities, there are major differences between Haraway and Williams which relate to the underlying questions of intellectual authority and patriarchy. In its first sentence, Haraway defines her essay as 'an effort to build an *ironic* political myth faithful to feminism, socialism, and materialism' (1991a: 190, added emphasis). The irony here is not cynicism, but rather a suspicion of any totalizing form of politics, reflecting two decades or more of feminist critiques of patriarchal authority. What Haraway, unlike Williams, is offering is not a resolved argument based on historical reality but a fiction, 'an ironic political myth', which works by appealing both to argument and to the imagination, in order to reformulate old debates and values.

For Haraway, however, this is not a pure exercise in imagination, but a fiction closely related to the conditions of social life, particularly those of women; it is a way of imagining those conditions differently and from the perspective of a different set of values. As Haraway puts it, 'the cyborg', which is the key mythical figure of her essay: 'is a matter of fiction *and* lived experience that changes what counts as woman's experience in the late twentieth century' (ibid.: 191, added emphasis). Haraway's vision is not so much grounded in a particular historical form of lived experience, like Williams' community of working-class life, as imagined against the grain of lived experience.

The cyborg, literally, is a creature that is a hybrid of machine and living being. In terms of Haraway's argument, the associations of the cyborg are more complex.[9] As an image, the cyborg makes concrete the close interactions between humans and machines in contemporary life, the complex dependence between human life and machine infrastructure. More than that, the cyborg represents an attempt to formulate imaginatively a reference point for debates about value, community, politics and intellectual work that *stands outside* the terms set by historical concentrations of power, above all patriarchy. It is an attempt to supersede two alternative political images: Marxism's image of revolutionary 'man' who will overcome the capitalist system which oppresses 'him'; and feminism's image of a female 'essence' which will be liberated in a gender revolution (ibid.: 198, 218).

In a discussion about cultural studies method, what matters is not the details of the cyborg fiction – that is a whole debate in itself, which has now extended to other questions such as artificial life (cf. Haraway, 1997) – but Haraway's strategy for developing a positive political vision without appealing to totalizing theories of any kind (whether of 'man', 'woman', 'race', 'nation' or whatever) (1991a: 196). The feminist philosopher Rosa Braidotti (1994) has conceptualized this more generally in terms of the importance of new imaginative 'figurations', which embody alternative values. Politics, for both writers, is not about preserving or restoring some mythical origin or essence but about valuing openness, connections, transformation. To understand this, it is important to appreciate that the cyborg is not a complete fusion of (wo)man and machine, but instead a metaphor for relationships between us and machines, or between us and other human beings, that are *not* unitary or complete. The cyborg embodies an openly partial perspective that values connections rather than closure, whether in politics or in intellectual or scientific work: a counter-image to undermine foundational narratives.

This offers an important advance in thinking about cultural complexity and difference, while at the same time continuing to address inequalities of power. For example, Haraway's notion of 'cyborg politics' (1991a: 218) is broad enough to cover cultural criticism, imaginative fictions, and political action in the more conventional sense: 'cyborg politics is the struggle for language and the struggle against perfect communication, against the one code that translates all meaning perfectly' (ibid.). Instead of any one political or cultural vision that captures in itself 'the whole truth', whether it is a patriarchal politics or an essentialist feminist politics, the point is to imagine new cultural connections – not in the hope of achieving some unproblematic common language, but to multiply possible dialogue (ibid.: 223). Equally, however, this is not a postmodern celebration of the play of differences for its own sake. Like Sandra Harding, discussed in Chapter 1, Haraway is keen to preserve a balance in cultural analysis between openness/scepticism and a critical edge.[10] A critical edge is essential in the face of the forces of cultural definition associated with science and technology, forces that continue to reproduce inequalities of power. The need is not merely to articulate, but to 'challeng[e] the informatics of domination' (ibid.).

Haraway's 'cyborg manifesto' may, therefore, be seen as an urgent meditation on the changing grounds for community in a culture which, at the end of the twentieth century, has been made radically more unequal through the concentration of power in scientific and informational institutions. It makes sense, therefore, to read it alongside Williams' earlier work, even if it differs in refusing any claim to a totalizing cultural authority. A paradox which Haraway expresses as follows:

> I do not know of any other time in history when there was greater need for political unity to confront effectively the dominations of race, gender, sexuality, and class. I also do not know of any other time when the kind of unity we might help build could have been possible. None of 'us' have any longer the symbolic or material capability of dictating the shape of reality to any of 'them'. Or at least 'we' cannot claim innocence from practising such dominations . . . cyborg feminists have to argue that 'we' do not want any more a natural matrix of unity and that no construction is whole. (ibid.: 199)

Instead, then, of relying (like Williams) on a notion of fixed, stable community, Haraway looks towards alliances *across* difference, communities of dialogue which are not simple or 'whole'. I develop these ideas in Chapter 7, the concluding chapter.

This is one way in which the values espoused in Williams' work have been transposed and transformed. I want to illustrate a similar possibility in relation to issues of 'race' and hybridity.

### 'Race' and hybridity

It should already be clear that, in one respect, Williams' concept of culture – focused on lived experience in particular locations – is simply not adequate to deal with cultures that are formed in movement, in the course of *disruptions* of location, whether voluntary[11] or involuntary. It is not adapted to the contexts that have provoked contemporary discussions of hybridity. It cannot, for example, help us understand the experience of the migrant workers who have lived in the Mexico–USA border region for the past two decades or so. Their cultural experience is no less important for the fact that it is not based on 'settled' social relations (as Williams might put it) and draws on a complex hybrid of US and Mexican sources, as well as international media culture more generally.

For a clear focus on these issues we need to turn to the Argentinian cultural theorist Nestor Garcia Canclini (1995) who has worked a great deal on the cultures of the US–Mexican border region.[12] The challenge, he argues, is to think about culture in the light of '*the loss* of the "natural" relation of culture to geographical and social territories' (1995: 229, added emphasis), exactly the natural relation that Williams seems to assume as his ideal. At the same time, this loss of connection may be cut across by new patterns, new 'natural' relations, based on shared media experience.

The conditions for cultural continuity have been disrupted: perhaps, border regions and other intense sites of displacement illustrate this most graphically, but they affect contemporary culture quite generally, because of the profound impact media narratives have on both private and public space. Garcia Canclini puts it as follows:

> Collective identities find their constitutive stage less and less in the city and in its history, whether distant or recent . . . Almost all sociability, and reflection about it, is concentrated in intimate exchanges. Since . . . even the accidents that happened the previous day in our own city reach us through the media, these become the dominant constituents of the 'public' meaning of the city . . . More than an absolute substitution of urban life by the audiovisual media, I perceive a *game of echoes*. The commercial advertising and political slogans that we see on television are those that we reencounter in the streets, and vice versa: the ones are echoed in the others. To this circularity of the communicational and the urban are subordinated the testimonies of history and the public meaning constructed in longtime [sic] experiences. (Garcia Canclini, 1995: 210, 212, original emphasis)

'Communication' in this context does not mean sharing a historically continuous set of experiences tied to a separate location. The connections between space, community, and culture have become more complex, but without that necessarily meaning that *community* is 'lost'.

Even more problematic is the issue of cultural conflict, and particularly ethnic conflict, which I touched on in discussing Ngugi's conception of culture in post-colonial Kenya. As Stuart Hall has eloquently argued (1997), it is precisely under the pressure of violence and displacement that the histories of identity formation are played out, and hybrid identities emerge. It is, above all, in situations of conflict that a critical understanding of culture is called for; more generally, we can say that cultures are *formed* in conflict. Let me illustrate this by drawing on some recent reflections on the prospects for black cultural criticism in the USA.

Once again, as with Williams and Haraway, these reflections address a sense of crisis, which the philosopher and cultural critic Cornel West has posed, perhaps controversially, in terms of 'nihilism' in black communities in America: 'nihilism not as a philosophical doctrine that there are no rational grounds for legitimate standards or authority; it is, far more, the *lived experience* of coping with a life of horrifying meaninglessness, hopelessness, and (most important) lovelessness' (West, 1992: 40, added emphasis). Whether or not he has Williams in mind, West's emphasis on 'lived experience' seems to turn Williams' arguments on their head. The lived experience in question is not one of 'settled' community, but one of facing daily the 'ontological wounds and emotional scars' of living in a culture marked by racism (ibid.: 42). This experience cannot simply be 'affirmed'.

What is needed, Cornel West argues, is 'prophetic criticism': 'a self-critical and self-corrective enterprise of human 'sense-making' for the preserving and expanding of human empathy and compassion' (West, 1993: xi). As with Williams, the emphasis is on 'the discovery of common meanings' (1961: 54), but in very different conditions from those Williams imagined. For black cultural critics in the USA, there can be no simple affirmation of the Euro-American intellectual tradition. At the very least, West argues, there must be a *double* consciousness', which is well aware of that tradition's implications in the material realities of imperialism and slavery (1993: xi),[13] and carries the impact of what Paul Gilroy has called 'the catastrophic rupture of the middle passage' (1992: 197). Nor, as we saw, can there be any simple affirmation of the 'lived experience' of place, given the continuance of racism. Instead, what cultural studies must address is something more like the experience of exile in time and space: what West calls a 'homebound quest in an offbeat temporality' (1993: xiii). In similar vein, Toni Morrison has called for a black cultural criticism that aims to discover: 'how to convert a racist house into a race-specific but non-racist home' (1997: 5).

Such prophetic criticism examines and judges the culture that surrounds it at a quite fundamental level. It is engaged in challenging the very categories of representation such as 'race' (West, 1993: 20), and asking how 'race' is embedded in hierarchical notions of who is a fit subject to speak and be heard, and who is not (Gates, 1986: 9–11).

Such criticism necessarily involves a complex relationship to collective experience and culture. It is, as West says, self-critical and self-corrective. A recent essay by David Lionel Smith expresses this powerfully:

> we [black cultural critics] must have the courage to risk alienating ourselves by challenging common sense, by being true critics and not mere celebrants of black culture, and by subverting the premises that define blackness . . . What then is black culture? No one can answer these questions definitively, because 'black culture' is not a fixed, single thing 'out there' in the empirical world. It is, rather, a complex and ambiguous set of processes and interactions, facts, and fantasies, assertions and inquiries, passionately held and passionately contested. (Smith, 1997: 188, 192)

There is a parallel, perhaps, with the interrogation of the place of black experience in 'British' culture during the 1980s: the work of Stuart Hall (1996a, 1997), Paul Gilroy (1987, 1992), the Centre for Contemporary Cultural Studies (1982), and Kobena Mercer (1994). At one level, the vision of Britain that was possible in the late 1980s was very different from that of the 1950s and 1960s. As Kobena Mercer put it:

> in relation to . . . global forces of dislocation in the world system as a whole . . . Britain . . . has been massively reconfigured as a local, even parochial, site in which questions of 'race', nation and ethnicity have brought us to the point where 'the possibility and necessity of creating a new culture' [quoting Gramsci, NC] – that is, new identities – is slowly being recognised as *the* democratic task of our time. (Mercer, 1994: 3, original emphasis)

At another level different writers within black British cultural studies (especially Hall, 1997) argued that the very notion of identity needed to be rethought to take account of widespread experiences of discontinuity (whether the historical catastrophes of colonialism and slavery and their aftermath, or contemporary forms of migration and displacement – even tourism). The very space of nations and cultures, organized around the assumption of mutually exclusive differences, was deconstructed by Homi Bhabha (1994) and others. And all these debates have extended into the wider space of post-colonial theory.[14]

These are debates to which we return from another direction in Chapter 5. For now, it is enough to reaffirm that if we want cultural studies to go on addressing the (changing) conditions of 'common culture' – and if we do not, what useful continuity has cultural studies as a subject to offer? – then we must transpose the terms in which Williams originally formulated the debate.

## Towards common ground?

At this stage I shall set out five principles, or values, which are important for the practice of cultural studies and which emerged from the preceding discussion. I am brief here because these principles are developed throughout the book (in fact, they were already implicit in the images of cultural studies suggested in Chapter 1). Taken together, they represent possible common ground on the basis of which cultural studies can stand, or fall, as a discipline.

The first principle involves valuing what *all* members of a 'culture'[15] – any culture – have to say, in their own voice and not as spoken for by others, about their experience of that culture and its productions. What matters is not the achievement of some unified voice that elides difference, but the multiplication of voices. So Donna Haraway in 'A manifesto for cyborgs' writes of a 'dream not of a common language, but of a powerful infidel heteroglossia', that is a mass of different voices and languages ('heteroglossia' deriving from *hetero* and *glossa*, respectively the Greek for 'other' and 'language': 1991a: 223).[16] bell hooks has made the same point, but emphasizing the danger that others' speech may already have been spoken for. Black cultural studies needs, she suggests, 'new ground': 'a counter-hegemonic marginal space where radical black subjectivity is *seen*, not overseen by any authoritative Other claiming to know us better than we know ourselves' (hooks, 1991: 22, original emphasis).

At stake here is much more than a universal right to speak (a tower of Babel without mutual understanding). Necessarily involved is a second principle: the obligation to *listen* to those other voices.

Cultural studies has to be a space for both speaking and listening. This second principle is often forgotten, but it is crucial. As the post-colonialist critic Gayatri Spivak has put it: 'for me, "Who should speak?" is less crucial than "Who will listen?"' (1990: 59, quoted in Mercer, 1994: 31).[17] This applies to politics, to academic writing, and to teaching. The classroom itself needs to be a space where each person can be confident that their voice will be recognized and valued (hooks, 1994: 186). Yet the practice of listening – of bearing witness (hooks, 1991: 133) – to each other's accounts of living inside culture is only now beginning to be theorized. There are, in spite of the limitations of Williams' position, continuities here with what he wrote forty years ago at the end of *Culture and Society*:

> A good community, a living culture, will . . . not only make room for but actively encourage all and any who can contribute to the advance in consciousness which is the common need. *Wherever we have started from, we need to listen to others who started from a different position.* (1958: 320, added emphasis)

This principle can apply to many different settings: from the interclass politics of 1950s Britain, to the cultural and racial politics of today's USA, to the complex negotiations in many parts of the world with globally distributed, commodified culture.

Cultural studies, however, should involve not only dialogue, but also *reflexivity* (this is the third principle), including reflection about the means through which all the voices in that dialogue have been formed, and the conditions which underlie the production of the space of cultural studies itself. That means reflecting both on ourselves and on the culture around us: does, for instance, that culture satisfy the principles of cultural democracy which the first two principles encapsulate? Critical reflection on shared culture, of course, carries risks: of being misunderstood as elitist or unconstructive.[18] The risk is unavoidable, but in taking it we must, as John Frow (1995) has argued, be fully self-reflexive about the institutional power which enables us to be publicly critical. Cultural studies is the work of critical intellectuals; it is not part of the popular domain which it discusses, and implying anything else is bad faith.

If such reflexivity is to be effective, it must be theoretically adequate for what it reflects upon. In looking at how voices and cultures are formed, it must adopt a *materialist* perspective (the fourth principle). Cultural phenomena – and this is a common thread throughout the history of cultural studies, wherever it has been practised – are always material processes, which are far from transparent. Who is represented in them and how? Who has access to them and on what terms? Who does not have access? Studying culture, then, means examining how hierarchies and exclusions, as well as inclusions, work in practice within culture – whether those of race, class, gender, sexuality, education, age or the relations of power that exist between large-scale cultural formations (colonialism, imperialism, economic domination). These questions apply on all social and geographical scales: personal, local, national and global.

It is here that cultural studies must draw on work in the political economy tradition, because of the way it addresses the impacts of economic as well as cultural processes of exclusion. As made clear in Chapter 1, I do not want to reproduce the division between political economy and 'culturalist' approaches.

Yet there are dilemmas: how are we to give adequate weight both to speaking and to listening, both to self-reflexivity and to critical analysis? How can we develop a materialist analysis which is respectful of the individual voice? How can we reconcile a sense of the complexity and difference within the real inequalities of power? These are issues and tensions to be explored in the rest of the book.

One further principle is worth stating: quite simply, the first four principles have to be actively defended through the work of cultural studies itself. There is no automatic consensus in their favour; cultural democracy – for which they are necessary conditions – is not a 'natural' state, even if we can argue for it on rational grounds. If it is to be more than fine ambition, cultural studies must be an *empowering* practice, a practice which acts directly upon the conditions of culture to change them.

As if to illustrate the need for this, when I began writing this chapter in April 1999, Britain was enduring a particularly prominent spate of racist and homophobic violence, which provoked Prime Minister Tony Blair to make an affirmation of a vision of community across difference:[19]

> In the past, patriotism, national identity was defined by reference to those excluded . . . Today we take pride in an identity, limited by the geography of the country, but within that country, open to all whatever their colour, religion or ethnic background . . . and the true outcasts today, the true minorities, those truly excluded are not the different races and religions of Britain, but the

racists, the bombers, the violent criminals who hate that vision of Britain and try to destroy it. (Blair, 1999: 6)

Fine words; but, before we draw too much comfort from them, the record of Blair's Government on such issues (punitive legislation on asylum seekers and immigration, for example) is hardly impressive. The undermining of cultural democracy can, in any case, take more subtle forms than bombs. Consider the celebrity among the American political elite of Samuel Huntington's recent book, *The Clash of Civilizations and the Remaking of the World Order* (1997).[20] That book argues that world order depends on the balance of power between separate civilizations ('the West' unsurprisingly being one). Huntington's balance of power, in turn, depends on a model where each separate civilization is stable in itself, focused around the leadership of a 'core state' (the USA in the case of 'the West'), and that core state must be stable in its commitment to its own civilization. This has quite drastic implications for the cultural dialogue for which cultural studies calls:

> The clash between the multiculturalists and the defenders of Western civilization and the American Creed [sic] is . . . 'the real clash'. Within the American segment of Western civilization, Americans cannot avoid the issue: Are we a Western people or are we something else? . . . Domestically this means rejecting the divisive siren calls of multiculturalism. Internationally it means rejecting the elusive and illusory calls to identify the United States with Asia. (Huntington, 1997: 307)

It is against the background of this and other rallying cries to cultural exclusion that cultural studies has to work, actively defending the values for which it stands.

## Learning (teaching) from experience

Values sound abstract, but they must always be redeemed in practice. Cultural studies' values must be translated into how we try to pass on the subject to students and, beyond them, to the wider culture. In this chapter, I have tried to radicalize Raymond Williams' vision of cultural studies' values and put it into dialogue with visions from other times and places, but in this final section I want to remember that Williams was concerned also with issues of how to teach culture in modern societies – and his writings have something to say to us about this even four decades later.

I have my own personal reasons for caring about this continuity, since my father worked as a young man in the same broad adult education movement as Raymond Williams. His own education was marked by injustice. He grew up in a working-class family, but at the age of 11 the scholarship place he had won on merit was awarded to another boy through nepotism. Because of lack of family resources, he left secondary school in London at 14 years of age, long before his educational abilities had been fulfilled. Yet he educated himself sufficiently to become a tutor in 1942 for the National Council of Labour Colleges (NCLC), which was affiliated to the trade unions rather than the universities (unlike the Workers' Educational Association (WEA), the wing of the adult education movement to which Williams belonged). The NCLC had traditionally put more emphasis on socialist education, which resulted in bitter institutional conflict with the WEA. It was, arguably, the NCLC which remained closer to the principle of workers' education, as Williams later recognized (1979: 79).

Looking back from this distance, the pedagogic principles shared by both wings of British adult education matter more than the differences: above all, there was the principle that education is central to democracy and must be responsive to the life experiences of those it teaches. Williams' explicit aim in the writings and teaching that later emerged as cultural studies was 'the creation of an educated and participating democracy' (1993a: 223 [1961]; cf. McIlroy, 1993). He saw democratic principles extending into the classroom:

> Popular education in any worthwhile sense begins from a conception of human beings which . . . insists that no man can judge for another man [sic], that every man has a right to the facts and skills on which real judgement is based, that, in this sense, all education depends on the acknowledgement of an ultimate human equality. (Williams, 1993b: 123–4 [1959])

This vision, as the American educational and cultural theorist Henry Giroux has seen (1992b: 163; 1994: 130), remains highly relevant today.

Giroux, like many writers discussed in this chapter, has developed his ideas of cultural studies' values in response to what he sees as a crisis – a crisis in educational and cultural authority in contemporary multicultural America as a whole: 'The emergence of the electronic media coupled with a diminishing faith in the power of human agency has undermined the traditional visions of schooling and the meaning of pedagogy' (Giroux, 1996: 73). Unlike many authoritarian attacks on American cultural collapse, Giroux is concerned to understand a real change in the conditions under which young people now make sense of the culture they live in: 'Youth . . . are faced with the task of finding their way *through a decentred cultural landscape* no longer caught in the grip of a technology of print, closed narrative structures, or the certitude of a secure economic future' (ibid.: 74, added emphasis). For example, we simply cannot assume any more that the book is the best (or main) route to cultural reflexivity in today's primarily visual, media-dominated cultures (ibid.: 51).[21] As a result, cultural studies in order to address these realities must open up possibilities for cultural production by the students themselves.

Doing cultural studies means being active as a cultural producer and doing your own theorizing about the culture around you (Giroux, 1996: 50, 52; cf. 1994: 132). This means as many people as possible getting critical skills, demystifying the processes of representation through examining how meanings are produced, and becoming aware of the underlying politics of representation. It means the possibility of 'cultural recovery' – recovering histories you have not heard before (Giroux, 1996: 89), including your own.

Seen in this light, the principle developed in the last chapter of recognizing the complexity of culture becomes 'political': it is part of expanding the possibilities for everyone to be active and critical participants in the culture around them, a question of *citizenship*. It means creating the cultural conditions for new forms of democratic political exchange: 'restoring the language of ethics, agency, power and identity' (ibid.: 53). This is the true moving force of cultural studies as a discipline. It means always listening to the experiences of others, and, as part of that, being ready for theoretical and methodological change. Raymond Williams, in a letter written at the end of his work for the WEA, reflected in these terms: 'The tutor . . . may not know the gaps between academic thinking and actual experience among many people; he [the tutor, as opposed to the student] may not know when, in the pressure of experience, a new discipline has to be created' (1993a: 224: [1961]. Cultural studies, of course, was that new discipline; and yet we are a long way from achieving, anywhere, the participatory culture for which Williams hoped.

There is no route forward other than through what Williams called 'the pressure of experience': opening up our experiences of living inside contemporary mediated, commodified cultures to reflection and dialogue, on terms that match both our need as individuals to speak and our collective obligation to listen. The result is that we cannot see culture – the space of a possible 'common culture' – as anything other than complex. Method is the route to making that complexity manageable.

The succeeding chapters look directly at the methodological challenges which cultural complexity poses.

# Notes

1 I use the term 'race' in quote marks in order to register the major critique of 'race' as a socially constructed form of difference that has characterized cultural studies and other subjects in the past decade or so: see, especially, Appiah (1986) and Gates (1986).

2 There are problems with the anthropological notion of culture, explored in Chapter 5. Some of these problems emerge implicitly later in Chapter 2, but they do not undermine the essentials of Williams' vision.

3 Ngugi (1986: 11–13); cf. Williams (1989b: 7) and see Chapter 1.

4 Cf. the early critique of Williams' *The Long Revolution* (1961) by Thompson (1961b) for its neglect of the role of conflict in the formation of cultures. Williams acknowledged this later (1979: 158).

5 See Gilroy (1992).

6 Cf. Williams (1979: 118–19). For the term 'internal colonialism', see Hechter (1975).

7 Williams does, in passing, allow for new forms of community formed around immigrant communities, but doesn't develop the point (1983: 196).

8 See Williams (1977), especially section II 3.

9 See Kember (1998: 114) for helpful discussion.

10 As Sarah Kember notes (1998: 110), there is a 'productive conflict' in Haraway between an 'allegiance to science and objectivity' and a separate allegiance to 'the politics of difference'.

11 Significantly Williams wrote critically about English writers such as Lawrence who chose exile: Williams (1958: 203).

12 This is to select drastically from a large tradition of work on the Mexican–US border: see Alvarez (1995) and more generally Chabram-Dernersesian (1999).

13 For the concept of 'double consciousness', see du Bois (1989) [1903] and Gilroy (1992).

14 For overviews of post-colonial theory, see Moore-Gilbert (1997) and Moore-Gilbert et al. (1997).

15 'Culture' is in quote marks because in Chapter 5 I re-examine the idea that there are such things as 'cultures', rather than something more complex. The principle that everyone's voice should be heard is not affected by this qualification.

16 The term 'heteroglossia' is in fact borrowed by Haraway from Bakhtin (1981).

17 For the neglect of 'listening' and 'hearing' in Western intellectual history, see Levin (1989).

18 Cf. bell hooks' important reflections on this issue (1991: 1–14).

19 For a usefully sceptical analysis of Blair's attempt at 'enlightened patriotism', see Davey (1999: ch. 1).

20 For discussion of the hostile reaction to this work in Asia, see Chen (1998: 16–19).

21 Cf. de Certeau (1993: 118–19 [1974]).

# 3  The individual 'in' culture

Where is the place that you move into the landscape and can see your-self?

Carolyn Steedman (1986: 142)

No social study that does not come back to the problems of biography, of history, and of their intersections within a society, has completed its intellectual journey.

C. Wright Mills (1970: 12 [1959])

[W]hen she realized what her situation in the world was and would probably always be she threw away every assumption she had learned and began at zero.

Toni Morrison, *The Song of Solomon* (1989: 149)

The individual self is formed within culture, and on the basis of shared cultural resources. That much is agreed across the humanities, although battles may rage about the balance between 'genetic' and 'environmental' influences on education, sexuality, and other aspects of our lives. By 'cultural resources', we can mean a vast range of things: from language, to how we hold and use our bodies, to ethical codes and imaginative horizons, right through, even, to the ways in which we imagine ourselves as distinct individuals – the social construction of 'the individual'.

While there may be broad consensus on this point, there remain a number of difficult issues. First, there is the question of the extent to which what we call 'the individual' – 'the individual self' – is in fact a single coherent entity. Questioning this has been a feature of post-structuralism, a challenge to one of the main tenets of modern thought in the West. I come back to this in Chapter 6, where my view, assumed here, that announcements of the 'death of the subject' have been exaggerated, is argued in detail.

A separate difficulty involves questioning whether the types of culture or cultural formation to which we assume individuals 'belong' are themselves stable, coherent entities. If not, our whole perspective on the individual-culture relationship must change. We can look at this problem on two levels. On one level: are there single entities called 'cultures' which are more or less attached to a particular place? This is a question, partly, about cultural flows; it is fundamental to any attempt to understand cultural experience across the world today, whether in anthropology, sociology, history, or cultural studies. I discuss this in Chapter 5.

Alternatively we can ask: what is the relationship between my cultural experience as an individual and the 'culture' within which I was formed? Can that experience be understood simply as forming 'part of' – that is, being fully encompassed by – a wider culture, or are the relations between the individual and wider cultural formations more complex, more uncertain? And if more uncertain, how far is it legitimate still to speak about the 'cultures' in which we live, as if they were single entities, cultural wholes? These questions are particularly important in understanding how cultural studies has developed and they are the subject of this chapter.

My argument is that cultural studies, until recently, has tended (although with some important exceptions) to study culture on the scale of wider cultural formations, even where it has emphasized the contradictions that operate there. This has meant paying too little attention to the scale of the individual's cultural experience (see particularly the first section below, Absent voices). As a result, cultural studies has provided relatively few insights into how individuals are formed, and how they act, 'inside' cultures.[1] Post-structuralist critiques of the subject have often only served to confuse matters.

In the second section (The problem of experience) detailed examples are used to show why ignoring the scale of individual cultural experience means missing crucial insights into what culture is. My main example comes from British cultural studies, Carolyn Steedman's biographical and autobiographical text from 1986, *Landscape for a Good Woman*, but I also draw more widely on American and European feminist work and on the recent work of the French sociologist Pierre Bourdieu.

In the final part of the chapter (Expanding the scope of cultural research) I look more broadly at the new empirical questions about culture that arise when we take seriously the complexity of individual experience. They include questions about the historical nature of experience, to which cultural studies has tended to give too little emphasis. In this and other ways, this chapter provides a preliminary working out of the methodological themes addressed more fully in later chapters.

## Absent voices

The complexity and range of people's cultural experiences is so vast that it could easily seem to defy description. Reducing that vast landscape to (more or less) functioning wholes – whether we call them 'cultures', 'mentalities', or whatever – is a dangerous undertaking for any social and cultural theory.[2]

Here, however, we need to focus only on the form that risk has taken in cultural studies, and the legacy with which it leaves us if we want to re-imagine cultural studies' method today.

### Subcultural theory

The problem of overemphasizing the unifying tendencies in cultural experi-ences and cultural production emerged in Chapter 2, when we discussed Raymond Williams. The whole burden of Williams' political and theoretical position was to emphasize that 'the making of a society is the finding of common meanings and directions' (1989b: 4 [1958]) and, therefore, to see 'the theory of culture as a theory of relations between elements in a whole way of life' (1958: 11–12). Although there is a complexity here – 'a theory of *relations between elements* in a whole way of life' (ibid., emphasis added) – the crucial point is that Williams always formulates the problem of cultural theory in terms of possible unity and coherence at the level of a whole 'culture'.

A similar formulation was shared by many other writers in early British cultural studies: indeed it was closely connected with the power and insights of the work. This can be illustrated, first, from the studies of primarily male, working-class cultural life generally known as 'subcultural' theory: for exam-ple, Cohen (1997a [1972]), Hall and Jefferson (1976) and Hebdige (1979). Initially, this body of work focused on explaining subcultural style (mods, rockers, skinheads, and so on) as a resolution, on the 'cultural' level, of conflicts experienced by British working-class youth at a 'material' level (declining opportunities for employment, conflicts with the parental gener-ation, and so on). From the outset, this approach depended on seeing cultural experience and expression as systematic unities (only if they were systematic, could they be understood as 'structural' responses to very general underlying conditions). Take, for example, the following passage from Phil Cohen's important study of working-class culture in London's East End:

> mods, parkers, skinheads, crombies are a succession of subcultures which all
> correspond to the same parent culture and which attempt to work out through

a system of transformations, the basic problematic or contradiction which is inserted in the subculture by the parent culture. So you can distinguish three levels in the analysis of subcultures: one is historical analysis which isolates the specific problematic of a class fraction, in this case, the respectable working class; and secondly a structural or semiotic analysis of the [cultural] subsystems and the way they are articulated . . .; and thirdly the phenomenological analysis of the way the subculture is actually lived out by those who are the bearers and supports of the subculture. (Cohen, 1997a: 100–101 [1972])

In this approach, the problem is not that individual experience is completely neglected, but that it only comes into the analysis *after* the key issues have already been defined at a structural level: in terms of the unities of 'subculture' and 'parent culture' and the relations between them. On this basis, then, individual experience is merely the place for working out wider structural patterns.

Dick Hebdige's analysis (1979) of popular style and music was more complex in some ways: first, because he emphasized the structural contribution to cultural expression in Britain's large cities not only of class, but ethnic relations; and, second, because he saw the connection between popular materials for cultural expression and underlying social conflicts as highly mediated – and to some extent arbitrary. Even so, Hebdige continued the tendency to discuss cultural issues in terms of wider structural unities, for example in this extract from his justly celebrated analysis of British punk:

This is not to say, of course, that all punks were equally aware of the disjunction between experience and signification upon which the whole style was ultimately based. The style no doubt made sense for the first wave of self-conscious innovators at a level which remained inaccessible to those who became punks after the subculture had surfaced and been publicized. Punk is not unique in this: the distinction between originals and hangers-on is always a significant one in subculture . . . different youths bring different degrees of commitment to a subculture. It can represent a major dimension in people's lives . . . or it can be a slight distraction . . . However, despite these individual differences, the members of a subculture must share a common language. And if a style is really to catch on, if it is to become genuinely popular, it must say the right thing at the right time. It must anticipate or encapsulate a mood, a moment. It must embody a sensibility, and the sensibility which punk style embodied was essentially dislocated, ironic and self-aware. (Hebdige, 1979: 122–3)

In this passage, Hebdige acknowledges a number of individual factors that complicate how we interpret punk experience, but they are contained in the wider narrative of what punk 'essentially' is, and that in turn is defined by reference to what its originators – not the wider range of people involved in punk – were doing.

The problems with the term 'popular culture' itself have been widely debated and there is probably a consensus that it no longer offers a useful way of identifying what cultural studies is about.[3] Rather than get lost in that debate, I want to bring out a more general point. Even at its most sophisticated, cultural studies' discussions of 'the popular' reproduced the approach that, in my view, is problematic. They formulated the important issues about culture exclusively at a broad structural level, with too little account taken of the complexity of individual cultural experience.[4] Stuart Hall, for example, in his important essay 'Notes on deconstructing "the popular"' (1981b) spelt out clearly the dangers of forgetting that what counts as 'the popular' is not a simple, natural category, but itself already a social construction. Even so, Hall argued that it was useful to think of culture in terms of a continuing and complex conflict between two large-scale structures: the 'popular' and the 'dominant' culture. This approach was rooted in wider debates in the Marxist tradition about culture's contribution to large-scale political change (the route from Marx's theory of revolution, to Gramsci, and then to Laclau and Mouffe's work of the late 1970s).[5]

Whatever the political importance of this work in its time, it creates a problematic legacy for us working in cultural studies now. It leaves little space for thinking about culture in terms of the *complexity*, perhaps even the *resistance*, involved in individuals' (apparent) accession to wider cultural forms. The Australian cultural theorist, Meaghan Morris, has formulated the difficulty very well in a critique of the British cultural studies tradition (and also, incidentally, the writings of Baudrillard). She argues that both fail to 'leave[] much space for an unequivocally pained, unambivalently discontented, or momentarily aggressive subject' (Morris, 1990: 25).

The relevance of this insight to Carolyn Steedman's work will become obvious in the next section. In Britain, Angela McRobbie (1991b [1982]) had already critiqued subcultural studies for neglecting girls and women, whose integration into male-dominated subcultures saturated by anti-female aggression was, to say the least, problematic. In fact, McRobbie's work during the 1980s was important in questioning the direction of cultural studies more generally and insisting on the need: 'to shift . . . interest *back to the living subjects themselves* . . . and to see how teenage girls interpreted some of the structural determinations of age, class, and gender in the context of their own lived experience' (McRobbie, 1991a: x, added emphasis).

This potential blind spot of cultural studies was summarized well in the mid-1980s by Richard Johnson, Stuart Hall's successor as head of the Birmingham Centre for Contemporary Cultural Studies. Here he is criticizing structuralist approaches to the media text, but the point has a wider significance:

> [in such work] there is no account of what I would call *the subjective aspects of struggle*, no account of how there is a moment in subjective flux when social subjects (individual or collective) produce accounts of who they are, as conscious political agents, that is, constitute themselves politically. To ask for such a theory is not to deny the major structuralist or post-structuralist insights: subjects are contradictory, 'in process', fragmented, produced. But human beings and social movements also strive to produce some coherence and continuity, and through this exercise some control over feelings, conditions, and destinies . . . [This] involves taking seriously what seems to me the most interesting theoretical lead: the notion of a discursive self-production of subjects, especially in the form of histories and memories. (Johnson, 1996: 103–4 [1986–87], original emphasis)

This passage contains, among other things, an important response to post-structuralist critiques of the subject, which I discuss in detail in Chapter 6. Most relevant here is how Johnson insists on looking at cultural cohesion not only at a broad structural level, but in terms of individuals' actual practices of making sense of the culture they inhabit, and, as part of that, their 'self-production [as] subjects'.

Stuart Hall's own later work was critically important in shifting focus onto the complexities of identity, provoked particularly by the highly ambivalent position of those who had grown up in the shadow of colonialism:

> Identity is formed at the *unstable* point where the 'unspeakable' stories of subjectivity meet the narratives of history, of a culture. And since he/she [the colonized subject] is positioned in relation to cultured narratives which have been profoundly expropriated, the colonized subject is always 'somewhere else': doubly marginalized, displaced always *other* than where he or she is, or is able to speak from. (Hall, 1997: 135 [1987], first emphasis added)

There is, in other words, a gap between the space from which the subject speaks and the discursive means available to him or her with which to speak. At the same time, identifying that gap allowed new identities to be formed – for example, within the ethnic, cultural and sexual politics of late 1980s Britain (as analysed in the work of Kobena Mercer (1994) and others). The foundations for empirical work on the individual's experience of culture had certainly, by the late 1980s, been laid.

It is all the more surprising, then, that little empirical work has since been done within cultural studies on 'the subjective aspects of struggle' (Johnson). I later suggest a way beyond this impasse, but it is worth first noting two issues: one relating to the 'politics' of cultural analysis and the other to underlying theoretical questions.

## Some objections to the individual perspective

The tendency of early British cultural studies to analyse cultural experience only in terms of wider cultural formations and conflicts was not a simple mistake, even if we now need to move beyond it.[6] It was a deliberate choice, based on the important desire to address issues about culture and democracy: the possibility and difficulty of constructing a 'common culture', that Raymond Williams had championed (see Chapter 2).[7] The challenge, then, is to retain that awareness of the political significance of culture without reducing its actual complexity.

That challenge works in two directions at once. On the one hand, it would be a mistake (politically, theoretically) to deny that there are very powerful forces in most contemporary societies that encourage a conformity of cultural judgement and, therefore, to some extent, of cultural experience: what the Australian cultural theorist John Frow (1995: 144–51) has usefully called 'regimes of value'. These are based, in part, on the central fact that cultural production is never 'free', but is bound into the workings of a capitalist economy, based on commodification. This directly leads on to important political issues about the unequal opportunities which people have either to participate in or to be represented by cultural production. On the other hand, it is equally a mistake (again with political consequences) to forget that individuals' relations to the highly structured cultural environment in which they live are *not* simple. These relations are full of contradictions, and the contradictions themselves are crucial to understanding wider issues of inequality.

This raises also the theoretical question of what *evidential* status we give to individuals' reflections on their experiences. This has become controversial because of influential arguments within structuralist and post-structuralist thought; these have argued that we cannot use individual testimony as evidence at all, since individual 'experience' is merely the effect of what Stuart Hall, in summarizing the structuralist position, called the 'categories, classifications and frameworks of the culture' (1981a). This is taken from Hall's well-known essay, 'Cultural studies: two paradigms', where he compares the structuralist paradigm of 'experience'(as structured from outside) with the 'culturalist' paradigm which gives more weight to 'authentic' 'lived' experience. But, as Hall points out, while there is a real conflict between the two positions, even structuralist arguments do not completely undermine an appeal to individual experience.[8] Quite the opposite is the case, in fact, since structuralism largely ignores the way that as individuals we reflect upon wider cultural forms. Of course, we can only reflect using the resources of a shared language and cultural assumptions, but that does not mean that our reflections are nothing but the 'effects' of those shared resources. The initial conditions for each person's reflexivity are, after all, different. The American sociologist and psychologist, George Herbert Mead long ago explained this relationship between the 'cultural' (or social) and the 'individual' perspective very clearly:

> The fact that all selves are constituted by or in terms of the social process, and are individual reflections of it . . . is not in the least incompatible with, or destructive of, the fact that every individual self has its own peculiar individuality, its own unique pattern; because each individual self within that process, while it reflects in its organized structure the behavior pattern of that process as a whole, does so from its own particular and unique standpoint within that process, *and this reflects in its organized structure a different aspect or perspective of this whole social behavior pattern from that which is reflected in the organized structure of any other individual self within that process* . . . the common social origin and constitution of individual selves and their structure does not preclude wide individual differences and variations among them, or contradict the peculiar and more or less distinctive individuality which each of them in fact possesses. (Mead, 1967: 201 [1934], added emphasis)

Each person carries with them an individual history of reflection which cannot be reduced to shared cultural patterns. Partly pure accident, and partly structured, this history is the trace of that person's perceiving, absorbing, interacting, reflecting, retelling, reflecting again, and so on, a sequence endured by that person alone. This very particular 'structure' is what we mean by 'experience'.

These are, of course, difficult issues, to which we return in Chapter 6. For the time being, it is worth keeping in mind a crucial distinction that is often forgotten.

There are two, quite different, ways in which we might think of wider forces (language, ideology, cultural frameworks, and so on) as influencing our experience as individuals. The first is as *determining* conditions, which would determine the specific content of experience, so that our experience would truly be reducible to those underlying conditions; it would be nothing but their working out. Alternatively, those wider forces might be merely *constitutive*, or *limiting*, conditions, which would impose some limits on the types of experience we might have (all experience, for example, is closely tied to our means for formulating it in a particular language, normally our first language), but would *not* determine specifically their content. In fact, no one has yet convincingly shown that those wider forces (ideology, and so on) are determining, rather than merely constitutive, conditions of what we experience.[9] (Indeed it makes very little sense to say that, for example, the English language 'determines' the experiences of those who speak it: how, if it did, could we go on speaking new sentences and thinking new thoughts?) Yet post-structuralist claims about the illusory nature of 'the subject' often talk in terms of how it is 'produced' (that is, determined), confusing this with the more limited and much more plausible claim that it is constrained by those forces. The confusion, or sliding, of terms is crucial since it leads to a drastic exaggeration of the influence upon us of shared language and cultural forms.[10]

## The problem of experience

### Carolyn Steedman's *Landscape for a Good Woman*

If we are serious about studying culture, we cannot avoid listening to the individual voice. I have argued this, negatively, against the grain of some early British cultural studies, but here I want to put the point more positively through specific examples of where the individual perspective on culture makes a difference.

A good starting point is Carolyn Steedman's extraordinary double biography (1986) of her mother's life and her own childhood. Steedman grew up in the 1950s in a reasonably comfortable, but unhappy working-class family in south London. Her parents came from an industrial town in the North-West of England and their relationship fell apart shortly after Steedman's younger sister was born, although for some time her father continued to live, estranged, in the house. Whereas her relationship with her father was distant, Steedman's often difficult relationship with her mother was intense, and is intensely remembered. Steedman's account of her own growing up is closely tied with her piecing together her mother's life from her own memories, supplemented by her historical research. It is Steedman's account of her mother on which I focus.

The book is far from a straightforward biography or autobiography, as Steedman makes clear early on: 'this is not to say that this book involves a search for a past, or for what really happened. It is about how people *use the past* to tell the stories of their life' (Steedman, 1986: 8, added emphasis). The book is concerned not just with a particular life, but with the conditions under which people's stories of themselves are constructed. As such, the book presents a fundamental challenge to cultural studies' neglect of the individual's relation to culture.

It is important, however, to point out that this is just one strand of debate within the book. Steedman critiques many other confusions: the superficial understanding of working-class consciousness in Britain (particularly the experiences of working-class women), oversimplified theories of patriarchy and psychoanalytic accounts of growing up, and myths about girls' and women's 'natural' relationship to motherhood. In particular, the book contains a detailed dialogue with psychoanalytic perspectives, which it would be interesting to explore in detail. However, as I mentioned in Chapter 1, there are deep-seated theoretical issues relating to the role of psychoanalysis in cultural studies which are beyond the scope of this book. To keep the discussion within bounds, those issues are put to one side.

With this qualification, we can analyse the challenge Steedman poses to cultural studies' method in terms of a number of elements. First, as she tries to show through the details of her mother's life, we need 'a sense of people's complexity of relationship to the historical situations they inherit' (1986: 19). People do not simply 'take on' the general narratives of their time, since each person is actively involved in the often difficult task of making sense of *their* life, *their* conditions, *their* failures. As a result, 'personal interpretations of past time – the stories that people tell themselves in order to explain how they got to the place they currently inhabit – are often in deep and ambiguous conflict with the official interpretative devices of a culture' (ibid.: 6). To give a specific example, Steedman discusses from many angles her mother's misgivings about bearing and bringing up children. Yet she also insists that her mother was a good mother, and that this was a role which her mother explicitly sought to play. This leads Steedman to comment on how people inhabit the stereotypical roles that are required of them:

> her presentation of herself as a good mother shows also with what creativity people may use the stuff of cultural and social stereotype, so that it becomes not a series of labels applied from outside a situation, but *a set of metaphors ready for transformation* by those who are its subjects. (ibid.: 103, added emphasis)

We should, then, be very careful about assuming that individuals inhabit easily, without contradiction, the roles and descriptions assigned to them within the wider culture: this applies as much to people's apparent engagement with popular culture as to anything else.

Another point on which Steedman insists is the significance, the non-triviality, of her mother's longing for some degree of material comfort. People's engagement with 'ordinary' material culture (everyday clothes, household goods, and so on) and their dreams of material prosperity have normally been downplayed in cultural studies compared to more exciting, more conventionally 'cultural' interests (music, films, books, the leading edge of fashion).[11] But, as Steedman convincingly shows (1986: 108–9), the longing for material goods of people who are poor, or feel themselves poor, is just as culturally and politically significant as those other areas. Far from being 'merely' materialistic, they express a desire to be included in wider society, to have what others take for granted.

This connects in turn with issues of politics. Steedman's mother came from a Labour background, but herself voted Conservative: on the face of it, the very opposite of cultural studies' favoured narrative of politically accented 'resistance' by those in subordinate groups. But Steedman argues that such resistance narratives miss completely the meaning of her mother's politics, leaving it only to be interpreted as self-seeking materialism. Voting Conservative, for Steedman's mother, was a way of expressing publicly her dissatisfaction at *not* being included in any wider political community and affirming her desire for a life that was different – a true 'politics of envy'. Conservatism gave her mother 'a public language that allowed her to want, and to express her resentment at being on the outside, without the material possessions enjoyed by those inside the gate' (1986: 121).

Two important implications follow from all of this. One is that people have to construct their lives and their sense of self from whatever means, and in whatever conditions, are available: we cannot understand an individual's cultural experience, unless we fully grasp this point.[12] For example, the sense people make of the culture around them is crucially affected by their awareness of inequality and *their* position in the social hierarchy: in Britain (notoriously) this is articulated through perceptions of class difference, which in turn (as Steedman and many other writers[13] have insisted) is closely intertwined with gender inequality. If you do not regard yourself as 'inside the gate' in Steedman's phrase, then your use of shared cultural resources is likely to be marked by tension, not simple identification.

Another implication follows. A crucial dimension of inequality, Steedman suggests, is precisely the fact of whether you are 'outside' or 'inside' the central narratives of your society and culture. Being of higher social status is, broadly, to be closer to those central narratives, to have a ready place in them; being of lower status is to know that your individual story, your most significant experiences, are more likely to be classed as marginal – or, at best, 'ordinary'. These are real exclusions, and they work right through to the question of whose experiences 'matter', whose lives count as significant 'stories'. As a result, Steedman argues that the stories she tells

> *aren't stories* in their own right: they exist in tension with other more central ones. In the same way, the processes of working-class autobiography, of people's history and of the working-class novel cannot show a proper and valid culture existing in its own right, underneath the official forms, waiting for revelation. Accounts of working-class life are told by tension and ambiguity *out on the borderlands*. The story – my mother's story, a hundred thousand others – cannot be absorbed into the central one. (ibid.: 22, added emphasis)

Individuals' relationship to cultural formations, including 'popular' culture, may then be profoundly ambiguous and uncertain, 'out on the borderlands' (cf. Giroux, 1992a). Taking seriously each person's reflexivity about their place in culture is a necessity, not a luxury; it may involve reassessing what we think of as the central 'stories' of a particular culture or time.

## Not identifying . . .

*Landscape for a Good Woman* is an original, and particular, history. But other important challenges to the familiar narratives of cultural studies have been developed by British feminist writers during the 1990s.

Valerie Walkerdine's (1997) important work on young girls and popular culture has argued against the assumption, implicit in some cultural studies work, that working-class lives are simply 'boring' (and, therefore, not worth commenting on) unless they can be interpreted as 'resistance' to wider power structures, for example because not involved in radical or spectacular forms of cultural expression (ibid.: 19). Making that judgement ignores the reality of people's lives away from the political 'cutting edge', the complex experience of 'coping and surviving' with material and symbolic inequalities (ibid.: 21). Think, for example, of how the fantasy of being included in some way in major cultural forms such as television or film – what Walkerdine summarizes in historical terms as the fantasy of 'getting on the stage'(1997: 142–3)[14] – is itself marked by class. For Walkerdine, the relations of individuals to widely available popular culture are anything but 'natural'; far from popular culture simply 'expressing' some pre-existing sentiments, it is the lack of other means of legitimated self-expression that makes people's uses of popular culture so important – and so difficult to research.[15]

The sociologist Beverley Skeggs (1997) has pursued parallel themes in relation to the issue of English working-class women's attempts to achieve social 'respectability'. Once again, the complexity of individuals' relationships to available cultural resources and stereotypes becomes clear, for example, in Skeggs' account of what she calls 'passing': in other words, working-class women passing, more or less successfully, as middle-class through various forms of performance. This is not simply self-directed social advancement, but a consequence of something deeper: the fact that those women did not have available to them narratives through which they could speak positively about themselves as working-class women (1997: 95). As a result, they worked on performing another class position. This represents not so much a desire to be middle class, as a desire *not* to be regarded as 'merely' working class (ibid.: 87):

> The women may make disidentifications from being positioned as working class but this does not mean to say that they want to take on the whole

package of being middle class. Whilst the imaginary middle class may represent elegance and sophistication, the real middle class may behave in ways the women do not want to be associated with . . . They cannot pass as completely middle class because they do not want to. They respect (and resent) the power of the middle classes but despise them for the power they affect. (Skeggs, 1997: 93)

Skeggs here raises the issue of *disidentification*: people's lack of fit with their ascribed social position(s). Although it is individuals who feel it, disidentification connects with something far beyond the individual: the unequal distribution of the resources through which people can describe themselves, which is itself related to inequalities of class, gender and age – and, in other contexts, 'race' and sexuality.

The issue of disidentification is relevant to cultural studies internationally, far beyond the British context and debates over class. The US feminist theorist Judith Butler (1993), for example, whose work is concerned with challenging inequalities around the naturalization of compulsory heterosexuality, has argued that our identities are formed at a fundamental level by reference to an 'order' which excludes certain sexual identities (particularly lesbian identities) as 'unspeakable', 'impossible'. At the same time, our fit to this 'order' is not complete; there are also potential countervailing forces: 'Does politicization always need to overcome disidentification? What are the possibilities of politicizing *dis*identification, this experience of *misrecognition*, this uneasy sense of standing under a sign to which one does and does not belong?' (Butler, 1993: 219, original emphasis). The French lesbian theorist Monique Wittig closes her influential book, *The Straight Mind and Other Essays* (1992), by emphasizing the uncertain position of each individual both inside and outside the available narratives of their culture. Yet we must retain, she argues, the dream of 'tear[ing] open the closely woven material of the commonplaces, . . . to continually prevent their organisation into a system of compulsory meaning' (1992: 100). It is clear, in other words, that what I am calling the 'individual' perspective is highly provocative for gender, sexual and class politics.

The complexity of the individual's relationship to cultural formations can also be pursued in the area of 'race' and ethnic difference. The late twentieth century has seen no reduction in the compulsory movement of peoples across cultural boundaries, not only because of war, but also due to the need to find work (usually matching the receiving country's requirements for cheap, unofficial labour) – the plight of what Avtar Brah (1996: 201) has called 'the undocumented worker', for example in Europe, the Middle East or on the Mexican–US border.

Stuart Hall's theorizations of hybrid identity in the late 1980s have already been mentioned as a way of opening up perspectives on such situations. An important recent source of individual narratives of displacement is the collection of interviews, *La Misère du Monde*, directed and edited by the French sociologist Pierre Bourdieu (1993). This collection is significant for cultural studies,[16] partly for the affirmation by one of the world's leading sociologists of culture that individual stories *must be listened to* and that without them our picture of the social terrain is inadequate (1993: 16–17). Its many interviews demonstrate beyond doubt what an indispensable resource individual voices are. Here, for example, is a retired factory worker, called Abbas, who emigrated to France from Algeria in 1951 and now has come to reflect bitterly on the consequences:

> How did we arrive here? Are we the same? The same creatures that we were on the first day [we emigrated]? What changed our state of being? [*meta-morphosés* – explained by the interviewer, as a transformation in the form of a 'curse'] When did this date from? We didn't see it coming, the change fell upon us when it was too late to react to it. One must accept it, as it is . . . [later in the interview] God is too strong . . .! There are moments when you must resolve to accept what can't be avoided: we went against it, pushed against it as much as we could. But the reality is there: we can't live alone in the world; we are in France: whether it pleases us or not, France is there, we're in its guts, and it's normal that it'll finish up in our guts, by entering our guts, even if it hasn't entered our hearts. As for me, France has never and will never enter my heart, and I don't hide it, I never stop saying it, I live it every day. (Bourdieu, 1993: 1272, 1297, my translation)

This interview is a powerful portrayal of exile (the difficulty, as Abbas puts it, of leaving one country, and not finding in the new country 'your place', ibid.: 1288). Bourdieu's collection contains many other stories – unresolved, subtly articulated – of displacement. It may sound as if Bourdieu is returning us to a naive individualism, where individual voices are taken at face value. But this is far from the case: the point of orchestrating these individual voices is to bring out the structural patterns working within the details of their lives, which a more general social theory (or equally empirical survey work) could never uncover (cf. Bourdieu, 1996).

Wherever we turn, then – whether below the surface of class or gender politics in one country, or to the experiences of those who have moved between countries – we find voices that cut across any simple notion of the individual as merely a 'part of' a cultural 'whole'. Addressing this is, fundamentally, a political question about who gets heard. The photographer Jo Spence, who did a great deal to challenge gender and ageist stereotypes in Britain in the 1970s and 1980s, expressed the issue eloquently in some reflections on her self-portraits:

By giving expression to this part of my history, I stand in contradiction to those who have the power to repress or deny the experiences of others. In so doing, they make our experiences appear ordinary, robbing them of any importance or potency. If I don't find a language to express and share my subjectivity, I am in danger of forgetting what I already know. (Spence, 1995: 134–5)

What are the implications of this principle for empirical work on culture?

## Expanding the landscape of cultural research

We live in societies and cultures where individuals are spoken *for*, much more than they speak in their own name – and they are not necessarily spoken for accurately. As Michael Pickering has put it, '"experience" remains analytically important because misinterpretations of the experiences of others abound' (1997: 178). When so many people's lives are standardly judged not 'interesting' enough to hear, cultural studies – informed by the values of cultural democracy (cf. Chapter 2) – should operate on the principle that *each person's* voice, and reflexivity, matters.[17] This seems straightforward, but I want to show how following through the implications of this principle transforms the landscape of cultural studies research.

### Whose cultural experience?

If our aim is to understand how cultures work, there can be no 'favouritism' in who we study. This means researching cultural experience on all sides of important social and cultural divisions.

Take the example of contemporary dance music. We need to understand the engagement with dance of both men and women, people of high social status and of low social status, and whatever their ethnic identity. Equally, of course, we need to look closely at how such social divisions are bridged, and how far they continue to be reproduced, through the consumption and production of this music. Although there has been important work which takes that responsibility seriously,[18] it is worth emphasizing that to study popular music consumption in this way – that is, *across* class status and other divisions – undermines the implicit assumption of much earlier cultural studies work that it was dealing principally, or even entirely, with the taste of *subordinate* groups. How can we possibly assume this, given the broad availability and popularity of dance music?

Alternatively, take cultural studies' work on television and film. This has rarely, if ever, considered the engagements of people with high cultural and/or economic capital. Some writers, rather unfairly, have argued that this is because media studies is complicit with a project of pathologizing the working class, maintaining it under surveillance (Hartley, 1987; Walkerdine, 1997). This ignores the potential practical difficulties in doing ethnography in the living rooms of the rich and powerful, resulting precisely from the fact that they *are* rich and powerful! This has been an issue as much for anthropology as for cultural studies (Lamont, 1992). But the gap in cultural studies research remains.

Perhaps the most intractable blind spot in cultural studies research has been age. Although never stated explicitly, there has been an assumption that the experiences of the old are just not worth studying. We need to be clear that the other side of the countless celebrations of 'youth culture' is *the silencing* of the cultures of the old. Cultural studies has failed completely to challenge the discriminations against the old which operate in British and many other societies (Hazan, 1994).[19] Perhaps this is one reason why cultural studies has given so little emphasis to studying social memory: that is, the passing of cultural material between generations.[20] Yet, if we are interested in understanding the complexity of individuals' experience of culture, then surely it is important to understand how those from one generation (the old) use the high proportion of cultural production directed at those younger than them – or if not, understand their lack of engagement with it. Are they alienated by it or do they find ways of engaging positively with it? The answer as yet is: we do not know.

In these various ways, we need to integrate into cultural studies' research the 'others' whom it has unconsciously excluded.

### What type of cultural experience?

There is also no justification for favouritism in what aspects of culture we study. Cultural studies cannot be about 'popular' culture alone; it must also encompass 'high' and 'middlebrow' culture (as Simon Frith argued more than a decade ago in relation to music: 1986). This applies even if we argue that these divisions are being destabilized to some extent – for example, in the area of music, by commercial pressures and the influence of television (an obvious example in Britain would be the limited popularization of classical opera in the 1990s focused particularly around 'the Three Tenors'). In fact, until we study in greater depth the full range of cultural materials that individuals consume, we cannot hope to deal theoretically with the changes to the landscape of taste that may, or may not, be occurring.[21]

Nor is it helpful to prioritize between different areas of cultural consumption on 'political' grounds. Even if in some cases we are sure that a particular type of music or film is more radical, more politically engaged, than others, that provides no special reason for studying its consumption. There is, in any case, always the question of how such material is absorbed by individuals *alongside* the less innovative, the less radical. Clearly, there are historical moments when large groups of people, for a time, make drastic choices about what they will and will not consume. It is important to understand those moments (punk in Britain in the late 1970s would be one such moment), but the normal flow of people's consumption may actually be rather messier and less consistent.[22]

I return to these issues in relation to 'texts' in Chapter 4.


## Historical dimensions

Studying the range and complexity of individuals' cultural experience means taking seriously its 'historical' dimension, the trajectory of people's tastes and their reflections on them.[23] Recall the passage quoted earlier from Richard Johnson on 'the self-production of subjects, especially in the form of histories and memories' (1996: 104 [1986–87]), or equally Carolyn Steedman's emphasis on 'personal interpretations of past time' (1986: 6). Each person's story of their life 'inside' culture is a significant history, however difficult it may be to disentangle.

If this is true for individuals, it must also be true on a larger scale. As part of the values discussed in Chapter 2, cultural studies has consistently engaged with the present realities of the cultural environments we inhabit, but there is a great danger of exaggerating the importance of present phenomena unless we apply a historically informed sense of the material processes which form our 'presents' and our 'pasts'. Cultural studies cannot do without a sense of history, an awareness of the historical production of the cultural surfaces with which it has to engage. As Meaghan Morris argues in a powerful and subtle meditation on the necessity for a historical dimension to cultural studies, we must avoid in cultural description 'a complicity between the aesthetic problematic of the exemplary object, the singular site, "the" text, and . . . a linear model of historical time in which the inevitable . . . is realized' (1998: 21).

One of the continuing functions of history – both traditional history and Foucault's genealogical history (1977b) – is to disrupt our naturalized sense of 'the present'. Steedman's work illustrates this in the case of personal narrative. Yet the uses of history in cultural studies are underdeveloped (C. Hall, 1992; Steedman, 1992; Pickering, 1997) and *comparative* historical research in cultural studies remains just a dream.

## The real politics of cultural analysis

Some of my suggestions may sound like a blueprint for a sociology of culture divorced from values or political commitment, which is exactly what I argued against in Chapter 2. But, as always, it is a question of *where* politics enters the analysis. An underlying argument in this chapter has been that, if politics enters at the level of dictating what forms of cultural experience – or what types of people – we study, then it can only distort our picture of the cultural terrain.

Politics must enter the analysis at a different point, in foregrounding the issues of power and inequality within all culture, and their bases in the material workings of culture: its exclusions, its inclusions, its contradictions, and in each case their basis in other structures (social, economic). If, as I've argued, we cannot ignore the individual's perspective on these processes, then we must look closely at how these power issues affect the individual's cultural experience: the resources which the individual does, or does not, have to exercise choice over what or whether she or he consumes or produces, whether she or he speaks or is spoken for. It is in insisting on these issues that so-called political economy approaches have been very helpful (for example, Golding, 1990), although they have no monopoly on them (Couldry, 2000: ch. 9).

We confront here starkly the issue of choice. It is definitely *not* the case that all people have an equal range of cultural activities from which to choose, and the reasons can be economic, social and/or cultural. Cultural studies has to take much more seriously than before the possibility that many people's 'engagement' with wider culture is less a matter of choice than the result of lack of alternatives.[24] The Australian cultural theorist Stuart Cunningham expressed this well, when he called for cultural studies to shift

> its command metaphors away from rhetorics of resistance, progressiveness and anti-commercialism on the one hand, and populism on the other, towards those of access, equity, empowerment, and the divination of opportunities to exercise appropriate cultural leadership. (Cunningham, 1991: 21, quoted in Bennett, 1993: 68 [1992])

This connects with broader issues of citizenship and community which are raised in Chapter 7.

The power invested in cultural studies intellectuals (to speak and write about culture) is itself, of course, an important part of the equation here; if we take seriously a commitment to cultural democracy, we should be suspicious also about that voice, using it tactically and cautiously. Empirical research, whatever its limitations, is one important tactic to open up what can otherwise easily become rather isolated theoretical positions. As Beverley

Skeggs put it in describing her own work: 'this book shows how theory can be radically transformed if others are let in on the conversation' (1997: 2) – that is, 'let in' through interview-based research.

This is no naive empiricism. Issues of power, for example, mean that we cannot simply take interview material at face value. This is not only because of the power relations involved in the research process itself, but also because we have to weigh our hopes for what our research will 'reveal', with the possibility of silence: the sheer difficulty of speaking about certain issues and from certain positions. As Valerie Walkerdine (1997: 43) has eloquently written, what is passed down through families is not necessarily 'a spoken history, but a silence'. The same is true of the wider culture. Culture and power are entangled even in the 'evidence' on which we base our cultural claims.

## The complexity of action and talk

I have not considered in any detail in this chapter what researching individual cultural experience might involve. The contentious issues lie at a more general level. Even so, it is worth giving a sense of the terrain.

Studying cultural experience must involve looking at a number of processes, which may or may not mesh neatly together. These are basically action and talk (a useful, if crude, division): see Figure 3.1. By 'action', I mean (a) the actual consumption choices people make, their tastes, their level of engagement, and (b) the direct interpretations people make of what they consume. By 'talk', I mean (a) people's talk about what they consume in its wider aspects and (b) their reflections, more widely, about their relationship with wider cultural formations. The last item can expand into many areas not directly related to cultural consumption, including people's own participation in cultural production.[25]

Both aspects of experience – action and talk – need further unpacking. It may seem simple, for example, to take people's tastes in music as a starting point and explore the associations which that music has for them. But the question of how identity connects with music is not straightforward. We cannot simply take individual tastes at face value, for a number of reasons. First, because they can be seen in terms of a strategy (which may not be consciously formulated) of social positioning and capital acquisition (Bourdieu, 1984). Second, because identity is not simply expressed in music but to some extent – perhaps even to a large extent – is found *through* music (Frith, 1996). We recognize an affinity with others through music which (without music) we might not have articulated at all.

People's talk about culture adds another level of complexity, because of the

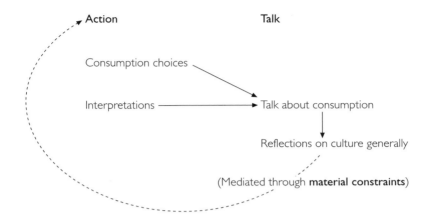

FIGURE 3.1  *Cultural experience*

complexity of talk itself, and the myriad ways in which power relations and ideology are reproduced through it. For a superb example of how to analyse this, see Michael Billig's study of people's talk about the British royalty (1992). Far from talk being a simple process of reproducing shared beliefs or attitudes, Billig shows convincingly that it is through the ways people argue, joke, and contradict themselves about royalty – the complex patterns of talk and 'rhetoric' – that an ideological form of thinking is reproduced. Studying the texture of individual voices, in other words, if done properly, brings us back inexorably to wider structural issues about power and the workings of social and cultural institutions – which is exactly where we should be.

In the next two chapters, I shift focus and look at the issues concerning the complexity of culture that arise when we take a trans-individual perspective – in relation, respectively, to texts and cultural flows.

## Suggestions for further thinking

1   Take as an example a particular object from popular culture: say, a dance music form, the music of a particular group, a particular film or television series, a fashion 'look'. Think back to the passage from Dick Hebdige's *Subculture* quoted towards the beginning of this chapter, and

how he distinguishes between different levels of engagement with punk style. With this in mind, think about the *different* types of engagement you might have with the object you've chosen, drawing on your own experience or that of people you know, but also on media representations of why people like it. Can these types of engagement with the same object be understood together – as forming a 'style' or 'taste' – or would this be to obscure important differences between them?

2  Think of the cultural tastes of anyone you know well. Can you see a coherent pattern to them? How can you relate them to that person's history? Find out if that person finds your account convincing; if not, think about where, and why, your accounts differ.

3  With the example of Carolyn Steedman's *Landscape for a Good Woman* in mind, read a biography or autobiography of a well-known figure, and think about what it reveals of that individual's relationship to the wider cultural formations in which they grew up and the possible difficulties of that relationship. You can choose a book of any sort, even if it is 'ghost-written'. In each case, think both about what is said, and what might have been omitted; think both about the individual narrative presented, and about the wider set of narrative forms *through which* that life has been told (or perhaps *not* told).

4  Keeping in mind the principles set out in the final section of this chapter, develop your own suggestions for researching culture which take seriously the perspective of the individual. Identify both what might be important about the particular topic and the further, comparative studies it might generate.

## Notes

1  In this chapter I deliberately use the term 'individual', rather than the less compromised term 'self' or the Foucauldian term 'subject', leaving until Chapter 6 discussion of the implications of post-structuralist critiques of the notion of individual experience. These are not, however, as devastating for the 'individual' perspective on culture as is usually assumed.

2  See, for parallel discussions in other disciplines, Lloyd (1990) and Sperber (1985).

3  See, for example, in defence of the study of 'the popular', Chambers (1986), Fiske (1987), and Schudson and Mukerji (1990); and for important critiques, Frith (1986: 53–8), Nowell-Smith (1987), O'Shea and Schwarz (1987), Morris (1990), McGuigan (1992), and above all the brilliant recent analysis in Frow (1995: ch. 2). Cf. also Chapter 1.

4  Cf. Hannerz (1992: 69–75) for penetrating comments on the concept of 'subculture'.

5  See Frow (1995: 75–80) for helpful discussion.

6  David Morley makes a similar assessment of cultural studies' early focus on 'the popular' (1998: 494–5).

7  Something similar could be argued for American cultural studies: see, for example, Grossberg (1992).

8  It is sometimes wrongly assumed that Hall simply opts for the structuralist view of the individual; in fact, as usual, his position is more subtle (cf. Hall, 1996a).

9  Cf. Seyla Benhabib's critique (1992a: 213–16) of Judith Butler (1990) along those lines. For helpful discussion of this debate, see Benjamin (1998: 82–8).

10  Joan Scott's well-known essay on '"Experience"' (1992) sometimes makes this slide: compare the passage at p. 25 ('we need to attend to the historical processes that, through discourse, position subjects and *produce* their experiences': apparently a determining condition) with her denial of linguistic determinism (at p. 34). Because of this slide, Scott's argument has been taken as a more drastic attack on the use of individual testimony in history, or equally cultural studies (see Appleby et al., 1994, ch. 6; Pickering, 1997: ch. 7), than perhaps intended. For a clear discussion of the distinction between determining and limiting (or constitutive) conditions, and its importance for assessing post-structuralist attacks on social research, see Bohman (1991: 112–32); and cf. recently Bowie (1997: 113).

11  For a similar critique, see Walkerdine (1997), who points out the connection with Raymond Williams' understanding of people's desires for better material conditions (Walkerdine, 1997: 11–12, quoting Williams, 1958: 310–11).

12  Compare Ulf Hannerz's concept of the individual 'perspective': 'people . . . manage meanings from where they are in the social structure' (1992: 65). I come back, in Chapter 5, to Hannerz's fascinating work.

13  See Skeggs (1997) and Walkerdine (1997), discussed below.

14  The issue of why people want to appear on television has been almost completely ignored by cultural studies, yet it is vital to questions of participation (or otherwise) in contemporary cultures: see Priest (1995) and Couldry (2000).

15  I have developed a similar argument about the apparent explosion of popular politics in the wake of Princess Diana's death (Couldry, 1999a).

16  There is, I admit, an irony in cultural studies drawing on the work of Bourdieu when he has recently written with great hostility about the very idea of cultural studies. Cultural studies, according to Bourdieu and Wacquant (1999: 47), is merely a production of the international publishing industry, although their knowledge of cultural studies' history and debates appears to be minimal. Thanks to Jim McGuigan for pointing out this reference.

17  In addition to the writers discussed in the previous section, there is important work in psychology that supports this position, inspired particularly by the Harvard psychologist Carol Gilligan: Gilligan (1982) and Taylor et al. (1995).

18  Thornton (1995), Hesmondhalgh (1998) and Sharma et al. (1998).

19  Very rare exceptions are Philo (1990: 88–94), Tulloch (1990: 42–7) and, in cultural sociology, Featherstone and Wernick (1995).

20  Recent work in Jewish cultural studies is an exception (Boyarin and Boyarin, 1997).

21  Clearly there is a need to update Bourdieu's (1984) monumental study of taste, which is based on surveys from the early 1960s.

22  One of the few works within British media studies seriously to study individual

tastes in television consumption was David Morley's *Family Television* (1986), but the idea would clearly be worth updating now in relation to television and other media.

23  Cf. the important argument of Pickering (1997).

24  Konrad Lodziak (1987), for example, has made this argument in relation to television.

25  On the importance of not isolating how people consume from how, in other contexts, they may be cultural producers, see Radway (1988).

# 4 Questioning the text

I don't read during the day. It's at night-time, when I go to bed . . . And
it is only magazines that I read . . . Just have trouble sleeping, which
everybody does, and that is what started me reading in bed . . . to put me
to sleep.

Mary Croston, interviewee quoted in Hermes (1995: 34)

the world is full of abandoned meanings

Don DeLillo, *White Noise* (1985: 184)

Our cultural life is saturated by texts, especially media texts. Cultural studies cannot, therefore, do without textual analysis; indeed many have argued
that textual analysis is the method which distinguishes it from, say, cultural
sociology.[1] As elsewhere, I do not spend time debating what is 'the' method
of cultural studies, since different methods have their advantages in different
circumstances and can, in any case, be combined: textual analysis with interviews, observations, and so on. Instead, I focus on the more general, and
more fundamental, question: what does it mean to do effective textual analysis in the context of contemporary cultural studies? More bluntly: what are
'texts'? At what level can we usefully analyse the textual environments we
inhabit? In contemporary cultures of exceptional textual density and complexity, serious doubts arise about these questions.[2]

The traditional literary model of textual analysis started out from a limited
selection of texts (the 'canon') and aimed either to elucidate their meanings
and debate their significance ('exegesis') or to find out how those texts produced their effects ('analysis'), or both. Both exegesis and analysis depend on
prior value judgements: obviously about the merit of texts themselves, but
also (more subtly) about the judgement of a particular type of reader – the
critic or (more recently) the semiotician, that is, someone who is assumed to
make correct or authoritative judgements. Cultural studies, emerging as it
did from literary studies, has always critiqued the narrowness of such value

judgements.[3] In response, as it were, some literary theorists such as Stanley Fish (1980) have admitted the purely rhetorical status of literary judgements, and refused to disguise them beneath claims about absolute values or cultural necessity.

That might seem to be the end of the matter, since critical discussion about literary value (provided it admits that it cannot be other than partisan and particular) would seem to be an important part of our cultural conversation. But in deciding whether literary models still have anything to offer to cultural studies, we have to ask a further question: what is the *methodological* function of value judgements about texts and readings? They work, I would argue, to limit the complexity and vastness of the textual field: selecting from the range of available texts those to which we have to pay close attention; selecting from the range of possible readings those which can serve as reference points for establishing meanings. Such value judgements are stabilizing devices[4] in textual fields which, in reality, are far from stable – or at least so complex that we have as yet few reliable means of describing where their stability lies.

Ask different, broadly sociological questions – what are the social or cultural effects of particular texts or what does it mean for a text to have social significance? – and these stabilizing or simplifying devices begin to look like part of the problem, not part of the solution. Surely, to put it crudely, we have to allow for the possibility that a particular text (whether a novel, a film or a TV programme)[5] may not matter much at all, or at least not matter in the ways that its 'expert readers' expect or think appropriate. The important question becomes not what is a text 'in itself', or for a community of expert readers,[6] but how does a text get taken up in particular social and cultural formations? Or in relation to the mass of media texts with which we are confronted: 'how and when [does] everyday media use become[] meaningful?' (Hermes, 1993: 493). This raises the interesting possibility that our uses of media texts may not always be 'meaningful' at all, in which case *textual* analysis can only ever be part of the point.

It is this sociologically informed approach to texts which, I would suggest, is most useful for cultural studies, although of course it can always draw on the alternative two approaches (exegesis and analysis) to establish the possible meanings and impact of, say, a film and to analyse how formally they are produced. If we are really interested in articulating the connections between culture and power, as cultural studies is (see Chapter 1), then we are simply required to ask: what effects does that text actually have on social practice, what types of cultural experiences are in practice associated with seeing it? This approach can, and should, abandon the older stabilization devices, because they obscure the wider question we want to investigate:

what type of order or coherence (at the level of what texts and whose readings matter) is there in the textual field?

This raises an ontological question (evaded by literary approaches): what is a text, when considered as a social object? It is this question which is so difficult to answer in cultures characterized by a massive proliferation of texts. I argue that cultural studies itself has often neglected this question,[7] and this neglect underlies uncertainties within cultural studies about other problems, whether epistemological (how are we in a position to know about texts?) or methodological (how best, in practice, should we analyse texts?). By focusing firmly on the underlying ontological questions – what is a text? what is a textual environment? – I explore how we can radicalize cultural studies' approach to textual analysis and make it more adequate to deal with the complexity of the textual cultures we inhabit.

This means de-centring[8] the position of 'the text' as it is normally understood (as a discrete unit of analysis: Ang, 1996: 67) – another reason why I am less concerned with which detailed method of textual analysis (say, semiotics or narratology) works better. First, we have to ask: on what terms can we go on thinking, and talking, about 'texts' *at all* in cultures where, in a sense, we have too many texts? This difficult question will be explored in each of this chapter's sections, drawing critically on the work of a number of authors.

## The challenge of too many texts

Early cultural studies, by rejecting the arbitrary barriers which had previously excluded the vast majority of texts as not 'worth studying', in a way made things worse – and the problem has intensified. Whereas 1950s cultural theorists addressed a handful of television and radio channels, popular music and novels, and advertisements, by the 1980s and 1990s the field of study was much greater: not only countless TV and radio channels but also video and computer games – and most recently the textual universe of the World Wide Web (with its associated phenomenon of the 'hypertext'). In addition, cultural theorists became increasingly aware of the phenomenon of *inter*-textuality:[9] the dense network of interconnections between texts, which, arguably, it is as important to understand as the texts themselves.

Let's take an obvious example. No serious textual study of the *Star Wars* 'prequel' *The Phantom Menace* (Lucasfilms, dir. George Lucas, 1999) can avoid analysing many other types of text apart from the film itself: the publicity narratives, the books of the film, the countless merchandising images, the computer games (*The Phantom Menace* and *Racer*), and many other texts constructed off the back of the film event. My favourite (as an illustration of how the *Star Wars* cover can be used) was an article in the high-circulation celebrity magazine *OK* promoting a visit by a British TV celebrity to the locations where *The Phantom Menace* was filmed: the article came with an invitation to compete for a holiday in Tunisia visiting the locations, itself promoting a travel company.[10] A high-profile media text such as *The Phantom Menace* focuses a whole field of proliferating texts, and this complexity is driven by obvious commercial pressures. If we place *The Phantom Menace* in its own wider context (the *Star Wars* series, all the associated fan literatures and practices, the whole history of cross-marketed merchandise-saturated Hollywood blockbuster films), it is clear that we need to understand not one discrete text but a vast space of more or less interconnected texts, and how that space is ordered. And this is just one of many interconnected regions of contemporary textual production.

In a vast textual universe, we must ask different questions about texts or, at least, address old questions in a different way. As a first attempt at handling the complexity of these issues, let's distinguish three levels: texts, textuality and tactics.

## Texts

We need to ask: On what scale is it really useful still to talk about 'texts'? In other words: What is the basic unit of analysis in thinking about textual production as a social phenomenon? Can we still talk here about '*the* text'? This may seem a strange question until we realize that, even in literary analysis, the apparent obviousness of treating the book, or play, or poem as the basic unit of analysis rests on certain conventions for thinking about authorship. These conventions continue to be influential of course; to treat the film *The Phantom Menace* as 'the text' 'created' by George Lucas is backed by a certain industry and marketing logic. The problem, however, is that since the actual textual field surrounding, say, a film is so complex and has so many participants, to treat the film text in isolation seems highly artificial from a methodological point of view.

If, as we saw, the canon of highly valued texts was a way of limiting the complexity of the textual field, and making analysis manageable, perhaps we need something similar for the wider textual environment, but based on more transparent criteria. What we need is a criterion for isolating those sites in the vast textual field which are useful 'units' of textual analysis. This is what I mean by the term 'text'; and, as a working definition we can call a 'text' a complex of interrelated meanings which its readers tend to interpret as a discrete, unified whole. To take a slightly flippant, negative example: the information and commentary on the side of the average cereal packet probably has little significance for anyone as a text in itself; it is merely a potential 'text', mattering only as part of its producer's wider textual strategies to promote the product. It is the wider textual strategy that would be the more useful 'unit' of textual analysis. Obviously it is still possible to treat the words and images on the packet as a text in their own right (like the mythical college professors in Don DeLillo's novel *White Noise* 'who read nothing but cereal boxes', 1985: 10), but it would be largely beside the point.

There is an effectively infinite number of objects which could be studied as 'texts' – from football shirts, to the film text of *ET*. But the important question is: on what scale do readers themselves regard textual order as existing? Put another way, what textual materials in practice function as texts? The more complex the textual universe we inhabit, the less simple our answers to these questions are likely to be, since we have to take into account not only critics' conventions for what is a unit for textual analysis but also the movements which the wider range of readers make across the textual field (see further on this below). Except perhaps in certain limited areas (Biblical or Shakespearean studies), we cannot assume as our starting point '*the* text' (cf. Bennett and Woollacott, 1987: 264).

## Textuality

This more functionally specific notion of 'texts' connects with questions of textuality. By 'textuality', I mean the different ways in which something can function as a text for its readers, what John Hartley (1996: 35) calls its 'phenomenal form'. Such differences are partly questions of convention, but they affect what expectations readers have of the text and of their own reading of it.

A basic, if oversimplified, example would be the contrast between films and magazines. Most films (or novels) are produced on the assumption that their audience will watch or read them with enough concentration to be aware of whether, and how, the plot is resolved at the end. By contrast, most magazines (and a great deal of radio, TV and press production) assume a quite limited, and discontinuous, degree of concentration in their audiences readerships.[11] Our textual universe comprises many zones of partly organized distraction.[12] As Joke Hermes in her path-breaking book *Reading Women's Magazines* has expressed it, they are 'putdownable' (1995: 32). When dealing with the second broad type of textuality as cultural analysts, we simply cannot make the same assumptions about how those texts are (should be) read as we would about, say, a film. 'Putdownable' materials are, of course, highly ordered textual productions, but that does not mean their readers treat them as '*texts*' in the same way as they do films or novels – or even that they treat them as texts at all.

Specific forms of 'textuality' have to be investigated in their own right. Inevitably, there are complexities and hybrid cases: not only magazines but also soap operas (at least British ones) can be viewed both as 'putdownable' television (they certainly assume that viewers will go in and out of a story-line) and as a series of programmes that are coherent in themselves. They work both as flow and as individual dramas. Soaps have, therefore, quite a complex textuality, and we cannot be sure (without investigating it further) that different viewers would necessarily agree about how a particular programme should be watched.

We also need to think about types of textuality which have not conventionally been regarded as involving 'texts' at all, yet are being created in vast numbers under various commercial and technological pressures. I've already mentioned the World Wide Web, which raises the question of whether websites should be understood as 'texts' and, if so, what sort of 'texts' are they? Another example (Bennett, 1995) is museum spaces. What are the conventions under which these 'texts' are read? Are they read as independent, self-sufficient entities, and if so by whom (other than professional cultural analysts and critics)? If not, how are they made sense of? Walter Benjamin's famous idea of art absorbed 'in a state of distraction' (1968: 240) is relevant here, as at least one side of the story.

Textuality in turn raises the question of inter-textuality. Certain types of inter-textual connection are specifically promoted and it is impossible not to be aware of them. I have already mentioned the merchandising extensions of *Star Wars* imagery and characters. There are countless others: for example, the cross-promotion of the *Tomb Raider* heroine Lara Crofts in advertisements for drinks (Lucozade, UK campaign, 1999). How are these inter-textual links interpreted by actual readers? Here too, of course, such inter-textual links may be ignored by most or all readers, remaining merely potential 'inter-texts'.

The point, at this stage, is that these questions of textuality and inter-textuality cannot be resolved in the abstract. It is not enough to study texts or inter-texts in isolation; we must look at the actual operations of the contemporary textual field.

## Tactics

If all of us negotiate a path across vast textual fields, how do we do this? The question has been implicit earlier, since 'potential (inter-)texts' and 'putdownable texts' are a familiar part of a world where readers have too much to read, and selection or screening out is at a premium.

This question was first theorized by the French historian and literary theorist Michel de Certeau in his book *The Practice of Everyday Life* (1984) through the notion of 'tactics'. He argued that in the space mapped out by texts with their 'strategic' patterns and order, actual readers make tactical journeys and crossings which are quite unpredictable when seen from the perspective of the texts themselves. Readers may inhabit the space of the text, they make it 'habitable', but they are not simply governed by it. De Certeau's concept of 'tactics' has, unfortunately, tended to be used in cultural studies only in the narrow context of the power relations between textual producers and consumers, with 'tactics' being seen as a form of resistance or alternative cultural production. While this may sometimes be important, it obscures the wider point de Certeau raises: *how do people interact not just with single texts, but with contemporary textual fields?* This is more of an 'environmental' question, than a matter of specific focused readings.

If people in actuality screen out the vast majority of images and texts around them, there will be a great difference between the total textual environment (the field of possible textual interactions for anyone) and the segments of that field with which particular individuals actually interact. One person's 'textual world' will only partially intersect with another's. Surely, therefore, we should know more about what individuals' 'textual fields' are like – how do people select from the myriad texts around them, what common patterns are there in how they select? Yet this is an area where cultural studies has done very little research.

We have moved here a long way from the idea of studying one particular text as a discrete unit in isolation (the literary model).[13] There is no choice, however, if we are to take seriously the complexity of the textual terrain we inhabit. Richard Johnson has characterized this necessary shift very well:

> The isolation of a text for academic scrutiny is a very specific form of reading. More commonly texts are encountered promiscuously; they pour in on us from all directions in diverse, coexisting media, and differently-paced flows . . . No subjective [textual] form ever acts on its own. Nor can the *combinations* be predicted by formal or logical means . . . The combinations stem, rather, from more particular logics – the structured life-activity in its objective and subjective sides, of readers or groups of readers: their social locations, their histories, their subjective interests, their private worlds. (Johnson, 1996: 102 [1986–87], original emphasis)

In thinking about 'texts' and their social effects, then, we have to address how the vast universe of potentially readable texts around us – and the even vaster universe of potential connections between them – are negotiated in practice. Our building blocks for textual analysis are, therefore, not only 'texts' but also the complexities of 'textuality' and 'tactics'.

## A note on structuralism and semiology

Before we explore these issues further, let us reflect briefly on how they probably could not have been formulated in these terms were it not for the intervention of structuralist approaches to literature in the 1950s and 1960s, which in turn took their main inspiration from the founder of semiology, Ferdinand de Saussure.

It was structuralism (most famously, Roland Barthes' essays 'The death of the author' and 'From work to text', both collected in Barthes, 1977) that changed the types of question we ask about texts. Instead of starting from 'the text' as a discrete object, created as a coherent unity by an author, Barthes reconceptualized the 'text' as a space where textual processes are at work. These processes are not controlled or directed by the author; they are processes that range across countless texts and are closely related to the competences of the reader as well. For Barthes, the site of textual order was not 'the author's text' but the textual culture as a whole and, increasingly in his later work such as *The Pleasure of the Text* (1990) [1973], the practices of actual readers. In that sense, Andrew Tudor (1999) is surely right to argue that the influence of structuralism marks a decisive moment in the historical development of cultural studies.

Why in that case have I not based this chapter more explicitly on structuralist and semiotic models (the same question can, perhaps, also be asked of Chapter 5)? For some writers (such as Tudor) it is precisely the adoption of structuralist insights that characterizes cultural studies, not only in relation to texts but cultural production generally. I believe, however, that it is unhelpful to place so much methodological weight on structuralism and semiotics, for two reasons. First, although I cannot go into the details here, Saussure's work (which is at the heart of such approaches) has come under quite fundamental attack as an incomplete and even incoherent model of how language works. Such attacks date back to the early work of Volosinov (1986) [1929] in Russia, but have recently been revived in various forms (Tallis, 1988; Jackson, 1993).[14] Their implications have yet to be fully absorbed;[15] for example, Andrew Tudor's recent and valuable summatory work (1999) on cultural studies and structuralism does not discuss them.

Second, structuralist and semiotic approaches to texts, while certainly an advance on traditional literary analysis, are themselves not immune from what I called 'the challenge of textual proliferation'. In fact, their analyses also rely on artificially stabilizing the actual complexity of textual fields. Whereas traditional literary analysis relied on 'the author-function' (Foucault, 1977a: 125) and the canon of valued texts as stabilizing devices, structuralist literary analysis relies on (a) an artificial concentration on those parts of the textual field where semiotic system seems most plausible, and (b) the value attached to the analytical brilliance of the semiotician.

Taking these points in turn, semiotics seems to be most effective where cultural production has systematic features explained by the industrialization of culture: for example, in the areas of fashion (Barthes, 1983 [1954]), novels produced for a mass audience such as the James Bond novels (Eco, 1981),[16] advertisements (Barthes, 1973), and news photographs (Hall, 1981c). The idea, however, that semiology is a general science for understanding all cultural production (as it is often presented) needs to be examined very critically.

Barthes said, in the 1970s introduction to *Mythologies* (his best known application of semiology to everyday culture), that he had aimed to write both 'an ideological critique . . . of the language of so-called mass culture' and 'an attempt to analyse semiologically the mechanics of this language' (1973: 9). Barthes' use of the term 'language' here is, I think, profoundly misleading, since it suggests that 'myth' is an order of signification which is compulsory, as the rules of language are. Elsewhere in *Mythologies*, however, Barthes makes clear that the huge variety of advertisements, stories and images which he so entertainingly dissects contains nothing like the order of language. 'Myth' according to Barthes, 'is experienced as innocent speech: not because its intentions are hidden – if they were hidden, they could not be efficacious – *but because they are naturalised*' (1973: 131, added emphasis).

This raises the question of what happens when certain standard associations (of ideas, of images) cease to be naturalized – that is, we see through them to something else. Clearly they then cease to be 'mythical', which implies that semiological analysis of the type Barthes performs can no longer work. But if myth were a system at all like language, that would be impossible. The rules of a language are always compulsory for those who speak or write the language and want to be understood; knowing explicitly the rules of a language does not stop us following them! The analogy between semiology and the science of language is itself a myth (encouraged by Saussure himself) – a myth enormously influential in installing semiology as, apparently, *the* method of cultural analysis. Even if this point is not accepted, we have to acknowledge how far semiology's 'method' has depended on the authority of its original and most brilliant practitioners, such as Barthes and Eco. Yet if we look closely, for example, at Barthes' *Mythologies*, 'semiology' is at best a cover for a wide range of interpretations of standardized texts; some may be completely convincing as objective analyses of naturalised meanings, but others are little more than personal associations (cf. Strinati, 1993: 123–8).

It is not a question of abandoning semiology entirely, but rather abandoning the myth that it is a total 'science' of cultural signs 'in general'. Rather, it is a locally useful way of analysing those aspects of contemporary cultural production which *are naturalized*. In that sense, the detailed uses of semiology are very much a secondary question. At the very least, we need also a method of analysing meanings which are *not* naturalized, and a theory of naturalization itself (how/why do meanings become naturalized, how do they become de-naturalized?).[17] The (only partly naturalized) complexity of the textual universe we inhabit lies, almost by definition, beyond the means of semiology, or indeed of any approach which *assumes* the systematic order at the level of meanings whose existence is precisely what we need to question and investigate.

## Textual analysis after textual proliferation

This discussion of structuralism and semiology has confirmed what was already suggested: if we are interested in textual analysis in an age of massive textual proliferation, our primary object of study is not a limited set of particular texts, but the whole textual environment – how it operates and how readers negotiate it. What conceptual tools do we have, or need, for that task?

### Re-employing the expert reader?

You can, of course, ignore the problem: take an isolated element from the textual field (say, a film) and analyse it as if it were a discrete object, coherent in itself, and as if the critic were in a privileged position to discern its meaning. Business as usual!

Provided such analysis does not claim to be more than it is – a particular reading of a particular text from within a particular institutional position – there is nothing wrong with it. The problem comes when analyses of a text claim to be more than 'exegesis' or 'analysis', and claim to contribute themselves to the analysis of wider social or cultural conditions. At that point, we are entitled to ask, along with the media theorist Justin Lewis: 'where's the evidence?' (1991: 49). Without evidence of whether, and in what way, the text is recognized as having those meanings by at least a significant group of readers, this is just social analysis using smoke and mirrors. Unfortunately it is all too common – and completely pointless.

Textual analysis which claims also to be social analysis assumes, among other things, that just because it reads a text one way, this tells us something about how the text is read by anyone else. A fundamental challenge to this occurred in the 1920s when a Cambridge Professor of English, I.A. Richards, published an analysis of the anonymous interpretations by his students of poems which he had handed out at lectures without any contextual information (1956 [1929]). Richards showed that a significant number of these relatively trained readers simply failed to understand the poem's literal meaning, and even if they did understand it, their response to it consisted largely of 'stock responses' (ibid.: 12–14). He explained this in terms of declining standards of literary appreciation in a world saturated by too much information (ibid.: 319), but it was equally evidence supporting the view that it is mainly through contextual clues (which Richards denied his student readers) that we interpret a text: the text 'in itself' is a myth. At least, Richards had showed the danger of cultural analysts *assuming* that they know how most readers read, or even perhaps how they read themselves.

Variations on the Richards test have emerged on other occasions. There is, for example, evidence to suggest that the way even trained listeners listen to classical music (if left to their own devices) differs radically from how musicology suggests they should listen if they are to appreciate the 'real' structure of the music: formal appreciation of key changes, and so on (see Cook, 1990: ch. 1). And when the social psychologist Sonia Livingstone investigated the variations in viewers' interpretations of a television soap, she found 'a problem in relating interpretations to textual structure' (1990: 187). Her empirical research led her to question, in fact, whether there *was* such a thing as the preferred meaning of a text, as opposed to a meaning which in some cases, but not others, people happened to agree on (ibid.).

There is, in other words, a measure of indeterminacy in moving from the text 'in itself' (as analysed by the critic) to how it is actually read. As a result, the individual text simply does not work as a stable reference point. Does that mean we should abandon close textual analysis, or perhaps switch the 'text' concept to another scale entirely where those problems become less apparent? The latter seems to be the strategy underlying the expanded notion of 'the text' in John Frow and Meaghan Morris' introduction to *Australian Cultural Studies*. The following passage is not necessarily typical of their writings elsewhere, but it is symptomatic of a wider problem:

> There is a precise sense in which cultural studies uses the concept of *text* as its fundamental model. However, in the working out of this metaphor (at its most abstract, that of the marking or tracing of *pure relationality*), the concept of text undergoes a mutation. Rather than designating a place where meanings are constructed in a single level of inscription (writing, speech, film, dress . . .), it works as an interleaving of 'levels'. If a shopping mall is conceived on the model of textuality, then this 'text' involves practices, institutional structures and the complex forms of agency they entail, legal, political, and financial conditions of existence, and particular flows of power and knowledge, as well as a particular multilayered semantic organisation; it is an ontologically mixed entity, and one for which there can be no privileged or 'correct' form of reading. (Frow and Morris, 1996: 355, second emphasis added)

'Ontologically mixed' is an understatement, since this expanded notion of the 'text' is much too broad to be useful. If a text is nothing more than 'pure relationality', almost any form of cultural order could be a text. In any case, does anyone except cultural analysts read a shopping mall as a text? We need surely *some* notion of text which is tied to how things functions as texts for actual readers.

An interesting attempt to grapple with the complexity of textual production while keeping some role for textual analysis is the work of the British media theorist John Hartley. Much of his work was done in Australia, whose universities have been an important focus for textual theory in cultural studies; not only Hartley, but also Frow and Morris (see above), Ien Ang (1996), and others are working out of Australian universities. I want to look at just one of Hartley's books, *Popular Reality* (1996). Hartley takes the challenge of textual proliferation very seriously. We cannot do textual analysis, he argues, by starting out from the individual text: we have to take account of the pervasiveness, the endless circulation, of meanings (1996: 2). Meanings circulate not just in one medium but in many, with countless connections between them (ibid.: 3); we touched on this point earlier in discussing *The Phantom Menace*. Contemporary textual production is 'a gigantic archive of textuality, a huge store of human sense-making' (ibid.). And yet, as Hartley forcefully argues, large regions of it have been virtually ignored by cultural studies – in particular, the world of the popular press. At the same time, Hartley sees a role for something like textual criticism – or 'practical criticism' (ibid.: 8) – in this wider field. This, he argues, should be able to identify 'emblematic texts or moments' of contact between producers, texts and readers (ibid.: 6). To his credit, Hartley takes a long-term historical view of the social centrality of modern media, drawing on material from and including the French Revolution.

Returning to the metaphor that has been used throughout this chapter,

Hartley's 'practical criticism' relies on two stabilization devices. It is these I now question: they are, positively, the concept of the 'mediasphere' and, negatively, a complete exclusion of audience research.

Instead of the individual text, Hartley needs some other (relatively stable) reference point which can anchor textual analysis. The 'mediasphere' (a concept he adapts from the 'semiosphere', as developed by the literary theorist Yuri Lotman, 1990) performs this function. The 'semiosphere' according to Lotman is the 'integrated unity' formed by particular semiotic systems, when considered in their relations to each other (1990: 273, quoted by Hartley, 1996: 1). The 'mediasphere' is Hartley's term for the mediated public–private space of connections which has replaced earlier public spheres: 'Journalism forms a mediasphere which connects readerships not only . . . with the public domain, but also with the culture at large – indeed journalism is one of the chief mechanisms by which different (and sometimes mutually incomprehensible) cultural domains are kept in dialogue with one another' (Hartley, 1996: 28). You do not need to take over Hartley's and Lotman's semiotic framework to see the general usefulness of this idea. Contemporary media do systematically produce connections between many different areas of life which otherwise might not be connected. They connect, for example, readers' possible reflections on their private family life and public issues about sexuality, health and education, whether directly or through the intermediary of celebrity life stories and media fictions such as soaps. In this way, they not only work as flows of texts, but contribute to the 'textualization' of the social world (ibid.: ch. 3). This is a kind of order in the textual universe, which Hartley is surely right to argue we must understand better. In addition, newspapers and magazines, for example, because they are widely available and shared, constitute their readerships as a public, focused around their texts; in that way, they create an ordered relationship between the readers themselves (ibid.: 72).

So far so good. But Hartley tells us nothing at all about how people negotiate the implications of all this. How many are people apathetic, or cynical about the contents of the mediasphere? More to the point, how much of it do they screen out? What types of connection do they make between the mediasphere and other spheres of social life? We must avoid the functionalist assumption that, just because the media apparently constitute an important 'mechanism' for the structuring of social life ('a technology of society', ibid.: 72), this is a mechanism that always works.[18] Actual readers are surely more than oil on the wheels of the media mechanism.

Yet Hartley rules out the possibility of researching the relationship of actual readerships to the mediasphere, except through assumed clues in the texts themselves. Developing a position he has argued elsewhere (Hartley,

1987), he claims that audience research always oversimplifies and patholo-
gizes those it studies, seeing them as in the thrall of media messages, rather
than recognizing that audiences are no less sophisticated than researchers
and researchers are members of the audience too. While of course these are
serious points, they provide no reason for stopping us *thinking* about how
people (all of us) read, or watch. If, for example, as Joke Hermes (1993,
1995) argues, a great deal of media use is casual, distracted – barely 'reading' at all – then Hartley's claims for the mediasphere's centrality to public
life would carry much less weight.

Hartley sees the potential problem (1996: 64) but does not resolve it. He
makes a lot of claims about the importance, and therefore implicitly the
social impacts, of media discourses on sexuality, health, gender, and so on
(for example in his chapter on the public profiles of popular models and
singers: what he calls the 'frocks pop'), but without any supporting evidence. That these discourses circulate in prominent media sites (which is all
he establishes) is significant, but it is quite unclear *how* significant.[19]
Hartley's work, then, offers at best a half-solution to the challenge of textual
proliferation, which omits a major source of complexity under the cover of
a new virtuoso 'reading' of the social world.

## A new place for textual analysis

To recap: there is no question of abandoning the idea of analysing texts; it is
a matter of rethinking how it fits into our understanding of the wider textual
environment. We have to take seriously the difficult question: what is a text
(considered as a social object)? That means investigating – not simply assuming – the status that texts have in the environment and the extent to which
there are systematic orders of meaning. (Perhaps there is less order than we
imagine.) This, in turn, means taking seriously the contribution to these
processes of actual readers.[20]

It helps to think of our textual environment as formed by at least three
patterns of movement: (a) flows of texts, (b) flows of meanings (across and
within texts), and (c) the movements of potential readers within (a) and
(b).[21] This complex interchange is represented in Figure 4.1. *There are in
principle as many perspectives on that overall pattern of flows as there are
readers*: each of us stands at a different point in the flow. We must abandon
the idea that there are particular, elevated vantage points (those of the critic
or virtuoso semiotician) from which the flow can directly be 'read'. That is
an illusion, based on thinking that the flow itself is a 'text' (with a 'creator'
underwriting its systematicity), when in fact it is only a flow, in which
myriad texts and textual fragments move.[22]

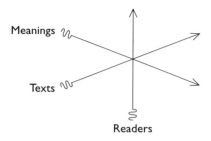

FIGURE 4.1  *The textual environment*

On the other hand, what make the world around us into a textual environment rather than a complete chaos are certain ordering processes, which John Hartley, for example, makes us think about. One is the inter-textual patterns through which texts draw on each other (similarly, each of us in conversation or reflection draws on material we have heard, seen or read elsewhere). I want to concentrate here, however, on the processes which organize the flows of texts and readers themselves. What are these processes? The following is a preliminary list:

1  The material structures of textual production (most obviously, the heavy concentration of production in particular institutions, rather than across whole populations).
2  The material structures of distributing texts (again highly concentrated).
3  The processes which tend to order how we read, what connections we make between texts, what texts we screen out, and so on.

The first two processes are familiar – they are central to any political economy of textual production – but the last is more difficult to envisage. How is our reading ordered? An image may help. There are countless switching processes (or, perhaps, gradients) which, in the overall textual space, make one set of connections more likely than another; they are repeated, resulting in various feedback loops – some small and some massive. Examples would be the authority given to particular 'expert' or prestigious sources (critics, commentators, celebrities, governments) or to particular sites where important 'themes of the moment' are defined (particular programmes or newspapers; particular events, such as major sporting events).

To understand the textual environment we need, therefore, to track not only texts, but also the processes of 'textualization': how particular complexes of meanings come to be treated as texts to be read, within the textual wider environment.[23] A helpful concept here was developed by Tony Bennett and Janet Woollacott at the UK's Open University in the 1980s, particularly in *Bond and Beyond* (1987), a study of the cultural and social impact of the James Bond story. This book contains a devastating attack on the old notion of studying the text 'in itself' (whether the Bond novels or the Bond films) rather than the inter-textual environment focused around the Bond story. In addition Bennett and Woollacott introduce the concept of the 'reading formation' – the process through which particular texts and particular readers come to be in an ordered relation to each other. The strength of their idea comes from being very clear that this process is not 'natural' or given, but part of what we need to explain: 'The reader is conceived not as a subject who stands outside the text and interprets it any more than the text is regarded as an object the reader encounters. Rather, text and reader are conceived as *being co-produced within a reading formation*' (Bennett and Woollacott, 1987: 64, added emphasis).

The 'reading formation', then, is what brings about a particular reading of a particular text within a particular set of inter-textual associations. This neatly brings together the range of processes listed above. What, in turn, produces the reading formation? '[I]t is the product of definite social and ideological relations of reading composed, in the main, of those apparatuses – schools, the press, critical reviews, fanzines – within and between which the socially dominant forms for the superintendence of reading are both constructed and contested' (ibid.: 64–5). The reading formation is, in effect, a working term for thinking about the quite abstract notion of textualization – that is, the processes which lead to certain complexes of meaning, and not others, being read as texts. Crucially, however, Bennett and Woollacott (unlike Hartley) are open to empirical research into readers and reading practices.

Two minor caveats are necessary. We should be sceptical about Bennett and Woollacott's suggestion that a reading formation is always associated with a more or less coherent ideological formation; their language reflects the heavy influence of both Gramsci and Althusser at that time in British cultural studies.[24] There is a danger of overestimating the degree of cohesion that exists even among those who go to see the same film in broadly the same historical and inter-textual context (compare with the argument developed in Chapter 3).[25] Second, we need to bring out a point which is implicit in their writing (ibid.: 44), but obscured by the term 'reading formation'. Their argument is relevant to many other practices, which would not naturally fall within our idea of 'reading', such as the influence of 'Bond' on clothes and fashion, talk, even people's everyday performances of identity.[26]

These details aside, the concept of 'reading formation' usefully points to the direction in which textual analysis in cultural studies should move. Our starting point has to be the actual complexity and fluidity of the textual environment, and from there the question of how certain texts come to be closely read as texts – how 'textual events', as we might call them, occur. We are now in a position to review cultural studies' agenda for text-related research in a post-literary framework.

## The future of text-related research

Broadly there are three main priorities for research: the textual environment, patterns of belief, and textual events. These are discussed in more detail below.

### The textual environment

If we picture the textual environment as the result of a number of flows (see Figure 4.1), then we need to study: (a) how far stable meanings and associations are produced; (b) what texts are produced and how they circulate; and (c) the various ways in which people use, or negotiate, the vast textual resources around them.

The first task is what cultural studies has always done, except that (as argued earlier) we cannot rely on the authority of semiology (with its quasi-scientific language of 'codes')[27] to legislate for order. A useful area for research would be to look in detail at those whose job it is to produce standardized, naturalized meanings (the marketing and advertising industry). Advertisements are, in effect, experiments with semantic order. It would be crucial, in relation to particular advertisements, to establish through audience research to what extent they were accompanied by a stable set of associations. The same idea could be applied to other areas also. Instead of the armchair science of semiology, we need a more active and open-ended research exploration of the possibilities of order in the field of meanings.

The second task – studying the flow of texts – is also a familiar part of cultural studies, except that our definition of where to look for texts has to expand to match the scale of our textual environment. If, for example, we are interested in discourses around masculinity and technology, or childhood and violence, it is artificial to study films and television in isolation from computer games, comics, toys, advertisements, and so on.[28]

The third task – studying how people actually negotiate the textual environment – should not be consigned to the 'too difficult' bin; it is an essential complement to the first two tasks. People's negotiations involve active processes. We may screen some material out entirely, and make a more explicit and considered choice about other material. Some texts we may read closely, working hard to connect them with other texts. Or we may read a text with limited attention, incompletely, without any great interpretative work. This is where questions of 'textuality' and 'tactics' come in (see above). There are also 'passive' processes, which affect what texts are available to particular people. These range from material exclusions (economic, educational) to other more subtle forms of exclusion (like people's sense of what is 'appropriate' for them, their 'taste'), which by endless repetition come to have an almost material force (compare Bourdieu, 1984).

Take the active and passive processes together, and you have a rough picture of the complex determinants of each person's perspective on the wider textual environment, their map of the wider space. Different people's maps may differ quite radically. After all, no one (not even the researcher) can claim even to be aware of the whole space – it is too large. It has been in media and cultural studies, if anywhere, that the pioneering work in researching these maps has been done.[29] But we still know surprisingly little, for example, about the many different textual maps with which people operate, and how forms of cultural production (such as music sampling or enthusiasts' collections) are themselves forms of 'remapping' the textual environment.[30] 'Postmodern' theory can, in a sense, be seen as an intellectual variant of such remappings, but as yet far too little attention has been given to the more interesting question of how 'postmodern' cultural environments are actually lived.

Whatever we already know may be transformed soon by a new device for reordering people's awareness of the textual environment: the Internet. I say 'soon', rather than 'already', because it is only when in some countries Internet access becomes widely popularized, probably through digital TV packages, that the Internet will become more than a highly specialized research problem (as usual, we should not believe the hype).

As a research agenda this may sound exhausting but, as argued in Chapter 3, we need to know more about people's competing cultural maps and perspectives, if we are to grasp how our shared textual environment is registered in people's lives. It is also, crucially, here that issues of power – the unequal distribution of the resources of cultural entitlement – emerge most clearly. We should not blithely assume that the textual environment is somehow simply 'shared' on equal terms. That is an old-style 'textualist' illusion that we can ill afford.

## Patterns of belief

Separate from the question of the contents of the textual environment is the question of how particular texts (for example, film texts) are caught up in wider patterns of belief: beliefs about films, of course, and more broadly the media industries, but also patterns of belief in apparently unrelated areas such as the worlds of school, work, sport and leisure, fashion, politics, religion, science, and (bearing in mind the arguments of Chapters 3 and 6) our narratives of ourselves and our families. This of course goes well beyond 'textual analysis' as it has been conventionally conceived, but it is a direct consequence of generating our research questions from the inter-textual environment itself.

Some work has recently emerged in this area: Hartley's (1996) book on 'popular reality' and the media's 'pedagogic' role (cf. also Miller and McHoul, 1998; Miller, 1998). None as yet amounts to a sustained programme of research into how, in practice, people integrate their readings of texts (say, the press or television news) into the formation or reinforcement of wider beliefs. Each tends to stay within a Foucauldian model of discourse analysis that is more comfortable with textual surfaces than social practice (the ghost of the 'expert reader' again). Particularly neglected is the question of people's varying beliefs in media outputs themselves. There have, of course, been many studies of particular types of media enthusiast (that is, fans), but little work done on other points along the scale of belief: indifference, cynicism, active dislike, mistrust or scepticism (about factual or moral claims), and so on.

Cultural studies' adoption – only sometimes and certainly not as much as its cruder critics claim – of a celebratory mode towards popular consumption has obscured the problem in an unhelpful way. For example, how are we to understand the following attitudes to television? The quotes are taken from a 1970s study of working-class San Francisco families (both speakers here are men):

> After the kids go to bed and things settle down, we're just here. I guess we watch TV or something. [angrily] What am I saying? It's not 'or something'; that's what it is. It's the same every night; we're just here.
> I'm watching, that's all. I'm not thinking about things or anything like that. I sit down and I'm just watching. That's what I do most nights. I come home and die in front of the TV. (Rubin, 1976: 185, 191)

Once again, these quotations raise questions about the differences in people's engagements or beliefs in the textual environment, which link inexorably to issues of cultural power.

## Textual events

It is against the background of continuing research into the first two areas that the analysis of particular texts should take its place.

There are, perhaps, two basic questions to ask of any text (although answering them is rarely easy). First, how did that text come to be one which significant numbers of people engaged with closely as a text? In other words, how has it come to function as a text? This involves looking at the features of the text (its generic features, plot, characters, associations), not in isolation but alongside the other factors which go to make up a 'reading formation': marketing and the producer's industrial strategy; the discourses circulating about the text and its themes; and so on. Second, how is the text read by actual readers (allowing for many different possible readings)?

This is to move away from studying texts as 'objects' (complete in themselves) to studying textual processes, or what the American film theorist Janet Staiger (1992: 9) has simply called 'events'. In vast, complex textual environments, texts which attract a great deal of close reading are not simply 'there': they emerge as part of a 'textual event' which needs to be studied (Pribram, 1988; Staiger, 1992). Think of the events surrounding the release of any major Hollywood or Bollywood film. Such events are themselves, of course, inter-textual (Bennett and Woollacott, 1987). Indeed, as Georgina Born (1991: 158) has pointed out in relation to music – but the point is a general one – many texts function through the mediation of (texts in) other media. The 'textual event' is inherently multitextual and involves multiple media.

At the same time, given the arguments above, we must remember that a function of the media industries (from publishing to film) is precisely to *create* textual events. We need to think about whether (beneath the hype) actual readers are engaged or not with those processes.

It is here also that the complexity of consumption has to be addressed. Countless texts are absorbed in a state of distraction, others are read carefully and then forgotten; but there are also moments when a particular text comes to be read closely and by many people as a coherent unity. Sometimes, at such moments, texts acquire resonances across the whole textual environment. They become agreed means through which history can be 'read', as it is formed – and, as such, important historical evidence (Geraghty, 1996).[31] The density of meanings that can be condensed into one text or set of texts has to be studied in its full cultural, social and historical context.

Having said all this, there must somewhere come a point where our questioning of the text stops and we recognize that particular texts *do* exercise power over us, and for reasons that sociological 'context' can only partly explain. We take pleasure in programmes, in films, in novels, music and dance, and these pleasures, while embedded in history[32] (the histories of our own taste and of wider cultural formations), contain something left over which sociology on its own has difficulty explaining: the realm of *aesthetics*.

Throughout this chapter, questions of aesthetics and pleasure have been left to one side, and this emphasis will be unacceptable to some.[33] My aim, however, has been to reorient – as far as possible – the way we think about texts in cultural studies. This has meant leaning heavily in the other direction in order to clarify what else has to be in place before textual analysis and questions of value and aesthetics can be pursued on a satisfactory basis. With this move completed we can perhaps, over time, work towards a wider synthesis of the sociological and aesthetic concerns to which texts give rise.[34]

## Summary

In this chapter, we have explored how the methodological and conceptual framework for conducting textual analysis must be transformed to take account of the actual complexity of textual production. Instead of the simple discrete text–reader relationship, we are looking at a textual environment comprising complex patterns of flows: flows of meanings, texts and potential readers. To understand the effects of that environment, we also have to understand the different levels of engagement that readers may have. And, finally, we have to understand the complex extra-textual conditions which create textual events: the situations where things function as texts for significant numbers of readers.

To read texts in this way, however, is to have de-centred textual analysis in the traditional sense. Instead of the text being the source of certainty, it has become the site of an enigma, or at least cautious exploration. But this is only as it should be: in the vast textual fields we inhabit, it is order rather than uncertainty that we need to explain.

## Suggestions for further thinking

1   Develop a map of your own 'textual world': what texts you consume, what connections you make between which types of text. Distinguish between texts which you think of as 'putdownable' and those with which

you engage more intensely. Compare your map with those of others. How significant are the differences and similiarities?

2   Take one text that is attracting current attention (an inevitable example at the time of writing in Britain would be *The Phantom Menace*). Using your own observations but also any electronic searches you can (for example, CD-Rom or Internet searches), develop a picture of the inter-textual field in which that text functions. Think about how far that field is ordered: for example, do particular texts have greater weight in generating other texts? (In the case of *The Phantom Menace*, one question would be: have publicity narratives about the film generated more texts about themselves than the detailed narrative of the film itself?)

3   Take a textual event and try to identify the range of factors which led to it, including any which have led to the text involved being regarded as having wider historical resonances.


# Notes

1   For example, Frow and Morris (1996: 357).
2   This chapter was virtually complete when I heard Martin Barker's stimulating reflections on texts and audiences at the University of North London 'Researching Culture' conference in September 1999, which drew on Barker and Brooks (1998). I was pleased to discover that we were asking similar questions, although pursuing them in different directions. I would also like to acknowledge the very helpful comments of Dave Hesmondhalgh on an earlier draft of this chapter, even though I am sure I have not answered all his objections.
3   For a review of the impact of the cultural studies critique on literary studies, see Easthope (1990).
4   Cf. Bennett and Woollacott (1987: 68).
5   I will use 'text' in the broad sense familiar in cultural studies, which includes not only written texts, but film, television, the visual arts, music – in fact, ordered complexes of meaning in any medium or combination of media.
6   There is also the need to ask where the interpretative authority of expert readers comes from: this question was an issue raised by a stimulating presentation by Deborah Chambers and Estella Tincknell called 'The problems and practice of researching culture' at the 'Researching Culture' conference (see note 2).
7   On the importance of ontological issues, if questions of method are to be clarified, see Tudor (1995) and, more generally, Archer (1995: 2–3, 20–6). It was Richard Johnson (1996: 96 [1986–87]) who, more than a decade ago, asked the essential question: 'What is a text?'
8   Again, see Johnson (ibid.).
9   Following Bennett and Woollacott (1987: 44–5), I use the hyphenated spelling

('inter-textuality') to refer to the relations between texts actually established in specific conditions of reading and production, as opposed to 'intertextuality' (Kristeva) which means the references to other texts which are purely internal to a particular text.

10  'The beautiful Gail Porter on the trail of the new "Star Wars" film in Tunisia', *OK*, 170, 16 July 1999, 31–9. For the significance of media locations, see Couldry (2000).

11  The example is clearly oversimplified, since magazines can be read both intensely and casually in different circumstances (McRobbie, 1991c: 142), but it is useful to get the discussion going.

12  Cf. Grossberg (1987) and Morse (1990).

13  Of course, literary analysis in one sense does not treat texts in isolation, but analyses them in the context of the rest of the author's work, and then compares that work to other authors'. Those links, however, always have as their reference point the idea that the text can usefully be treated as a discrete unity 'in itself'.

14  This is without even considering Derrida's deconstructionist attacks on Saussure and structuralist analyses of literature (1976, 1978).

15  On the neglect of Volosinov's critique of Saussure, see Williams (1989c) and Barker (1989: ch. 2, especially page 311, n. 2). As Martin Barker points out, while some acknowledgement of Volosinov was made early on in cultural studies, the trenchantness of his critique of Saussure has not been adequately addressed.

16  As we shall see below, even the Bond case is not simple: see Bennett and Woollacott (1987: 68–90) for a critique of Eco's analysis.

17  Alternatively, you can argue that semiology is simply wrong, and the naturalized system it assumes is imaginary: Barker (1989: 152–5). That goes too far, I believe, but Barker's analysis of the problems in semiology's claims to systematicity is convincing.

18  The functionalism of Hartley's work is a little similar to that of Paddy Scannell's work on radio and television (especially, 1996). For discussion of the problems, see Couldry (2000: ch. 1).

19  There is a broader problem here, common to all Foucauldian or quasi-Foucauldian analyses: their inadequate notion of the reflexivity of the subject. I touch on this again in Chapter 6.

20  There is an echo here of important debates in 1980s feminist media analysis between proponents of an essentializing Screen Theory (based on abstract psychoanalytic models, such as Mulvey, 1975) and writers who insisted on the need to study actual women audiences (Brunsdon, 1981; Kuhn, 1984).

21  I am influenced here by the Swedish anthropologist Ulf Hannerz; this connection is developed explicitly in Chapter 5.

22  By interpreting the flow as a sort of 'text', 'textual' readers of the social repeat (in subtly disguised form) precisely the error Bourdieu once identified in anthropological practice: mistaking the way the social world *must look* to analysts in order to be systematically interpreted, with the way the social world actually *is* (1977: 2).

23  Hartley, certainly, is well aware of this (1996: ch. 3). But by ruling out research into readers, he excludes a major part of the process.

24  Since then, however, Bennett has shifted from a Gramscian to a Foucauldian position: see Chapter 5, note 1.

25 Cf. more generally the debate in sociology about the dangers of overestimating the extent to which societies share common values (Wrong, 1961; Mann, 1970).

26 On media-related performance, cf. Chaney (1994), and Abercrombie and Longhurst (1998).

27 For a critique of the slippery notion of 'codes', see Corner (1986). Corner's argument concerns Hall's work, but it applies (perhaps more fairly) to semiology in general.

28 For such a broader approach, see Kline (1993).

29 The best study (dealing with television consumption) remains Morley (1986). For a general precedent, in terms of how people map the cities they live in, see Lynch (1960).

30 An important book which opens up a framework for thinking about some of these areas is Willis (1990).

31 Note also that to fulfil this function you do not necessarily need a 'text' as such, but only an event or series of events which become textualized (such as the O.J. Simpson trial in the USA). Cf. Couldry, 1995.

32 For excellent reflections on the complexity of such histories, see Gilroy (1992: 105).

33 For a very different approach to the case of music, see Frith (1997).

34 For an interesting discussion exploring these possibilities, see Born (1991).

# 5 Beyond 'cultures'

In a society where the cultural flow is varied and uneven, it is an open question which meanings have reached where and when.

Ulf Hannerz (1992: 81)

A culture that cannot be tied to a place cannot be analytically stopped in time.

Anna Lowenhaupt Tsing (1993: 66)

In Chapter 4, we took a seemingly technical question ('what is a text?') and showed how, by carefully unpicking its implications, we might rethink what textual analysis involves. In this chapter, our starting question has a similar form ('what is a culture?'), yet just by asking it we enter one of the most contested debates in the humanities and social sciences today. It is an urgent question: How can we think about cultural life, yet think beyond the assumption that there are, necessarily, such things as 'cultures'?

Here, as before, we see that questions which are apparently only methodological also have political implications, and vice versa. The political (or ethical) requirement to listen to the cultural experiences of others introduces an irrevocable degree of complexity to cultural analysis. As a result, cultural theory which seems mainly methodological in orientation (the work of Ulf Hannerz) has implications which are profoundly political; and cultural analysis whose political emphasis is very clear (the work of Paul Gilroy) threatens entrenched methodological assumptions.[1]

We approached some of this territory earlier. Chapter 3 began to unsettle claims about 'cultures' from the perspective of the individuals who apparently belong to them. But it left unresolved the crucial question with which I deal here: if cultural life is more than the sum of individual perspectives, what is this 'more'? This chapter also makes explicit a dimension latent so far: the external relations between cultures or nations – the international or global scale of cultural life. We see that the idea that cultural life must be understood in terms of separate, coherent entities called 'cultures' is structurally unsound on both 'inside' and 'outside'. I argue that we may still study what goes on culturally (to put it loosely for now), but without necessarily ascribing 'cultures' to others or to ourselves. First, however, we look at the problems with the concept of 'cultures', problems which cut across various disciplines: cultural studies, anthropology, and sociology. There is a lot at stake. Let me introduce some of the issues here (for more detail, see the next section).

Mapping the 'cultures' of others is now generally understood within anthropology to be an instrument not of science but of power, heavily implicated in the practices involved in, and in some respects still continuing after the formal end of, colonialism (the discourse of Orientalism analysed by Edward Said (1978) is only the most well-known example). As Lila Abu-Lughod has put it: 'culture is the essential tool for *making other* . . . anthropological discourse gives cultural difference (and the separation between groups of people it implies) the air of the self-evident' (Abu-Lughod, 1991: 143, added emphasis). Or in a slogan: divide, *categorize*, and rule. Applied to 'ourselves', a belief in a distinctive, shared culture is the touchstone of nationalism, even if the evidence for what it is we share is often problematic or absent (Schudson, 1994). For some writers, a shared national 'culture' is always the projection of a mythical unity, desired but never possible (Zizek, 1990; Bhabha, 1994).

In any case, constructing a particular national culture in a particular territory generally involves excluding others, who also have a stake in cultural life there. This is the price of what Paul Gilroy calls 'cultural insiderism', for which, as we saw in Chapter 3, he critiques Raymond Williams and early British cultural studies:

> The essential trademark of cultural insiderism . . . is an absolute sense of ethnic difference. This is maximised so that it distinguishes people from one another and at the same time acquires an incontestable priority over all another dimensions of their social and historical experience, cultures and identities. (Gilroy, 1992: 3)

The idea that there are 'cultures' attached to a particular location underpins the idea that cultural differences correspond to ethnic differences and (usually also) differences of 'race': English versus Irish, white British versus black British, and so on. Worse, the 'racial' implications of cultural insiderism are generally invisible to those on the 'inside', because the insider culture is naturalized. As Ruth Frankenberg argues about the USA, there are 'continual processes of slippage, condensation and displacement among the constructs "race", "nation", and "culture" [that] continue to "unmark" white people, while consistently marking and racializing others' (1997: 6). The legacy of the 'cultures' concept is, to say the least, problematic.

I explore later in the chapter (Rethinking cultural coherence) what it may mean to study culture without relying on the notion of 'cultures' – that is, stable, coherent, localized 'units' of cultural analysis. This requires a new model of culture, a new way of formulating the research issues. I draw in detail on Hannerz's work and his conceptualization of, first, cultural flows and, second, the importance of mechanisms of transmission and representation (in a word: 'mediation') in the far from transparent world we call 'culture'. Hannerz provides a useful theoretical framework for working with cultural complexity and making accountable descriptions of it, which fits well with the broader trend of cultural studies' work on cultural institutions.

I make this more concrete in the final section (Working with cultural complexity) by discussing various recent examples of cultural research, including work dealing with identity and cultural exchange in contemporary London and with the Internet.

Having mentioned the Internet, I must say a word about a fashionable but, for cultural studies, unhelpful form of complexity theory. A number of scientific and technological developments – chaos theory, new popularizations of Darwinism, the study of large computers involving massive parallel processing, new theories of neurological development – have converged around models of 'emergent order'. They suggest that order in both natural and artificial systems does not result from a specific number of predictable steps, but emerges unpredictably from a massive complexity – an unimaginably large number of connections.[2] An influential application of this so-called 'connectionism' is to the workings of the Internet – a system of enormous complexity without any formal centre.

I personally find these ideas exciting. The problem, however, is when they also become the basis for a loose metaphor of how cultural and social processes might work, as in a frequently referenced article by Sadie Plant (1996) (cf. de Landa, 1994). Connectionism here is merely a licence for thinking about culture as an ineffable complexity involving humans and machines, which produces order that cannot be objectively analysed, although presumably we know it when we see it:

> cultures are parallel distributed processes, functioning without some transcendent guide or the governing role of their agencies. There is no privileged scale: global and molecular cultures act through the middle ground of states, societies, members and things. There is nothing exclusively human about it: cultures emerge from the complex interactions of media, organisms, weather patterns, ecosystems, thought patterns, cities, discourses, fashions, populations, brains,

markets, dance nights, and bacterial exchanges . . . you live in cultures and cultures live in you. (Plant, 1996: 214)

This simply repeats what we already know (things are complex and inter-related) without beginning to explain *what sort* of order cultures involve, and where and on what scale we should look for it.

The vague metaphor of complexity (or 'connectionism') simply obstructs us from thinking concretely about what the complexity of culture might mean, and how to investigate it. This is now, perhaps, the central task for cultural studies, and one that has only recently been taken seriously enough. In this chapter, I map out some starting points. Inevitably the journey is at times quite difficult and abstract, but the result, I hope, is to make much clearer what it means to study 'cultures'.

## Cultural space: the traditional model

What, exactly, is the model of culture that we need to move beyond? Imagine we have a blank sheet and are trying to picture the space of culture (cultural experience, cultural production, cultural life). The older model pictures that space primarily in terms of a series of separate 'cultures', with the interactions between them being of secondary importance. Each 'culture' is understood as a natural unit: coherent (so that hybrid cultures are an exceptional case), and associated with a particular shared place and time.

This model has been formulated, perhaps most clearly, by its anthropologist critics: it is the model on which classical anthropology depended. As Ulf Hannerz puts it, it is 'the idea of culture as something *shared*, in the sense of homogeneously distributed in society' (1992: 11, added emphasis). This 'holistic' model is supported by various metaphors which James Clifford (1988) has done much to excavate. There is the organic metaphor of culture as *growth*: 'a coherent body that lives and dies', or alternatively survives, provided it remains uncontaminated by outside influences (1988: 235, 338). Closely linked with growth is the metaphor of *place* (since every body occupies one, discrete place): the 'place' of culture is the site where its reality is lived, the focus where all the possible lines of diversity in a culture intersect in a unity (Auge, 1995: 58). They intersect there so that they can be 'read', a third metaphor: 'culture as *text*' (ibid.: 49–50), a text with finite boundaries. All these metaphors are naturalized; they exclude other metaphors emphasizing discontinuity, the connections between multiple cultural sites, or the opaqueness of culture. The standard metaphors encourage us to look for less complexity in cultural phenomena: they are stabilization devices (to use the term introduced in Chapter 4).

This 'holistic' model of culture has been extremely influential: it crosses not only anthropology but also sociology (it was at the root of functionalist models of social integration, such as that of Talcott Parsons) and cultural studies, where its influence on Raymond Williams' early account of culture as a way of life is obvious.[3]

This cultural model, however, faces problems from many directions. First, the massive increase in inter-cultural flows of people, images, information and goods (brought about by improved communications technologies and intensified pressures for economic integration) makes the idea of cultures separated by hermetically sealed borders impossible to sustain. The model was already in crisis by the 1920s (Clifford, 1988: 14) and since then the crisis has greatly intensified. This remains true, even if we doubt whether the model of sealed-off cultures was ever strictly true. As Gupta and Ferguson have argued: 'people have undoubtedly always been more mobile and [cultural] identities less fixed than the static and typologizing approaches of classical anthropology would suggest' (1992, quoted in Schudson, 1994: 37). Leaving aside this complication, globalization (as everyone now calls it) has brought about 'the increasing transnationaliza-tion of economic and cultural life', creating 'a new global–local nexus' (Robins, 1997: 12, 30). Wherever we look, cultural life involves adaptations (often very recent ones) of materials from elsewhere: from music, clothing and food to images and ideas. 'Local' cultures are everywhere made up, in part, from translocal elements; local culture incorporates 'transculturality' (Welsch, 1999).

An influential analysis of these processes is the anthropologist Arjun Appadurai's theory of '-scapes'. Appadurai (1990) argues that we live in 'imagined worlds' which are complex amalgams of elements from all over the world (he divides these types of flow, abstractly, into 'mediascapes', 'ethnoscapes', 'technoscapes', 'finanscapes' and 'idioscapes'). The details are less important here than the point that these '-scapes' are the result of com-plex flows *across* cultural borders, and are not necessarily coherent; they are just flows, crossing many locations, often working in contradictory direc-tions.

The *second* threat to the older model of cultural space follows directly from the first: if our experiences of culture are increasingly marked by trans-border flows, then the ties of culture to place would seem to be loosened. At the least, the idea that culture is necessarily tied to a place can be seen for what it always was: an assumption. If we challenge that assumption, then many new objects of cultural research come into view:

1  Cultures formed through the shared experience of movement across borders (for example, cultures of diaspora, see Gilroy, 1992, ch. 6; Clifford, 1997: ch. 10).

2  The spaces of passage between nations that have not been recognized before as associated with 'cultures' at all (such as the Black Atlantic theorized by Gilroy, 1992).

3  The 'cultures' of ordinary places of transit, such as airports, tourist zones, and the like (which Auge (1995), perhaps too simply, has dubbed 'non-places').

4  People's loyalties (whether political or cultural) across, and sometimes in defiance of, national borders (what Appadurai (1996: 164), again too simply perhaps, calls 'postnational formations').

There is no space here to follow up these fascinating leads, but the central point should be clear: the links between culture and place are complex, not automatic, and the very idea of 'the *place* of culture' needs to be questioned. Added to which, 'place' itself has been deconstructed by geographers such as Doreen Massey (1994, 1997). No place, she argues, is reducible to a simple narrative, a coherent set of meanings. Places are points where many influences, operating on many different scales (up to and including the global), intersect. Instead of a traditional notion of 'place' as bounded locality, we need 'a global sense of the local' (1997: 240).

If the relations of cultures to place are constructed, so too is their relationship to time, although this point is less often emphasized. A third challenge to the old model has been to argue that our sense of living in coherent, unified 'cultures' is itself enhanced by fictions of 'national time' (the nation's history, present, and future). Instead, as Homi Bhabha has argued, we have to foreground 'the essential question of the representation of the nation *as [itself] a temporal process*' (1994: 142, added emphasis). This process operates through mechanisms of representation, such as television and radio. We are used to the idea that national 'traditions' are invented (Hobsbawm and Ranger, 1983), but the same is true of our cultural 'present' – what Charlotte Brunsdon and David Morley call 'the myth of "the nation, now"' (1978: 27; cf. Couldry, 2000: 50–2). The problems with the traditional model of cultures do not, then, derive only from the assumptions of earlier anthropologists; they are intimately related to how culture – all culture – is refracted through power, in particular *mediated power*. This point is crucial later.

In addition, the traditional model has been damaged by the critiques mentioned at the beginning of the chapter. There is a dangerous link between essentializing notions of 'culture' and essentializing notions of 'race' and ethnicity; if cultures really are naturally separate and spatially discrete, that is the perfect alibi for other forms of separation (that is, exclusion and discrimination). Paul Gilroy's work (1987, 1992, 1993) in particular has challenged the naturalness of such assumptions. At the same time, the intellectual and moral authority of cultural analysts to describe and assess 'whole cultures' has been challenged (Clifford and Marcus, 1986), partly because they were not accountable to the perspectives of those they wrote about: a clear case of methodological and political issues intersecting.

The traditional model of cultural space – an order of unified cultures linked by a secondary level of connections – simply does not work. Does that mean that cultural experience is entirely de-localized? The answer must be no, and it is important to see why.

There is now a consensus among theorists of globalization (Robertson, 1990; A. Smith, 1990; Hannerz, 1992: ch. 7) that globalization does *not* mean homogenization. While global flows may be intensified, it does not follow that we are heading towards a single global culture, with the same cultural flows everywhere. That would be to move from questioning the boundaries between cultures, only to reinstate the idea of a unified culture (with its own vast boundaries) at the global level. Nor does it follow that, just because some cultural experience is related to global flows, all cultural experience must be. Similarly, because we are beginning to understand the experiences of diaspora better, it does not mean it must be the model for all experience. As Sidney Mintz has put it: 'most people in almost any community do not migrate . . . [even if they do] the community is what the migrants come back to; it does not disappear in their absence' (1998: 120). We must be equally careful in thinking about the increase in global tourism: 'not all experience of travel fits so snugly into the protocols of circulation. Some are forced to stay at home, others are forced to run' (Kaur and Hutnyk, 1999: 3). There is also the question of how global cultural flows are received locally. As many writers have pointed out, we must not underestimate the degree to which cultures can adapt imported material for 'local' ends (Lull, 1995). A striking recent example comes from a study of McDonald's in Asia (Watson, 1997) which shows the various ways in which the McDonald's 'service' has been adapted to cultural practices in China, Japan and elsewhere, so that it almost comes to seem 'local' – or so the argument goes.[4]

Clearly this is a complex and wide-ranging debate. The key point, however, was made by Ulf Hannerz (1992: 226). Surely it is time to move beyond a polarized choice between 'homogenization' and 'localization', and return to the underlying question from which we started: *the nature of cultural space*. Instead of searching either for unified cultures or proclaiming their abolition, we must investigate the nature of cultural flows, and the space within which they work: how is that space (more or less) structured, how is it (more or less) ordered?

We can recognize provisionally in a 'transcultural' world: (a) the existence of (relative) homogenizations of cultural experience in particular places within (relatively) firm boundaries – call them for convenience, and with caution, 'cultures' – but also see (b) that in some cases cultural exchange is intensified and the exclusive ties of culture to place become much less clear. In addition, (c) global flows (of news, fashion, images, fictions, and so on) work to homogenize the materials in terms of which cultural *difference* (as well as similarity) is expressed. As Richard Wilk has neatly put it, globalization creates 'structures of common difference': 'we are not all becoming the same, but we are portraying, dramatizing, and communicating our differences to each other in ways that are more widely intelligible' (Wilk, 1995: 142, quoted in Robins, 1997: 43).[5]

Cultural space can no longer be pictured primarily in terms of an order of separate, autonomous 'cultures'. A more useful concept might be cultural flows, or rather a structured space of flows. Yet a great deal is still invested in the old model. We cannot leave it in limbo, wounded but still front of stage, as James Clifford (1988: 10) appears to do: 'culture is a deeply compromised idea I cannot yet do without'.[6] Instead we must examine more closely what cultural analysis would look like if we replaced the old model with a different one. What new questions have to be asked, and what new issues resolved? And how, methodologically, do we set about doing so?

## Rethinking cultural coherence

We have already seen the problems with the older model of cultural space that arise from the relations between a culture and its 'outside': the world of 'other' cultures. The best route to a new model of cultural analysis is to look closely at the additional problems the old model faces on the 'inside'.[7] We need to ask: To what extent is there coherence even within cultures? What do we mean by 'coherence' anyway?

### Hannerz on cultural complexity

A good way to focus these questions is to consider in some detail the argument of one theorist. None is more suitable than the Swedish anthropologist, Ulf Hannerz, whose fieldwork in West Africa and the USA is as wide-ranging as his theoretical writings. He is also rare among anthropologists in appreciating the importance of the media, and mediation, in the production of culture. He therefore shares common ground with cultural studies' recent reconceptualizations of 'culture' such as the following:

> culture [is seen] not as the organic expression of a community . . . but as a contested and conflictual set of practices *of representation*. (Frow and Morris, 1996: 356, added emphasis)

> Culture [should not be] seen as monolithic or unchanging, but as a site of multiple and heterogeneous borders where different histories, languages, experiences, and voices intermingle amidst diverse relations of power and privilege. (Giroux, 1992b: 205)

Hannerz's work (1996) on flows between cultures is relatively well known, but the radical implications of his work on the complexity within cultures (1992) have still not been sufficiently appreciated.

The starting point is deceptively simple: 'culture . . . is the meanings which people create, and which create people, as members of societies' (Hannerz, 1992: 3). The crucial emphasis is not on an abstract notion of culture as a unity, but on people's actions in making meanings, and the complex processes to which they give rise (ibid.: 17–18).[8] Culture is not a completed 'object' or 'text', but an open-ended process (ibid.: 3). The initial similarity with Raymond Williams' work is striking.

Hannerz, however, stresses not the unity of culture, but its duality. Culture is not just a set of meanings, which can be analysed for their structural unity, but two things: a set of meaningful forms *and* human interpretations of them (ibid.: 3). This is crucial, since these two things do not necessarily cohere. Unless we assume that everyone makes the same interpretations (and why assume that?), cultures are intrinsically dual, not unified, from the start. This in itself is, of course, too simple. 'Complex societies' (ibid.: 7) for Hannerz are distinctive in two ways. First, the meanings which exist in such societies do not just exist 'in themselves' (as thoughts or ideas of specific people), but quite separately they are translated into external forms for public consumption. Thus royal ritual in Britain is not just the meanings and ideas of those who participate in it directly, but also the externalized form which royal ritual takes for a whole society through the mediated forms in which it is publicly communicated. Second, those meanings (whether externalized or not) have to be distributed to the members of a complex society, who inevitably are dispersed across space. There is no reason to assume that the distribution is even; on the contrary, the unevenness of distribution is one of the main things to be investigated.

Hannerz, therefore, analyses complex cultures in terms of three interrelated dimensions:

*and modes of thought* . . . the entire array of concepts, propositions, and the like which people within some social unit carry together, as well ⅽ various ways of handling their ideas in characteristic modes of mental ⅰon;

2 *forms of externalization*, the different ways in which meaning is made accessible to the senses, made public; and

3 *social distribution*, the ways in which the collective cultural inventory of meanings and meaningful external forms – that is, (1) and (2) together – is spread over a population and its social relationships. (Hannerz, 1992: 7, original italics)

We can also represent this diagramatically (see Figure 5.1).

The most original aspect of Hannerz's approach is to show that what happens along dimensions (2) and (3) (questions of form and distribution) also has major implications – in the reverse direction – for how we interpret what happens along dimension (1) (questions of meaning and content). Any individual will have access to only some of the meanings circulating in the society. The distribution of meanings cannot be taken for granted: it is a crucial part of what we think a 'culture' is. Remember the quotation from Hannerz which heads this chapter: 'In a society where the cultural flow is varied and uneven, it is an open question which meanings have reached where and when' (1992: 81).

Nor are people monads taking inputs from the wider culture in isolation from everyone else; they are also engaged in making sense of other people's meanings and interpretations (ibid.: 14). This adds a further layer of complexity to the distribution of meanings. Returning to the example of royal ritual, there is no reason to assume that everyone interprets a particular ritual the same way. In addition, everyone interprets what others think – the meanings those others make of the ritual – and obviously each person's perspective on that interpretative landscape may be different, depending on

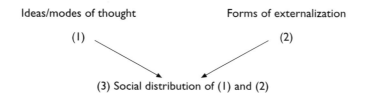

FIGURE 5.1    *The dimensions of complex cultures (after Hannerz)*

what their own interpretation of the ritual is. The complexity of the distribution of meanings, therefore, feeds on itself.

As a result, the idea of cultural 'holism' – that cultures comprise principally the meanings that people *share* – becomes untenable. As Hannerz puts it:

> we must recognize the real intricacy of the flow of meaning in social life. As each individual engages in his [sic] own continuous interpreting of the forms surrounding him, how can we take for granted that he comes to the same result as the next fellow [sic]? There is nothing automatic about cultural sharing. Its accomplishment must rather be seen as problematic. (ibid.: 44)

The assumption of cultural coherence must be questioned; this is true for any culture, regardless of its relations with other cultures. Hannerz reinforces the point by bringing out how individuals' involvement in all aspects of culture is affected by factors which divide, rather than unite, them: taste, education, income, occupation, and all the divisions in knowledge and status they imply. 'Contemporary complex societies', he concludes, 'systematically build *nonsharing* into their cultures' (ibid.: 44, added emphasis).

Even so, this sceptical approach raises issues of its own: how are we to explain the coherence within cultures which does exist? This is where Hannerz's profound scepticism on the question of cultural order fits well with cultural and media studies' historic concern with the industrialization and commodification of culture. We can explore this through the case of the media.

The media externalize ideas and images for public consumption, which otherwise would be available only privately. They therefore expand massively the quantity of meanings circulating in society. But this process of externalization is not 'transparent'; it involves distortions and imbalances (ibid.: 81). There are inequalities in who makes an input into media messages (few people, even in the days of 'reality TV' and talk shows, have actually appeared on TV let alone contributed to the decision making underlying it). In addition, of course, media messages are unequally distributed across a culture; they reach only some of its members. So working with Hannerz's model, the media, in externalizing the meanings of a culture (dimension (2) above), create asymmetries along other dimensions (in the inputs – dimension (1); and in the eventual distribution – dimension (3)). The external 'reality' of a culture – what passes for its 'surface' – is inseparably linked to inequalities of distribution and power.[9]

There is a further factor to be considered here, which is usually only implicit in Hannerz's account but which has emerged clearly from critical geography and cultural studies influenced by it. Complex societies involve not only social differentiation, but regular spatial separation or segregation. The result, paradoxically, is that situations of difference where mutual incomprehension would occur are, to a significant degree, avoided. To simplify drastically in order to get across the basic point: the rich tend to work, rest and play in different places from the poor (except when the poor serve the rich). The 'gated communities' and 'Common Interest Developments' (CIDs) of the USA (McKenzie, 1994; cf. Soja, 1992; Judd, 1995) and the high-security housing developments of white urban South Africa are only the most formalized examples of a more pervasive process. In addition, people are differentiated in terms of their mobility (where, and on what terms, they can move). There is what Doreen Massey (1997: 234) has called an uneven 'power-geometry' in contemporary societies, even as they appear to become faster moving and more interconnected. Cultural order – even when it *seems* to be present – carries with it a hidden degree of differentiation and disorder, which is spatially reproduced and spatially disguised.

I have shown, I hope, that Hannerz's work can help us develop an alternative way of thinking about cultural order, one which fits well with analyses of how cultural institutions such as the media work. It might be objected that Hannerz tells us little about the social and psychic power which certain cultural flows, in practice, have over us: the claims of nation and community, and of cultural and ethnic identity, the implication in 'culture' of our fears and desires, our sense of belonging and responsibility, or (to return to the debates of Chapter 4) our strong engagements with particular texts in the context of textual events. But, as we see in Chapter 6, the whole question of subjectivity remains unresolved in cultural studies, so we can hardly blame Hannerz for not supplying a solution. It is achievement enough to have clarified the terms on which we can speak about 'cultures' as such.

Cultures do not in any simple sense 'cohere'. Cultural coherence in complex societies is not so much a matter of shared perspectives, but of 'more people's perspectives mak[ing] sense of other people's [different] perspectives' (Hannerz, 1992: 168): it is a matter of 'a network of perspectives' (ibid.: 62) – or, to use Wilk's phrase, 'structures of common difference' (1995: 142, quoted in Robins, 1997: 43). By making this very clear, Hannerz gives us a more workable notion of 'cultures': as the possibility (not necessity) that certain large groups of people share in common many meanings, but also many structures of difference. Often (but again, not necessarily, in the age of dense trans-border media flows) such groups will share a common territory. But there is no basis for assuming that their 'culture' is necessarily a unity. Instead, cultural order (to the extent that it exists) becomes part of what we have to explain, just as order was in the textual environment.

Having abandoned the assumption that cultural space is simply the order of separate, authentic cultures, we are freer to examine the many forms of cultural experience which fall outside or between exclusive cultural boundaries. The complexities of tourist culture and other forms of cultural 'sampling' such as food or dress fashion are important cases, as are the hybrid inter-cultural spaces suggested by music.

What makes Hannerz's work fit so strategically with cultural studies is not that its implications are entirely new (echoes of Stuart Hall and Raymond Williams, among others, can be found in the past few pages) but that it is entirely free of organicist assumptions about culture (which were present even in Gramsci's theory of hegemony, so influential in the 1980s).[10] Following Hannerz, we can see clearly how forces of order *and* differentiation, symmetry *and* asymmetry, sharing *and* nonsharing, work together to produce the complex flows we reductively call 'cultures'.

### A new set of cultural facts

There is nothing simple, then, about a 'culture'. A culture is not a surface off which we can simply read the 'facts' of some 'inner' life; nor (as we saw earlier) does it fit neatly within spatial or temporal borders. Cultures are complex structures of flows whose (relatively ordered) workings have to be gradually pieced together, without assuming their coherence in advance.

We must get away from the idea that the 'primary data' about a culture are a set of 'shared' meanings, rituals, beliefs, ideas or images, or even the semiotic or semantic structures that may connect them. That is the old model at work, which thinks of culture as a 'place' where certain things are collected together and ordered. But there is no such place (it is just a worn metaphor). Our primary data are not so much particular meanings, which we imagine to be shared, as patterns of flow and the structural forces which shape them. Equally part of our primary data (and recognized, if only abstractly in Hannerz's model) are the structures which underlie the industrialization and commodification of culture, which political economy work has done so much to explore. We return here, but in a new and clarified form, to cultural studies' founding insight: that the 'facts' of culture are already marked by inequalities of power.

This methodological point makes a big difference to how we interpret the apparent realities of cultural life.[11] Consider the events in the week in 1997 following Princess Diana's death (cf. Couldry, 1999; McGuigan, forthcoming). In Britain (and elsewhere) there was a vast number of individual and collective expressions of grief: the laying of flowers, the signing of remembrance books, the writing of messages to be pinned to trees and gates. From there it seemed a small step for the huge majority of public commentators in Britain to read off a message about 'the state of the nation in grief'. Before our eyes, a national text of grief was being written, or so it seemed. Very few, at the time, asked the basic questions which the flow model of culture requires: Who exactly was mourning, and who wasn't? Who was visiting the public sites of mourning, and who wasn't? (How, in other words, was the phenomenon distributed?) And how much was the impression of 'a nation in grief' influenced by the way particular messages and images were externalized by the media? What, in turn, were the reactions of audiences to that externalization of the grief which undoubtedly many felt? It was only some months later that evidence emerged of a significant minority (perhaps more) who dissented or felt no involvement at all (cf. Couldry, 1999: 85). Even when they seem most secure, old-style 'cultural facts' are treacherous.

This links to the question of discourses about culture itself: claims about the state of Australian or American culture, the uniqueness of French culture, and so on. We have to investigate too how these claims are produced and distributed, and the asymmetries built into those processes. There is nothing transparent about them. As Meaghan Morris points out in discussing 1980s debates about the 'Ordinary Australian' (1992: 470), we have to be very cautious when '"everyday life" has become – in the name of "culture" – an object of bureaucratic fantasy, policy desire, and media hype, as well as a subject of seemingly unlimited cultural production'. Hence the distance Morris advocates keeping from discourses about 'the popular', including cultural studies' own popularizing rhetoric (see also Chapter 1).

If we operate outside the descriptive language of 'cultures' (as being 'expressed', 'preserved', 'declining', and so on), we can afford to be quite sceptical about the variously motivated claims made on their behalf. Changing our method of thinking about 'culture' changes the reality from which political debate begins.[12]

## Working with cultural complexity

In the rest of this chapter, I look more concretely at how the agenda of cultural analysis is already being changed by this shift of models (Hannerz is only the clearest example of a process under way in many writers' work). As we would expect, this is occurring in many disciplines: cultural studies, sociology and anthropology.

## The feel of the new model

Working with cultural complexity means 'working *against* culture' (Abu-Lughod, 1991), against the older model of culture(s), that is. There is no reason any more to suppress or reduce the complexity all around us. Why not focus closely on the places whose 'meaning' cannot be summed up in a single narrative; the lives which are stretched across many sites and many roles, without necessarily cohering into a unity; the communities which are not tied to a single nation-state, but are informed by the experience of moving between many? We must take seriously 'identities that resist classi-fication' (Kearney, 1995: 558), which of course may mean working at odds with the definitional strategies of states or markets.

Culture emerges 'on a differently configured spatial canvas' (Marcus, 1995: 98) where the connections between sites matter as much, and sometimes more, than the sites of imagined closure (the village, the city, the nation state, or even the globe). This is the canvas which, for a decade or so, cultural anthropology has begun to address; I am unable to do jus-tice here to the range of this work,[13] which is partly the point. There *is* no vantage point from where an accurate map of 'the world's cultures' and all their interconnections can be drawn up, although that does not stop powerful economic and political forces – from News Corporation to Microsoft – from speaking as if they had one. There can be no map either of what the new agenda of cultural analysis is achieving around the world.

With this caveat, one interesting example is Anna Lowenhaupt Tsing's impressive book (1993) about her time with the Meratus Dayak people from the mountainous forest regions of south-east Kalimantan in Indonesia. They are in various ways managed and marginalized by the central Indonesian government, but at the same time engage in a complex set of negotiations of their identity with many 'centres', not just Jakarta, but more locally and globally also. Tsing found there were no 'villages' to study, but rather a shifting network of cultural dialogues across scattered populations, between which she moved. In a powerful passage, Tsing describes how her own movements across cultural space made irrelevant the attempt to reduce it to a closed cultural order:

> As I involved myself with a network that stretched across the mountains, I moved increasingly further from structural models of local stability and came to recognize the open-ended dialogues that formed and reformed Meratus culture and history. My own shifting positioning made me espe-cially alert to continual negotiations of local 'community', to the importance of far-flung as well as local ties . . . Moreover, a culture that cannot be tied to a place cannot be analytically stopped in time. As I observed communities

in flux, it became difficult to avoid the fact that local agreements about
custom, ritual, language, and livelihood were also open for renegotiation.
(Tsing, 1993: 66)

In this vision of 'postcolonial anthropology' (1993: 14), the aim is not to
define the cultural lives of others, but to study the processes by which
people are defined, through or against their will: the processes of 'cultural
heterogeneity, power and "marginality"' (ibid.). 'Marginality' is in quotation marks, because there is no absolute 'marginality' – any more than
there are 'masses' in Raymond Williams' view – only the unequal processes
through which some (more or less successfully) marginalize others. Note
how well the early concerns of cultural studies fit with this new anthropology; in stating her vision, Tsing speaks of 'cultural studies' and 'postcolonial
anthropology' interchangeably. Certainly, divisions between historic disciplines matter less here than the genuineness of the shift in thinking about
culture.

Freed from the compulsion to find cultural order, the new approach can
address alternative spaces of imagination, which do not fit into wider strategies of inclusion and exclusion. This is one implication of the sociologist Paul
Gilroy's powerful analysis of 'black' music in multi-ethnic Britain and
America as a '*counter*culture of modernity' (1992: 36). In one way, Gilroy
follows British cultural studies' tradition of analysing the links between
music and social dissent, but his work marks an important break because it
seeks to transcend the essentialism endemic in cultural description. He rejects
the idea that cultural forms are ever 'essentially' expressive of one 'race' or
tied to one place: an exclusive set of roots. He focuses instead on patterns of
movement and exchange, the 'crossroads' rather than the 'centre', sites of
connection and hybridity rather than boundaries. But like Hannerz, he
rejects the naive idea that cultural flow is free and unconstrained, as if our
cultural investments could ever be innocent of the bitter history of conflicts
about who belongs and where.[14]

Gilroy's work raises new questions about cultural experience and in the
process suggests dimensions of 'culture' which are not reducible to definitional strategies and exclusions.

## New directions in empirical research

Rather, however, than explore the theoretical implications of Gilroy's
work, which would take us too far afield, I close this chapter with some
further examples of what is at stake in doing cultural analysis beyond 'cultures'.

First, we should be clear that we are talking about something quite different from the politics of 'multicultural*ism*'. Although, superficially, there is a similarity (both reject the explicit entrenchment of dominant cultures), a profound difference is that 'multiculturalism' fails to challenge – in fact it reinforces – the idea of essential cultural difference. Since it is a small step from there to reproducing discourses of ethnic and 'racial' difference as well, multiculturalism poses dangers in both its political and academic guises (Chow, 1993; Zizek, 1997; Bharucha, 1999). The current 'multiracial' policy of the Singapore state illustrates some of the issues (Ang and Stratton, 1997; Chua, 1998). While affirming tolerance between three 'races' (Indian, Chinese and Malay), the Singapore government is seeking to reduce the actual complexity of the 'cultures' which 'correspond' to them; thus, for example, Singaporeans of Chinese origin are encouraged to speak Mandarin, regardless of their actual first language (Ang and Stratton, 1997: 63; Chua, 1998: 190).

The wider importance of distinguishing between the cultural flows model and multiculturalism emerges in the context of fierce US controversy over the political impacts of multiculturalism (Gitlin, 1995; Glazer, 1997). If the new model (which I believe to be central to cultural studies) is in fact incompatible with the political discourses of multiculturalism, then cultural studies cannot simply be blamed for America's 'culture wars' within its own boundaries or its political crisis (as Todd Gitlin implies: 1995: 146). We are not required to choose between cultural studies and an adequate democratic politics.[15]

More positively, recent work on multi-ethnic London has shown the value of listening closely to what 'sceptical young voices' have to say about questions of cultural identity (Back, 1996: 2; cf. Baumann, 1996).[16] Les Back's work is on discourses of racism and community in south-east London (including areas with large populations of Afro-Caribbean origin and a smaller Vietnamese population); Gerd Baumann (cf. also Gillespie, 1995) writes about the town of Southall in west London (which has a majority South Asian population). Both pay close attention to the complexity of people's language. Back's main theme is how racialized attitudes can be reproduced at the same time as multi-ethnic community is legitimated and 'black' culture (in the form of music and fashion) identified with. In what he calls 'urban multiculture' (1996: 15), 'transcultural production' can coexist with racism (and its implied claims to ethnic and cultural exclusivity) (ibid.: 7). Baumann concentrates on the unresolved tension between two types of discourse about culture within everyday talk in Southall: the essentializing 'dominant' discourse which assigns everyone to a different culture, community and ethnic identity – and reifies the differences; and a second, popular discourse which emphasizes the flexibility of cultural differentiations.

Both writers are sensitive to the complexity of people's talk and actions about culture and identity, while showing how reifications of 'culture' are reproduced. Both also discuss how musical forms may allow new identities to be expressed. Back analyses bhangra as a new space for expressing a common identity for all South Asians in Britain (1996: 219–20; cf. Baumann, 1996: 156–7); whereas jungle in its musical form and in its very relations of production affirms an identity which is explicitly trans-ethnic, transcultural:

> Jungle demonstrates a diaspora sensitivity that renders explicit the Jamaican traces within hiphop culture along with a radical realignment of national images. Black, white and Asian junglists all claim that the music uniquely belongs to Britain . . . For these citizens, jungle is a music 'to feel at home in', profoundly heterotopic and simultaneously local, national, and transnational. (Back, 1996: 234)

There is always the danger, however, of tying the impacts of a musical form too closely to discourses about cultural difference. If Hannerz is right, we have to think not only about cultural inputs but also their externalized forms and their distribution. When cultural interchanges are so fast, and the technology for adapting image or sound samples from 'elsewhere' so readily available, the 'meaning' of hybrid forms – even to their producers, let alone their audiences – needs very careful unpacking; it may even be quite ambiguous and uncertain.[17] The scepticism we developed in Chapter 4 in relation to texts is useful here when analysing cultural production more generally.

The final example here concerns a very different type of cultural interchange: that between humans and machines. It is important that cultural studies not only adopts the new non-unified model of culture, but also expands the range of cultural phenomena to which it applies that model. As argued in earlier chapters, there are many important areas of cultural life that have been neglected so far in cultural studies, including the cultures of science. Disregarding the flood of attempts to mystify these matters, there has recently been serious theoretical and empirical work exploring the impact of 'virtual life' on our notion of culture itself (Turkle, 1984, 1996; Morse, 1998). As Margaret Morse (1998: 17) points out, cyberspace and the Internet are only the last in a series of 'fictions of presence' (beginning with radio), which have accustomed us to interacting with persons who are not physically present. However, the Internet takes the detachment of 'culture' from 'place' (embodied place) one stage further:

> the gathering places and sites of experience in electronic culture are increasingly situated in what amounts to *nonspace* and in which humans not only

interact with human agents but also with the semiautonomous agency of machines . . . what else is cyberspace but *metaphors* made virtually perceivable by means of a display system? (Morse, 1998: 17–18, original emphasis)

'Virtual' culture is disturbing for Morse, not so much because it is de-localized, but because it is a 'space' which, much of the time, does not involve interacting with humans at all. The social psychologist Sherry Turkle is prepared (perhaps rightly) to treat the Internet (and particularly the interactive multiuser games called MUDs , the abbreviation for 'multiuser domains') as new cultural spaces of human interaction in their own right. But whatever your view on the ontology, Turkle asks a vital question: 'I want to know what we are becoming if the first objects we look upon each day are simulations into which we deploy our virtual selves' (Turkle, 1996: 22). Perhaps this is a little sweeping (at least, it does not apply to me!), but this is clearly an area of 'culture' where more research is vital.

Instead of lapsing into the idea that all cultural life is changing at once – becoming virtualized and disorientated (Virilio, 1995) – we should think of this as a useful opportunity for testing out the questions generated by the new cultural flows model. We have learnt not to take a pool of texts, such as those which circulate on and about the Internet, at face value. We have to ask about the distribution of those texts: who exactly is participating in this virtual world, and who is not? (Which immediately suggests a further little-asked question: what are the views of *non*-participants on the Internet's significance?) How are those texts integrated with the flow of other meanings (from media and face-to-face communications)? What wider status is given by MUD-users and others to the virtual texts that circulate in MUDs? Do MUD-users, for example, think of co-participants as belonging to a separate 'culture' in their own right, or do they assume they are members of the same 'culture' as themselves? (This might make a great difference.)

We should not treat 'virtual culture' as if it were coherent and bounded (tied to a definite, if virtual, place) when we no longer regard non-virtual culture that way, nor should we reify the boundaries between them. The complex and unresolved relations between the 'virtual' and the 'real' are already part of daily life, as the recent comment of a Bangladeshi community leader in London brings out:

I can surf the Internet, I can phone my relatives around the world, but I am afraid sometimes to go out of my front door in the morning to go round the corner to the paper shop in case I get attacked by a gang of racist thugs, who happen to live across the road. (Quoted in Cohen, 1997b: 14–15)

## Summary

In various ways, then, through theoretical explorations and empirical research, a new approach is emerging that listens to, rather than reduces, the complexity of culture. In explaining all this, I have kept to the broad methodological question – what type of entity is culture? – rather than detailed questions of which specific method of cultural analysis we should use for what purpose. My strategy is the same as in Chapter 4. There is simply no reason to legislate for the use of one particular method in cultural studies. Each method has different uses. Textual analysis is necessary to explore the sheer range and density of cultural production (textual, inter-textual), but it must operate with an understanding of the textual environment that fits with our picture of culture itself as a space of flows. Research methods that focus on cultural participants (studying their actions or talk or both) are vital in generating insights into how people are positioned within, and contribute to, cultural flows (see also Chapter 3).

As with the question of 'texts' and 'textuality', so with the question of 'culture': what matters is not which detailed method you choose, but whether the wider analytical framework within which you apply those methods is adequate to the complexity of what you are trying to understand. I hope to have established what that framework should be.

The new model of culture(s) begins from complexity. It regards cultural space not as a group of separate, coherent entities called 'cultures', but as a vast space of flows whose order and coherence cannot be assumed. The role of cultural analysis is to understand the structural forces which generate such order and regularity as exists, without assuming that order is 'natural' or 'built into' cultural space. The new model reckons with our sense of cultural, ethnic and social differences – Geertz must be right to say that we still need to go on 'imagining difference' (1994: 464) – but without essentializing them. It gives no priority to assumptions that culture is localized and, therefore, it is ready to study cultural forms that flow across many sites, with and beyond national borders.

At the same time, culture is not pictured as a free flow of meanings and forms. On the contrary, because it does not assume in advance that cultural order exists, the new model investigates directly *how* order is constructed, how flows are structured, and the inequalities and asymmetries they entail; in short, it investigates 'culture' as the complex and uneven working out of power.

This is a model of culture to which, as recognized by Hannerz (1992: 274, n. 27; cf. Marcus, 1995), cultural studies – through its work on mediation and representation – has made a vital contribution. Yet who 'owns' the model is not the point. Its effectiveness does not depend on being appropriated behind one disciplinary boundary or another, whether cultural studies, anthropology or sociology. The new model represents the emergence of a new way of investigating culture which replaces the essentialist models that have marked all three disciplines, opening onto a space that is available to them all. There is no turning back.

## Suggestions for further thinking

1   Sharma et al. (1998: 1) open their important book *Dis-orienting Rhythms: The Politics of the New Asian Dance Music* with a quotation from Asian Dub Foundation's track 'Journey'[18] that begins:

Now we're Nomads
That stay in one place
Not a country
Not a face . . .

What are the implications of this quotation for our model of culture(s)?
2   Would you describe yourself as belonging to a culture, or perhaps more than one culture? Can you develop a unified narrative of your cultural allegiances in this way, and if not, does it matter? To what extent is your 'culture' related to the physical places where you spend your time, and to what extent is it detached from them?
3   Survey the statements or claims made about 'culture' in the media over a period of a week (you might also like to think about related terms such as 'community' and 'identity'). Consider the distribution and sources of these statements, and any asymmetries of power that might have contributed to their prominence. How might these statements be taken up by individual media consumers (cf. Chapter 4)? How much weight, in the light of all these factors, should we give to these statements and claims?

## Notes

1   In the early 1990s in cultural studies this link between methodology and politics emerged in a very specific form. Working from The Institute for Cultural Policy Studies at the University of Queensland, Tony Bennett (1992, 1993, 1998a) argued that 'culture' (in the sense of a 'way of life' that we might or might not

share in common, as explored by Raymond Williams) is not a given, but the effect of a particular form of 'governmentality' in Foucault's sense. If, as he argued, 'culture' itself is merely 'a historically produced *surface* of social regulation' (1992: 27, added emphasis), then the prior question for research inevitably lies elsewhere: in 'the programmatic, institutional, and governmental conditions in which cultural practices are inscribed' (ibid.: 28). On this basis, Bennett called for a complete reorientation of cultural studies, focusing on policy rather than 'the more immediately perceptible qualities of texts or lived cultures' (ibid.). But this drastic move begs the question of what it means to say that 'cultural practices *are inscribed*' in government conditions or anything else. Whatever its value in other respects (see note 12), Bennett's new programme for cultural studies prioritizes one (Foucauldian) picture of how the cultural field works to the exclusion of other possibilities. It is precisely the underlying question of what *constitutes* 'order' in the cultural field on which I want to concentrate. Although there is no space to argue it here, I believe Hannerz offers a more useful account of cultural order than Foucault, although that does not mean the insights of Foucault are not valuable (see Chapter 6). Your position on all this depends, partly, on what emphasis you give to the reflexivity of cultural agents.

2 See for example Dawkins (1976), Lovelock (1979), Gleick (1988), Edelman (1992), and, for a summary, Turkle (1996: 130–45).

3 This lies behind Tony Bennett's critique of Williams' influence on cultural studies' notion of 'culture' (see note 1). But, as I argued in Chapter 2, there are more important dimensions to Williams' vision than his 'anthropological' notion of culture, even assuming that he adopted it quite so naively as Bennett suggests (which I doubt).

4 Not that arguments about cultural imperialism and Western 'hegemony' are closed off so easily. On the contrary, as one quotation from a Beijing resident illustrates: 'The Big Mac doesn't taste great; but the experience of eating in this place makes me feel good. Sometimes I even imagine that I am sitting in a restaurant in New York City or Paris' (quoted Yan, 1997: 49). Why exactly should this be a good thing to imagine, except within an asymmetrical relationship which McDonald's help to reproduce? For a parallel study with very different implications, see Mitsui and Hosokawa (1998) on global forms of karaoke.

5 Cf. also Appadurai (1995) and Ang (1996: 153).

6 Whereas Clifford's early work (1988) successfully deconstructed the old 'cultures' model, his later work (1997) has not clarified where, in its absence, the direction of cultural analysis should lie. For critiques of Clifford (1997) from different perspectives, see Geertz (1998) and Hutnyk (1998).

7 As Homi Bhabha (1994: 150) has argued there is a close link between the problems of 'inside' and 'outside': 'the threat of cultural difference is no longer a problem of "other" people. It becomes a question of [the] otherness of the people-as-one.'

8 There is a similarity here with Dan Sperber's 'naturalistic' model of culture (1996). Sperber, however, deals less directly with issues of power and mediation.

9 I develop a similar argument in relation to media aspects of culture in Couldry (2000: ch. 3).

10 See, for example, Gramsci (1971: 181–2). For a survey of Gramscianism in British cultural studies, see Harris (1992).

11  Cf. Grossberg (1997d) for a parallel argument.

12  It is here that Tony Bennett's arguments about culture as 'social surface' become highly relevant (see note 1). You do not, however, need a Foucauldian model to generate them.

13  For useful general discussions, see Marcus (1995) and Clifford (1997: ch. 3).

14  Hence Gilroy's insistence not on anti-essentialism, but 'anti-anti-essentialism' (1992: 99–103).

15  Indeed cultural studies, and the new model of thinking about 'cultures', is already opening up new complexities within white US 'culture', for example the conveniently forgotten perspectives of the 'White Trash' or the white rural poor (Stewart, 1996; Wray and Nevitz, 1997).

16  For an important parallel study on the identities of young Chinese people in Britain, see Parker (1995).

17  For useful scepticism, see Gilroy (1992: 107) on hiphop, and Sharma (1998: 34–8) on bhangra.

18  Nation Records, 1995. Words by Dr Das, Pandit, Savale, Zaman. Published by QFM/Warner Chappell Music.

# 6 Accounting for the self

the strangeness of the Other is that the Other is an 'I', the Other is the same as 'me'. Without this moment of universality, the otherness of the Other can be only too easily reduced to mythical projection.

Drucilla Cornell (1992: 55, quoted Benjamin, 1998: 100)

A reflexive sociology can help free intellectuals from their illusions – and first of all from the illusion that they do not have any [illusions], especially about themselves.

Pierre Bourdieu in Bourdieu and Wacquant (1992: 195)

The analysis of culture must take account of the complexity of the individual's experience, the cultural practices of the self. This point will be familiar from earlier chapters, and has been traced indirectly through the complications that arise with the notions of 'text' and 'culture'. In this chapter, I look at a further aspect of these issues, asking what it means to take full account of the complex self-reflexive life which each of us leads. We must recognize the value for cultural theory, as Elspeth Probyn puts it (1993: 3), of 'thinking the social through [the] self':[1] this, as we will see, is a two-way process involving reflections on both the social and the self, and their mutual conditioning.

Let's be clear at the outset, however, what an emphasis on 'the self' does *not* involve (in such a contentious area, there is huge scope for misunderstanding). First, it does not involve advocating autobiographical writing or speaking as necessarily valuable in themselves, as a hurdle everyone in cultural studies has to pass. We need to be very careful, in Britain and the USA for example, to avoid celebrating acts of self-disclosure for their own sake, when many forces (economic, social, media, governmental) are encouraging us to tell others about ourselves. I remain sceptical about the value, or necessity, of such self-speaking; at the very least, we must respect the 'refusal to speak' (Visweswaran, 1994: 51). My emphasis instead is on *thinking* the social through the self: the accountability of our thinking, not necessarily what we disclose in public.

Second, I am not arguing for any unqualified affirmation of 'the self' as a simple 'unity' or guarantee of authentic 'truth'. A crucial part of my argument is to emphasize the complexity of the self and the uncertain outcome of reflecting on our 'experiences'. To that extent, my argument reflects post-structuralist debates, but many other influences as well, including Ulf Hannerz's work (1980) on the multiplicity of roles people perform in complex societies. There is no problem in acknowledging, as Ann Gray (1997: 99) puts it, that '"experience" [is] a non-unified category which can be mobilized in a number of ways, for different purposes and with different epistemological outcomes'. This is, arguably, now the consensus both within and beyond post-structuralist approaches. It is quite different, however, from proclaiming 'the death of the subject' (see below).

Third, I am not claiming that reflecting on the self – let alone speaking or writing publicly about those reflections – is a simple human fact, that we can universally affirm, without giving it further thought. We have to recognize how historical forces – of racism, class conflict, and other forms of oppression – have systematically distorted the conditions in which selves are able to reflect, and speak, in their own name. Put another way: reflexivity, although it is to some degree intentionally directed, is not a simple matter of 'free will', as Lisa Blackman points out in her work on how the reflexivity of people who 'hear voices' is denigrated (Blackman, forthcoming). The distortions that structure the possibilities of reflexivity emerge with awful clarity from the memories of living with racism in America and France, recounted by W.E. du Bois (1989: 2--3 [1903]) and Frantz Fanon (1986: 109–16). Recalling how a young white girl recoiled before his black skin, Fanon writes:

> I am given no chance. I am overdetermined from without. I am the slave not of the 'idea' that others have of me but of my own appearance . . . already I am being dissected under white eyes, the only real eyes. I am *fixed* . . . they objectively cut away slices of my reality. (Fanon, 1986: 116, original emphasis)

It follows that the reflexivity of those who are privileged in structures of racism will often also be distorted, since they will be blind to the sources of the privilege of their own voice. It was the need to get beyond this blindness that motivated Ruth Frankenberg's important interview-based study of white US women's relation to their own whiteness (1993: 9). These distortions of the material conditions under which we speak as 'selves' are a central part of what we have to examine.

Arguing for the importance of the 'personal' perspective, then, does not mean affirming a simple universal subject; it is rather a question of insisting that particular selves – with all their uncertainties and contradictions – should be recognized, listened to and accounted for in the types of claim we make about cultures and cultural experience. Once again, issues of method work hand in hand with issues of ethics and politics. In 'Thinking the cultural through the self', I discuss in detail Elspeth Probyn's work (1993) since Probyn, more clearly than anyone else in recent cultural studies, has shown what is at stake in 'thinking through the self'.

Before that ('Beyond "the death of the subject"'), I address the highly problematic legacy of post-structuralist thought, especially Foucault, which on one reading rules out any positive valuation of the personal perspective within social or cultural theory. I argue that the post-structuralist position (in so far as it has taken the dogmatic form of proclaiming 'the death of the subject') is contradictory and unhelpful – a poor basis for thinking about how we can live with difference and analyse the realm of the intersubjective (cf. Benjamin, 1998: ch. 3). *Readers less interested in the philosophical debates underlying my approach to reflexivity can safely skip this section.*

Moving beyond post-structuralist formulations, I want to explore the possibility that the self's reflexive life is an important, non-trivial, dimension of culture *and* that by taking proper account of it, we can strengthen – not weaken – our commitment to empirical work about culture. There is a dialectic – a continual and necessary exchange – between the requirements of (reflexive) subjectivity and objectivity. I explore the links, for example, with Bourdieu's reflexive sociology (see 'Reflexivity'), and at the end of the chapter ('Accountable theory'), I focus the discussion through a two-way principle of accountability which should guide all cultural research.

## Beyond 'the death of the subject'

The work of Michel Foucault has altered how we think about the links between us as individuals and the social and cultural sphere. Foucault (especially the later Foucault of *The History of Sexuality, Volumes 1–3*: 1979, 1987, 1988a) raised a new set of historical issues, which complicate any historically informed view of our present. They concern the genesis – at specific times and under specific institutional conditions – of the practices (including, but not limited to language) through which each of us comes to regard ourselves *as selves*. The common-sense view might be that individual 'experience' is an unproblematic object, a 'thing' all humans – now or in the past – have had. But Foucault became concerned in his histories of sexual practice in ancient Greece and Rome to track the development of what he called 'forms of subject*ivation*' (1987: 29), the 'forms with which individuals are able, are obliged, to recognize themselves as subjects of . . . sexuality' (ibid: 4). His attempt to write 'a history of *the experience of* sexuality' involved reconceptualizing 'experience' itself as something more general, historically variable, and problematic: 'the correlation between fields of knowledge, types of normativity, and forms of subjectivity in a particular culture' (ibid.).

This is a crucial insight, taken as a statement about broad levels of historical and social change; it underlies my scepticism about the usefulness of psychoanalysis as a model for understanding 'the self' or for integrating sociological and psychological theory.[2] That, however, is not the point here. I am concerned, instead, with the wider implications of Foucault's work, particularly as applied by other writers, or when it reflects the affirmation within post-structuralist thought more generally of 'the death of the subject'.

Foucault's insight can, quite naturally, be taken to mean that 'experience' and 'the subject' are *nothing but* the 'effects' of certain historically shifting practices and 'technologies'. This is the position of the British sociologist Nikolas Rose, who puts the position very clearly in his important book *Inventing Our Selves*:

> I suggest that all the effects of psychological interiority, together with a whole range of other capacities and relations, are constituted through the linkage of humans into other objects and practices, multiplicities and forces. It is these various relations and linkages which assemble subjects; they themselves give rise to all the phenomena through which, in our own times, human beings relate to themselves in terms of a psychological interior: as desiring selves, sexed selves, laboring selves, thinking selves, intending selves capable of acting as subjects. (Rose, 1996: 172)

This seems already an astonishingly wide claim, but if our 'psychological' accounts of self are necessarily implicated with bodily practices, then it can be extended still further to question the idea of the 'embodied subject':

> the very idea, the very possibility of a theory of a discrete and enveloped body inhabited and animated by its own soul – *the* subject, *the* soul, *the* individual, *the* person – is part of what is to be explained, the very horizon of thought that one can hope to see beyond. (1996: 171–2, original emphases)

If so, each 'individual', each embodied 'subject', has to be understood as merely the site across which various practices of subjectification flow; it is those practices, not the 'individual', with which we should be concerned. The idea that each of us has an 'interior' – a privileged personal perspective on the world – would be an illusion on this view. Rather 'persons are *addressed as* different sorts of human being, *presupposed to be* different sorts of human being, *acted upon as if* they were different sorts of human being' (Rose, 1996: 35, added emphases), and nothing more than that.

This version of Foucault's thought (representing undoubtedly one strand in his late work, particularly as seen through the perspective of the philosopher Gilles Deleuze) results in an impasse. First of all, if the space of the self is collapsed into the 'effects' of external practices in this way, key issues of value become impossible to answer. Where *are* we to look for the values on which any ethics, any politics can be built? As Best and Kellner point out (1991: 64–5), Foucault's late work lacks any 'social ethics or theory of inter-subjectivity'; in other words, any broad basis for motivating political practice. Indeed what are the values on which Foucault's own intellectual enquiry is based?[3] The best attempt at defining what value ultimately motivates Foucault's work is some sense of 'freedom', 'a space of freedom' (Foucault, 1988b: 17, quoted in Probyn, 1993: 132). But freedom for what, freedom of what? Not the 'subject' clearly, according to this view of Foucault's work.

Secondly, Rose risks committing the error we identified in Chapter 3 of confusing two, quite distinct types of 'condition' for the existence of the self. These are, on the one hand, determining conditions (which determine the nature of the self, at least in all its significant details) and, on the other hand, limiting – or constitutive – conditions (which merely impose certain limitations or external constraints on the possibilities of the self, but without closing them down to one, predetermined result). Although his language seems to slide a little,[4] the implications of Rose's position are fairly clear: '*all the effects* of psychological interiority . . . are constituted through the linkage of humans into other objects and practices, multiplicities and forces' (1996: 172, added emphasis).[5] The determining conditions are the 'language and norms' (ibid.: 96) in terms of which our selves are formulated, and these are regarded as entirely exterior.[6] We might well ask: if that is right, how can Rose explain the possibility of *his own* (or Foucault's) critique? His answer seems to be that: 'the vocabularies that we utilize to think ourselves arise out of our history, but *do not always bear upon them the marks of their birth*: the historicity of concepts is too contingent, too mobile, opportunistic and innovative for this' (1996: 39, added emphasis). But what is this 'historicity of concepts' if not the result of particular people using those concepts – reflecting on them – in particular ways? If we allow for the flexibility of concepts, how can we ignore the practice of individuals reflecting upon the languages through which their 'selves' have been formed, and perhaps even challenging those languages? But this means seeing practices of 'subjectification' as merely limiting, not determining, conditions on the self. If so, then Rose's picture of subjectivity becomes contradictory.

There are in fact significant tensions within Foucault's late work on this point. His own definition of 'technologies of the self' would seem to allow for the causal effectiveness of individual agents. Such technologies are practices: 'which permit individuals to effect by their own means or with the help of others a certain number of operations on their own bodies and souls, thoughts, conduct, and way of being' (Foucault, 1988b: 18, quoted by Best and Kellner, 1991: 61). This passage suggests that 'technologies of the self' involve the agency of individuals in a significant (not trivial) way, and it is this interpretation which has inspired Probyn and other writers. Either Foucault is inconsistent here with his wider position, or he points to a position beyond the dogma of the 'death of the subject'. The latter is less difficult to accept, if we distinguish two levels of argument. Certainly Foucault (at the level of 'whole' cultures and societies) is right to argue that the types of practice through which individual experience becomes constructed are historically specific and socially formed. But it does not follow from this that the actual self-reflexive practices of particular individuals are reducible to those types, unless we assume that everything else about those individuals (all the events they live through, all the connections they make between those experiences, and so on) are reducible in the same way – which is absurd.[7] If we avoid that reduction, we can argue *both* that Foucault is broadly right at the historical level *and* that individual experiences or reflexivity are causally significant. Indeed, after Foucault, one of the things individuals have to reflect upon is the historical shaping of our emergence as selves of a particular sort: not only my emergence, but the emergence of the other selves around me.

What is missing from post-structuralist claims of the death of the subject – for example, as worked out theoretically by Rose and Deleuze – is any sense of what it is like to be an active, reflexive self. Few would now claim that the self is a simple 'object' rather than an open-ended process; one of the key elements in that process is reflexivity, reflecting back on our past, on the conditions which have brought us to be what we are.[8] Few would deny that this process necessarily involves contradictions and complexities, or that the origins of some of those contradictions lie in the social processes which contribute to the formation of selves. However, unless we confuse determining and limiting conditions, none of this means that the self is reducible to generalized, exterior processes.

The psychological 'interior' – the self's reflexive life – is not causally trivial and this is quite consistent with seeing the self as complex and contradictory. Why? Because the self is best understood as an open-ended practice of *narration* whose coherence is not that of an object but 'a narrative unity', which, if it succeeds as a narrative, can integrate contradictions into a complex and distinctive perspective on the world.[9] At the risk of stating the obvious, each such narrative is (at least potentially) distinctive simply because it is the narrative produced by the consciousness carried by a particular body that is born, as it dies, separately.

If we reduce the self – and what it does – to the effects of language or discourse or external practices, then we lose any sense of the processes through which particular selves are formed, through and against wider structural forces (Benhabib, 1992a: 215–18). We lose any basis for understanding resistance, except as the effect of discursive systems. We also undermine any basis for recognizing others, as independent selves.

As the psychoanalyst Jessica Benjamin has put it in a powerful attempt to move beyond the dilemma posed by post-structuralist critiques (1998: 93) – the details of her psychoanalytic framework matter less here than her general point[10] – it is a matter of still 'questioning the subject, while considering the problem of *recognition*' (ibid.: 82). We cannot 'leave the subject merely decentered and dispersed', without undermining our basis for recognizing others as selves in their own right (ibid.: 86). Since respecting difference in its many forms – class, gender, 'race', ethnicity, sexuality, age – is central to the practice of cultural studies, the inference is clear: cultural studies itself must move on from the post-stucturalist critique of the self.

Remember the quotation from the philosopher Drucilla Cornell which opened this chapter: unless we see 'others' as having something in common with us – something that requires recognition – how can we respect their 'otherness' except in parody form? What else can that 'moment of universality' be, except the recognition that they too are (complex, fractured, contradictory) *selves* – and (why not say it?) *individuals* – like us? I return to some broader implications of this in Chapter 7, the concluding chapter.

## Thinking the cultural through the self

Elspeth Probyn's book *Sexing the Self* (1993) is probably the most extended discussion in cultural studies of the self's contribution to thinking about the social and the cultural. Probyn's book is important for bridging the gap between post-structuralist theory and Raymond Williams' early work on the experience of living in complex cultures. At the same time, it attempts to move forward from the impasse in standard post-structuralist positions; to do so, it relies on the tensions within the late work of Foucault discussed in the last section. To some degree, however, it remains caught within those tensions.

For the purposes of my wider argument, I shall therefore have to interpret

Probyn slightly against the grain. I will also have to abstract from another aspect of her argument. As is clear from its title (and subtitle: *Gendered Positions in Cultural Studies*), the 'self' for Probyn is a 'sexed' self, a 'gendered' self. Probyn here draws on the work of philosophers such as Elizabeth Grosz. Grosz in recent work (1994) has argued that: (a) subjectivity can be entirely explained on the basis of the workings of the body (without any need to refer to an 'interior' consciousness) and (b) that bodies are always already gendered, from which it follows (c) that subjects are always, and fundamentally, gendered as well. While (b) is uncontroversial, (a) is highly controversial, which means that the conclusion (c) is also in doubt. Is it true that the self is 'sexed' or 'gendered', in the sense that no account of it is possible, unless formulated in terms of sex or gender? The risk here is not forgetting difference, but rather entrenching difference so far that there is no basis left for recognizing others *across* difference. This, however, is an issue I must leave unresolved.[11]

With those caveats out of the way, we can turn to the more general question: how does Probyn understand the methodological significance of 'the self' in cultural studies and cultural theory?

Probyn's starting point is that, although the self and its experiences comprise no simple unity, we need nonetheless to recognize what she calls 'the positivity of experience' (Probyn, 1993: 5). Probyn sees this as a necessary step for feminist writing after post-structuralist critiques of the subject, which risk either having no place for 'experience' or too simple a place. By recognizing the significance of experience, Probyn has to work with the tensions discussed in detail in the last section. She tries to resolve them by arguing that, although the 'self is an ensemble of techniques' ('technologies of the self' in Foucault's phrase), the self 'is *reworked* in its [the self's] enunciation' (ibid.: 2, added emphasis). In other words, although the self can only come into being by working through a series of practices that are socially shared (and therefore transcend the individual), there is a significant causal input from the self: the self is active in that process.

This seems very much like a recognition of the agency of the individual, even if not a simple unitary individual without contradictions. Probyn's post-structuralist scruples, however, prevent her putting things that way:[12] instead, she looks for 'ways to talk about individuation [i.e. the making of individuals, NC] without going through *the* individual' (ibid.: 3, added emphasis). This seems like a distinction without a difference, but it is an example of the tensions within the post-structuralist position with which Probyn has to deal: 'I want to enable a use of the self which neither guarantees itself as an authentic ground nor necessarily rejects the possibility of a ground' (ibid.: 30). Probyn's underlying position (when disentangled from post-structuralist debates) would seem to be that the space of the self –

experiencing as a self, reflecting as a self, speaking as a self – is real and important; it is a significant dimension of culture and cultural studies. But we continually need to be vigilant against assuming that the self is a unity which straightforwardly explains 'me', or grounds 'me', as an individual. Instead, the self is a complex process – or rather, a complex mass of processes – whose origin lies largely in social discourse, social practice. This is not very different from the conclusion reached in the last section.

The next and crucial step is for Probyn to argue that our (necessary) questioning of 'the self' opens up important questions about the social and cultural field. Here Probyn usefully draws on Raymond Williams' analyses of the tensions between 'experience' (or 'practical consciousness' as he calls it – culture as it is *lived*) and the forms through which it is lived. For Williams, it is because there are experiences not recognized in the fixed forms of a culture that culture is always more than those forms: it is a complex 'structure of feeling' (see especially Williams, 1977: 128–35; Probyn, 1993: 14–26). It is essential for both writers that the dimension of 'experience' is not lost from cultural theory. (Probyn incidentally brings out how early British cultural studies was sometimes more open to the individual's perspective than I allowed for in Chapter 3.)

If I ask 'in what conditions did a self (like me or you) emerge?', then this is a question about society and culture. It requires a critical perspective on the cultural field, because we have to ask about the forms of experience and identity which were socially available (gender roles, expectations about sexuality, class differentiation, and so on), and their impact on the fundamental question of: 'who speaks for whom, why, how, and when?' (ibid.: 2). Questioning 'the self' – how was 'I' produced as a self? – means challenging the assumption that societies of individuals emerge without tensions or exclusions, without regulating how/which people may speak in their own name. As Probyn notes, Carolyn Steedman is an important reference point here. 'The self' in this sense is a privileged site for asking important questions about the social.

The purpose of 'thinking the self' for Probyn, as stressed earlier, is not self-disclosure or self-affirmation; it is to think about the social and the cultural at the point where their tensions hurt us most and most need to be articulated – to 'think the social through my self'. As Probyn emphasizes, there is nothing easy about this. Each of us emerges from social and historical conditions which pre-exist us, conditions which in advance have limited the types of selves we can become. And these conditions affect each of us differently. There is no overarching perspective which can either guarantee our status as unitary individuals or integrate the differences between us.

We are incomplete subjects, yet also subjects who can be transformed through how we speak about ourselves (our 'practices of the self' in Foucault's phrase). As Probyn suggests at the end of her book, we may be transformed by sharing our self-reflections with others – a vision of *mutual* transformation: 'The self is not an end in itself, it is the opening of a perspective, one which allows us to conceive of transforming our selves with the aid of others' (ibid.: 169). I develop this vision of a discursive community of incomplete selves in the concluding chapter, Chapter 7.

To summarize: Probyn (in spite of some tensions, which reflect the tensions of post-structuralist writings about 'the self' generally) develops an inspiring account of how critical reflections on our formation (as speaking/writing/thinking/reflecting selves) are productive for cultural theory. She traces this insight back to Raymond Williams' work, which of course long pre-dates post-structuralist critiques of the subject. In effect, although Probyn would not use these terms, she insists on the value of individuals' reflexivity about themselves and their place 'inside culture'.

While Probyn's specific concern is with the gendered and sexualized conditions in which 'selves' emerge, her argument encompasses all of the material conditions which position us differently from each other. Reflecting on these conditions, and sharing those reflections with others, alters the terrain on which cultural dialogue and analysis takes place. Henry Giroux's description of his practice of 'border pedagogy' (see also Chapter 2) brings the general point out very well:

> the concept of border pedagogy suggests not simply opening diverse cultural histories and spaces to students, but also understanding how fragile identity is as it moves into borderlands crisscrossed with a variety of languages, experiences, and voices. There are no unified subjects here, only subjects whose voices and experiences intermingle with the weight of particular histories that will not fit into the master narrative of a monolithic culture . . . this is not a call to romanticize such voices . . . There is . . . the issue of making visible those historical, ideological, and institutional mechanisms that have both forced and benefited from such exclusions. (Giroux, 1992a: 174–5)

Thinking the social, and cultural, through the self means developing a practice of reflection which, from yet another angle, makes apparent the contested and non-transparent nature of 'society' and 'culture'.

## Reflexivity

There are parallels between Probyn's work and much other work in sociology and anthropology on the role of reflexivity in cultural analysis.

Post-structuralist thought certainly has no monopoly on reflexivity. It has been a major theme of European philosophical thought within modernity since Kant's fundamental examination, two centuries ago, of the preconditions of perception and knowledge (cf. Best and Kellner, 1991: 257–8); and 'reflection' (on the conditions in which knowledge about the social world is possible) was central to the critical theory of Adorno, not generally categorized as a post-structuralist thinker.[13]

The necessity of reflecting on the status of sociological knowledge has been explored for almost three decades by Pierre Bourdieu (1977 [1972], 1990, Bourdieu and Wacquant, 1992). Just as Probyn asks what are the conditions under which I (the cultural analyst) come to speak, so Bourdieu's 'reflexive sociology' foregrounds essentially the same question, but with an emphasis less on the production of selves, and more on the production of social analysts and theorists. More pointedly, Bourdieu asks: how is the distance from the social (which sociologists require in order to do their analysis at all) *itself* socially produced? From early on – and anticipating by some years the development of postmodern ethnography – Bourdieu has tried to explode the illusion that the cultural analyst's privilege is innocent (see especially, 1977).

Reflecting on the distortions built into the position of cultural analyst has, since the mid-1980s, been the central theme in postmodern ethnography (for example, Clifford and Marcus, 1986; Rabinow, 1987). We touched on this theme in Chapter 5. Here I simply note one extension of this work which gets close to Probyn's concern with 'thinking through the self'. Kamal Visweswaran, in developing a specifically feminist ethnography (1994), has argued for the importance not of 'fieldwork' (in some distant place, to which the anthropologist secures the privilege of travelling), but '*homework*' (1994: 101–6), a sort of 'anthropology in reverse'. This means questioning the process by which she came to be in a position to write about culture: the process of schooling, the various negotiations that her education involved with her wider cultural and social environment (she discusses growing up in the USA as a girl of South Asian parents). Above all, 'homework' means for Visweswaran grasping 'the illusory nature of home as coherence' (ibid.: 104): questioning the very idea that the analyst has a simple, unified place of origin that 'authorizes' or 'authenticates' her speech.

There is a danger, of course, that too much self-reflexivity on the part of the analyst can obscure the wider issue, which is always to clarify our understanding of the wider cultural environment in which the analyst is situated. Remember, however, that the speaking position of those we write about is no less complex than ours. If sociologists or cultural studies practitioners can question the conditions under which they come to speak, so too can everyone else. It is just as important, if not more so, to think about the reflexivity of others, as it is to think about the analyst's reflexivity. But this adds a major new level of complexity to cultural analysis, as explained by the anthropologist Anthony Cohen:

> I realised . . . that, as an anthropologist who pursued an explicit interest in culture, and culture theory, I was nevertheless dealing ethnographically with individuals, whose engagement with each other was problematic and fraught with misunderstanding, and who were reserved about their own generalisation into 'societies' or 'communities' in ways to which anthropologists seemed insensitive. (Cohen, 1994: ix)

If most models of culture underestimate cultural agents' reflexivity about their position within culture, then they massively underestimate the complexity of what cultures *are*.[14] Similarly, Ann Gray, within the tradition of feminist epistemology (cf. Chapter 1), has argued that the reflexivity of the analyst can only be 'genuine' if it respects the reflexivity of those it studies:[15] 'Whilst I would argue that cultural studies and feminists need to continue working towards more sophisticated methods which engage with 'lived cultures', those subjects must be allowed to be the knowledgeable and knowing subjects [that they are, NC]' (Gray, 1997: 103). We should not credit those we study with less reflexivity than we credit ourselves; *all* speaking positions are, in a sense, problematic.

This fundamental point works more than one way. From one perspective, consider the tradition of social research which has explored how people resist the social categorizations that are applied to them, more or less self-consciously (Sennett and Cobb, 1972, on class labels; Gilligan, 1982, on gender-related evaluations of individuals' reflexivity). A vivid illustration comes in the autobiographical texts collected by Andrew Garrod and others (1999) from African American, Afro-Caribbean and 'biracial' college students in the USA. Some of the 'biracial' students, in particular, reflect on the pressure which a racially segregated society exerts on them to define their identity in one ethnically marked direction or another. Here is 'Susanna', daughter of a white Swiss mother and an African American father:

> There is a certain paranoia built into my consciousness, bred from years of explanations and condemnations. 'What are you?' they ask, as if my race defines me. If I say I am African, Swiss, and Cherokee, does the listener gain some intimate knowledge of my mind or heart, or do they simply know my genealogy? How does my genetic code set up my realities? I've grown accustomed to the questions, and most answers are by now memorized and routine. (In Garrod et al., 1999: 135)

Here, strikingly, 'Susanna' questions the labels applied to her, while apparently reproducing the myth that 'racial differences' are genetically based. That aside, it is clear that any analysis of cultural and 'racial' politics in contemporary America must take account of some Americans' questioning of the racialized discourses that have shaped them (cf. end of Chapter 5).

The reflexivity of those we write about is not something that we can safely hold at a distance. The anthropologist Renato Rosaldo (1993: 46–8) has told (against himself) the story of trying when visiting his potential in-laws to apply to them the type of systematic observations and analysis that he had practised as an anthropologist in 'the field'. Not only did his in-laws not agree with his interpretations, they laughed them out of court. What makes this example disturbing – and for cultural studies as well as anthropology – is that the problems arose when the artificial distance between the reflexivities of researcher and potential research objects was removed, when they faced each other in the single space of a family meal.[16] As a result, the idea that the researcher's self-reflexivity is special, or privileged – one of the intellectual's illusions (see the Bourdieu quotation at the beginning of this chapter) – collapsed. The open-ended self-reflexivity of all agents is revealed as a normal dimension of cultural complexity. All agents can think the social and the cultural through the self.

What are the consequences of this for cultural research?

## Accountable theory

At the risk of sounding formalistic, I want to set out a principle of consistency or, perhaps better, a principle of accountability, that should guide all cultural research. Quite simply: the language and theoretical framework with which we analyse others should always be consistent with, or accountable to, the language and theoretical framework with which we analyse ourselves. And, equally, in reverse: the language and theoretical framework with which we analyse ourselves should always be accountable to the language and theoretical framework with which we analyse others.

The reversibility of the principle is crucial: it is this that prevents us from falling into a spiral of endless self-interrogation, never to resurface. There must be a dialectic between the way we think about others and the way we think about ourselves; what we say about one must reflect what we know about the complexities of the other. Writing against the background of positivist social science with its neglect of self-reflexivity, Adorno argued that 'the objectivity of dialectical cognition needs not less subjectivity, but more' (Adorno, 1973: 40 [1966]). Equally, and with post-structuralist inspired critiques of social science in mind, we can perhaps put things the other way round: the subjectivity of cultural commentary needs not less objectivity, but more. The two positions, in fact, complement each other. They come together in a vision of a dialectical and sceptical form of cultural enquiry in which: (a) every attempt to speak in one's own name is tied to an obligation to listen to the voices of others; and (b) every attempt to describe others must allow them the complexity of voice that one requires to be acknowledged in oneself. This, in the broadest sense, is what going beyond the 'dominative mode of thinking' about culture (see Chapter 1) means.

How, then, does this two-way principle of accountability work? We need to take each direction in turn.

### The perspective of the self

One direction – the need to make our accounts of others (and the wider culture) accountable to the way we understand the self – is relatively straightforward and has been anticipated in previous chapters. Since this book has been written mainly against the long-term background of the neglect of the individual perspective – whether in holistic notions of culture, oversimplified models of the textual environment, or over-regulated pictures of subjectivity – this is the direction I have had to emphasize most.

The argument has been made in stages. In Chapter 3, we saw how notions of culture within cultural studies have often failed to take account of the non-conformity of the individual voice – the dissenter, the person who works against the grain, the person who is angry, confused, hurt by the ways in which he or she is addressed by wider cultural forces. In Chapter 4, we explored the consequences of taking seriously the real complexity of textual environments and our movements across and within them: this involved a complete re-evaluation of the methodological status of textual analysis. In Chapter 5, we saw the inadequacy of the standard model of 'cultures' as unified, coherent objects to which each of us is exclusively attached; we explored a way of thinking about cultural flows and cultural attachments, which could replace that older model. Finally, in this chapter, we have seen how the implications for cultural and social analysis of everyone's self-reflexivity have been neglected.

The answer, in each case, is to integrate into our accounts of culture an awareness of what people 'inside' culture actually do: what cultural flows reach them, what they actively consume, what they feel or think about the wider cultural space they inhabit, and so on. The point is not simply that everyone's perspective on culture is as valuable as everyone else's; of course it is (that is a fundamental value of cultural studies, see Chapter 2), but it does not get us very far in explaining how cultures work. The point, rather, is that without empirical analysis of the types of complexity which individuals' relations to culture involve, we cannot even begin to understand what sort of process 'culture' is.

Our understanding of culture has to take account of the messiness of individuals' situations 'inside' culture. I can love a range of musics (from Western classical to jungle to Javanese gamelan); I can identify (loosely, but consistently) with musics, art, fashions, cultural positions that I only partly understand and have little time to follow in detail; I can be hostile to the way I am addressed by the marketing campaign for a particular product, yet for unconnected reasons buy that product (so that others may judge me as the 'type of person' who responds to that type of campaign); I can be disillusioned about the conditions under which politics in my country or locality is conducted, but lack any sense of what effectively I can do to change it; and I can reflect a great deal over time about my changing relationship with what gets defined as 'mainstream' culture – all of this without any clear resolution. It is obvious that the cultural experience of such a self is hardly a non-contradictory unity, and it involves a significant and open-ended degree of self-reflexivity. Each of us is a cultural agent; we have no pre-set 'position' within culture, since what we do and think constitutes a continuous self-reflexive process. Culture is the more or less systematic ordering of all those processes on a large scale. At every level, then, we need to think about cultural experience and cultural effects as processes, not 'things', as *necessarily* complex, not simple. That is what thinking the cultural through the self means.

That, however, need not prevent us grasping the real processes which reify and naturalize the social world: the processes which produce the impression that cultures/identities/persons are fixed, unified 'things', and thereby limit, or at least disguise, cultural complexity. Here, however, we have to make our thought accountable from the other direction.

## The materiality of the self

What does it mean to say that our accounts of 'selves' must be responsive to our understanding of 'others', or (more precisely) to our understanding of the cultural space within which we interact with others?

In Chapter 2, for example, we saw the importance of studying how material conditions constrain who, and on what terms, can speak and be heard, as coherent selves, as full members of a culture, and so on. Such conditions are of course the basis of differences between individuals, but crucially these conditions are processes that stretch far beyond the individual. They are conditions not of our making, yet they limit the types of selves we can become. They work, not once and for all, but through continuous adjustments, in part through the self-adjusting processes of reflexivity itself.[17]

Developing this point means studying the discourses and the practices of self-reflexivity, self-formation, and identification. We re-enter here the territory explored, for example, by Nikolas Rose, but with greater allowance made, first for the variability and complexity of how such discourses and practices are worked out in particular individuals and, second for the uneven material forces which condition their circulation (the work of Steedman, Walkerdine, and Skeggs discussed in Chapter 3 is important here). Any complete account of the formation of 'selves' in complex cultures would have to include not only the available discourses and practices of self-speaking, but also matters closer to political economy:

(a)  the concentration of cultural production, more or less, in particular cultural industries, governed by forces of economic competition and aggregation; following on from that

(b)  the concentrations of symbolic and cultural authority in particular sites which constrain people to identify in certain directions and not others;

(c)  the unequal distribution of individual access to the range of cultural goods;

(d)  the impact on identification of differences in material conditions (for example employment and status).

The principle of accountability requires us, then, to take seriously not only our reflexivity as selves, but the *material* conditions under which we are addressed as selves, citizens, members of this or that culture, consumers, and so on. It goes without saying that these conditions will vary, perhaps drastically, between different 'cultures'.

Any answers here must be specific, not universal, and they must always look in two directions at once. On the one hand, there are the forces of *concentration*, which constrain and limit the frameworks, the discourses, the images, and the practices that are available to individuals in their struggle to function as individuals. It is crucial to grasp that these forces involve much more than the organization of discourses themselves (the 'historicity of concepts', as Rose calls it). They include the material structures through which cultural production is organized: the organization of most aspects of culture on an industrial scale and on economic principles. The ways in which we are addressed as members of a cultural space are closely tied to the economic organization of that space (how cultural production is concentrated in particular sectors, including the media through which most societies now regulate access to cultural production): for seminal arguments here, see Miege (1989), Garnham (1990), Golding and Murdock (1991), and Schatz (1993). On the other hand, there are the forces of *differentiation* which cut across boundaries, multiply options for cultural allegiance, and disrupt the effectiveness of centralized forms of address (self-reflexivity being just one of those forces).[18] Culture, as worked out in the formation of individuals, involves the interaction of these two types of force.[19]

Major institutions (such as the media) focus identities and reflexivity, but at the same time disaggregate people, making it difficult for them to identify with particular others. We need, paradoxically, to think more about the reverse side of culture: the 'cultures' and cultural encounters we do *not* have. That means, in turn, thinking seriously about the processes of naturalization which protect disorder, uncertainty, and unevenness from being articulated, from becoming visible. How is the sense of a coherent cultural 'inside' created and maintained?

Cultural studies – through its engagement with the realities of mediated culture, and its historic concern with the interconnections of culture and power – is well placed to contribute to these questions, provided it maintains the *two-way* accountability of theory outlined here.

There is a danger, however, following post-structuralism and in the light of important intellectual and political pressures to articulate new identities, that cultural analysis will take to celebrating disorder and differentiation for their own sake, at the expense of rigorous empirical work. I am thinking, for example, of Elspeth Probyn's recent (1996) advocacy of a sociology of 'surfaces'. The problem is not so much with this as a philosophical vision, but rather that a philosophical vision is a poor guide to understanding the real processes that continue to order the social and cultural world, and give it 'depth'. Even if Marx was right to rebuke philosophers for interpreting the world when 'the point is to change it' (1977c: 158), distorting how the world looks is a poor starting point for changing it. Cultural studies cannot afford to drop its commitment to accountable empirical investigation, if it is to contribute to the central issues of social and cultural theory.

## Summary and wider perspectives

In this chapter, I have used the double question of 'the self' – How do we explain selves? How do we allow for their complexity in explaining culture? – as a means to bring into focus from a wider angle the central problem for cultural studies (as I referred to it in Chapter 5): the nature of the relative 'order' of contemporary complex cultures. The result has been not a full resolution, but a clearer sense of the basis on which we should research our lives 'inside' culture.

How 'selves' and 'subjects' are formed and how exactly they interact with cultural flows – these are issues currently unresolved right across the humanities and social sciences (Hall, 1996a). We should not close off the disciplinary directions in which we look for such a theory (see also Chapter 1). While psychoanalysis by itself is in my view inadequate to account for the social formation of selves, some combination of psychoanalysis with post-structuralist thought (Foucault and or Derrida) may be productive: see the work of Judith Butler (1993) and Jessica Benjamin (1998).[20] Equally, discourse analysis by itself is unlikely to generate an overall theory of subjectivity (see Shotter, 1993, for an unsatisfactory attempt); it needs to be supplemented at the very least by accounts of the institutional conditions of discourse production (from cultural studies). However, the close study of everyday language and practices of 'subjectivity' is an important task (cf. Chapter 3, and see, for example, Billig, 1992, 1995; Miller and McHoul, 1998). Geography can provide important insights, in terms of how spatial boundaries and segregations contribute to the formation of identities (Sibley, 1995). So too can historical research, for example, on how identification has been institutionally focused in the past (the history of Nazism, the rise of ethnic nationalism in the former Yugoslavia, and so on). In relation to such vast questions, the role of cultural studies is less to provide an overall theory, than to contribute insights linked to its special concerns: the relations between culture and power, the materiality of culture (production, distribution, reception), and the complexity of cultural experience.

Thinking the cultural through the self – and from two directions, correcting both for the irreducible complexity of the individual and for the structuring power of the social – brings together in a single question the various methodological issues discussed in this book. Whereas other approaches (whether Foucauldian or liberal individualist) have attempted to solve the problem by simplifying one side or the other, it is the *tension* between the different sides of the problem that is crucial. The two-way principle of accountability helps us keep in mind both sides at once.

In the commitment to account for our thinking about self and others, methodology and ethics converge. In the concluding chapter, Chapter 7, I ask what concept of community we need as the context for such a commitment.

## Suggestions for further thinking

1   How has your own voice – as a commentator on the culture around you – been formed? Answering this means reflecting, perhaps, on your

schooling (cf. Visweswaran (1994) on 'homework' above), on your own and or your family's investments in your education, your own involvement as a producer or interpreter of culture, and so on.

2   Think about the types of language you and others use that helps define the type of 'self' that you are. Do you see any analogies between your own position and that of 'Susanna' (discussed above) who feels at odds with how the language of others has the effect of defining her in a particular, and limiting, way? How can such definitions effectively be resisted?

3   Take something in the cultural domain with which you consider yourself to identify strongly. Think about the wider conditions which have shaped your identification (that is, by de-naturalizing it). To what extent might reflecting on those conditions weaken that identification, and if not, why not? Answering the last question may in turn help you to see other, less obvious, conditions which shape your identification: reflect on those in the same way, and repeat the last question . . . Do you reach an underlying identification which you cannot explain further?

## Notes

1   An earlier (probably overelaborate) version of aspects of this chapter's argument can be found in Couldry (1996). I am particularly indebted to Angela McRobbie for the encouragement she gave me in writing that earlier article.

2   To this extent, I am greatly in sympathy with the overall project of Rose (1996), in spite of the criticisms made below.

3   There is part of a wider problem in the whole trajectory of Foucault's work; it depends on successive acts of unmasking certain cherished values and perspectives (the 'truths' of madness, power, sexuality), yet the values which motivate those acts of unmasking ultimately remain unclear or contradictory (Taylor, 1985).

4   By 'slide', I mean Rose's use of the term 'constituted' rather than 'determined'. Rose is no doubt aware (like Butler, 1992: 12) that 'constituted' leaves room for agency. However, as we see, for Rose the 'agency' lies entirely at the level of discourses and practices, not individuals, so that there is nothing about psychological 'interiority' which for him is not already determined from the outside.

5   There is a parallel with Diana Fuss' (1989) argument that constructionist (that is, anti-essentialist) arguments of the self in post-structuralism contain a far higher degree of essentialism (about the forces which 'construct' selves) than they like to admit. Cf. also Benhabib (1992a: 218).

6   This takes us to the argument (Rose, 1996: ch. 8, following Probyn, 1993: 128–34) that the apparently 'interior' activity of the individual consciousness is in reality only an 'exterior', folded back upon itself so as to produce the effect of an interior. This is Deleuze's (1988: 94–123) metaphorical gloss on Foucault's

late work, which attempts to save Foucault from the 'mistake' of admitting the interiority of the self. It relies, however, on a weak argument – known as the genetic fallacy – which assumes that origins necessarily define outcomes, confusing again constitutive and determining conditions. Note that, if we strip Deleuze's 'fold' of its metaphorical exaggeration, there is nothing very new about it. It was, after all, Kant who wrote that 'internal experience itself is possible only mediately, and through external experience' (1929: 246). In any case, are we really to believe that our individual experience of facing death (because mediated by discourse) is merely an *exterior* event?

7  Cf. my discussion of Mead in Chapter 3.

8  See, for example, within social psychology, with or without a psychoanalytic perspective, Craib (1998); Harre (1998).

9  There is considerable philosophical support for this approach: MacIntyre (1981: 202–3); Benhabib (1992a: 198); Honneth (1995: 270).

10  There is common ground here between Benjamin and other non-psychoanalytic work in political philosophy (Habermas, Benhabib). For useful discussion, see Stevenson (1997).

11  In fact I would argue that its relationship to Probyn's (1993) argument is not fully resolved: it is important in ch. 1 and the conclusion, but less prominent elsewhere. Probyn's own position appears to have moved somewhat since 1993: see Probyn (1996).

12  This tension also motivates Probyn's discussion of Deleuze's theory of 'the fold' as 'a model of individuation without an individual' (1993: 130). As mentioned in note 6, I don't find that model convincing.

13  For a clear account of 'reflection' in Adorno's work, see Geuss (1981). See Dews (1987) for a re-evaluation of Adorno's relationship to post-structuralism.

14  Compare Hannerz's arguments discussed in Chapter 5.

15  Cf. Sandra Harding's concept of 'strong reflexivity' (1991: 163).

16  For an important and courageous exploration of those problems, as they surface in studying white racism in Britain, see Back (forthcoming).

17  For a clear argument for a link between reflexivity and social structuring, or 'structuration' as he calls it, see Giddens (1984).

18  Some will see here an echo of Deleuze and Guattari's (1988) vision of the open-ended struggle between forces of territorialization and de-territorialization. As a general metaphor, this is useful, although not entirely original to them (see, for example, Doreen Massey's quite independent work (1994) on 'place' in geography). Not only are there problems with uncritically applying philosophical metaphors in social or cultural analysis – see below – but also Deleuze and Guattari's vision of an open-ended struggle fails to capture the pressures by which certain types of order become *naturalized*, so that they are inaccessible to articulation or challenge, insulated from 'de-territorialization'.

19  For interesting explorations of these tensions in specific industries, see McRobbie (1998) on the British fashion industry, Negus (1999) on the global music industry and Burston (1999) on the megamusical.

20  We shouldn't, however, underestimate the difficulty, or uncertainty, of what Paul Gilroy has called the 'wild frontier between psychological and sociological domains' (1996: 227). Recent surveys (such as Woodward, 1997) completely fail in my view to resolve matters.

# 7 The future of cultural studies: community without closure

cultural studies must be committed to a 'politics of difference' that recognizes the importance of making space where critical dialogues can take place between individuals who have not traditionally been compelled . . . to speak with one another.

bell hooks (1991: 133)

we improve the clarity and bite of declarations of difference . . . by enlarging the basis of shared (translatable) language or of shared opinion.

Donald Davidson (1984: 197)

This book has tried to re-imagine the space from which cultural studies as a subject speaks, clarifying both the methodological focus and the value commitments which are central to it. Throughout I have emphasized how questions of method are inseparable from questions of value. This is to be expected in a discipline distinguished by its desire to grasp the interconnections between culture and power.

In this final chapter, I look back briefly over the trajectory of my argument, and then contextualize it within the visions which compete today to define the nature of democratic politics and democracy's contribution to education. Although I do not wish to close off other visions, I draw particularly on the work of the political philosopher Seyla Benhabib and the educational theorist Henry Giroux, because their visions contextualize best the commitment to a sceptical, empirically grounded, politically engaged cultural studies for which I have argued.

## Overview of the argument

We began by asking: what is the space from which cultural studies speaks? More literally, what is the general range of issues with which it is concerned? Like many other authors, I defined this first in terms of a concern to investigate the relations between *culture and power*. I argued that this involves a commitment to two things: respecting the actual complexity of culture and reflecting systematically on our own formation 'inside' culture. Following these principles through, however, means being rather more critical of cultural studies' achievements to date than we might like.

I made clear in Chapter 1 that my aim was not to legislate for the use of particular detailed methods or the addressing of particular detailed issues – in a global and truly multi-centred subject, these must be left open – but instead to argue that doing cultural studies means recognizing that we are mutually accountable to each other for our work. The only effective basis for accountability is a shared concern with *method*: that is, the paths of reasoning we have to travel to understand the complexity of culture. In effect, this means acknowledging cultural studies as a *discipline*. This is quite consistent, however, with cultural studies (like many contemporary disciplines concerned with aspects of culture and society) adopting an eclectic ('multidisciplinary') approach to specific methods developed elsewhere.

At the end of the first chapter I formulated the distinctive methodological stance of cultural studies more precisely in terms of three principles: materialism, anti-positivism, and a pragmatic eclecticism towards theory. Chapter 2 then specified these principles still further – particularly those of anti-positivism and materialism – by trying to define a set of *shared values* central to cultural studies. The difference between cultural studies and positivistic cultural sociology is here particularly clear. I drew on Williams' notion of 'common culture', but emphasized that this must be transformed to take account of crucial dimensions of difference (particularly gender and 'race') and history (particularly the history of colonialism) if it is to serve as a useful basis for thinking about cultural dialogue today. In addition, following Donna Haraway, we need to be clear that 'common culture' does not mean closure around any one specific located 'culture', but rather an aspiration towards dialogue and exchange across difference. More specifically, the vision of 'common culture' can be formulated as the values of: (a) democratic speech (a voice for everyone); (b) the obligation to listen to the voices of others; (c) the commitment to understand the conditions in which each of us speaks (reflexivity, materialism); and (d) a recognition that these values must be actively defended (a practice of empowerment and critical pedagogy).

Chapter 3 put these values to work by thinking about the perspective of individuals on culture and criticizing the limitations of how 'culture' was mobilized as an analytical tool in early cultural studies. Drawing particularly on the critiques of feminist cultural studies writers (such as Carolyn Steedman) but also drawing parallels with recent sociology (Pierre Bourdieu), I argued that 'the individual' is a useful focus, methodologically, for thinking about how cultural studies could *expand* the range of cultural experience that it studies – always keeping in mind the material forces which differentiate individuals' positions 'inside' culture. More research needs to be done, for example, into the cultural experiences of the old, the alienated, those who are on the margins of society's cultural 'centres' – and, paradoxically, those with the highest cultural and/or economic capital. More work also needs to be done on the historical dimension of cultural experience. Cultural studies needs to explore a much wider range of cultural experience, as reflected in the details of action and talk.

In this way the idea that cultural experience is complex and highly differentiated was introduced. Chapters 4 and 5 then analysed in more detail what we mean by the complexity of culture. Chapter 4 looked critically at the nature of textual analysis, rejecting the automatic authority of the textual critic who can 'magically' read the nature of society off the surface of certain privileged texts, and insisting instead on looking realistically at what textual analysis can tell us in today's vastly complex textual cultures. The key move, I argued, is to shift our starting point from specific texts to the wider *textual environment* – the flow of texts around us, and our movements within that flow – but retaining a sense of the important role which analysing specific texts can have under certain conditions. Drawing on the work of Tony Bennett and Janet Woollacott and (more critically) John Hartley, I explored the main priorities for text-related research in today's textual cultures, as I perceive them: the study of the full range of the textual environment and an individual's varying positions within it; the study of people's different levels of beliefs and engagement in the textual environment (from enthusiasm to complete alienation – cultural studies must be more than a mouthpiece for cultural enthusiasms); and the study of the complex circumstances where particular texts come to be read closely *as texts* (what I called 'textual events').

Chapter 5 addressed directly the status of 'cultures' themselves. Linking with the debates on this topic which have raged across cultural studies, anthropology and sociology – and drawing particularly on the work of Ulf Hannerz – I argued for the importance of working with the realities of cultural complexity. This means moving beyond the discredited, but still lingering, model of a world of autonomous, coherent, localized, ethnically specific 'cultures'. We need a model of *cultural flows* rather than cultural unities, cultural complexity rather than assumed coherence, cultural processes rather than cultural objects. Applying these principles means being ready to grasp a completely new set of cultural facts which (reinforcing the argument of Chapter 4) cannot simply be 'read off' from the textual surface of cultures, but can only be reconstructed by understanding the material processes through which cultural flows are structured. This principle is as relevant to the lived complexities of multi-ethnic cities (such as London) as it is to our growing interactions with machines through the Internet and the World Wide Web.

Chapter 6 returned to the principle of *reflexivity*, both about the methods of cultural analysis and about the conditions under which each of us as a speaking and writing self is formed. At this point I made explicit a difficult issue, which had underpinned the arguments of all the preceding chapters: the need to challenge the devaluation of the individual's experience in post-structuralist thought. Instead, it was argued, we need a clear grasp of the self as a reflexive agent whose experiences of, and reflections upon, culture are not only not trivial, but provide crucial insights into the material conditions in which we become selves. The work of Elspeth Probyn is particularly important in showing how 'thinking the social through the self' can open up important perspectives for cultural studies, but there are links also with developments in sociology and anthropology (including the 'reflexive sociology' of Pierre Bourdieu). I argued that our cultural theory must be *accountable* in two directions: to the complexity that derives from the fact that culture always works through self-reflexive individuals; and to the uneven forces that shape the common materials out of which particular 'selves' are formed.

All this, I hope, has shown why cultural studies needs an expanded range of sceptical, accountable and methodologically sophisticated empirical research, which respects not only difference but the real complexity of culture. The result is a greatly complicated sense of how we can talk of a 'common culture' (Raymond Williams' phrase).

## Visions of community

In the final pages, I turn to a broader question and revisit why Williams' vision of a 'common culture', and similar visions of cultural democratization,[1] should matter to us today. As Stuart Hall (1992b: 278) argues, cultural studies is always something more than the analysis of how cultures work; it has something *at stake* in the question of how far cultures are infused by power; it has a stake in the eventual democratization of culture and (inseparably from that) politics. This is a way of putting into context the methodological commitments for which I've argued: the commitment to empirical research and accountable theoretical generalization; respect for complexity; reflexivity; and, finally, a commitment to the unmasking of inequalities of power. If cultural studies has a disciplinary focus along the lines discussed, what notion of intellectual – and political[2] – community does this focus imply?

A useful way into these issues is to think about the notion of community that is implied in scientific work more generally. The philosopher of science Michael Polanyi in his book *Personal Knowledge* (1958) argued, at that time courageously, that science requires a community of individuals (ibid.: 266) personally committed to the risks of producing accountable claims about the world. This is a commitment to truth as an ideal, which is personal, but not subjective:

> The thought of truth implies a desire for it, and is to that extent personal. But since such a desire is for something impersonal, this personal motive has an impersonal intention. We avoid these seeming contradictions by accepting the framework of commitment, *in which the personal and the universal mutually require each other.* (Polanyi, 1958: 308, added emphasis)

This was written some time before critiques of mainstream science contested the apparent objectivity of much scientific practice, but the idea of personal commitment remains useful. Polanyi makes clear that, properly understood, there is nothing imposed or arbitrary about striving for objectivity. It is a personal commitment which we can maintain, even after particular models of 'objective' method have been deconstructed: in fact, it is precisely such a commitment that gives deconstructive critique a point at all.[3] Without a *universal* commitment to the ideal of objectivity in this sense, it is difficult to see what reason we have to talk to each other about culture, science, or anything else. As Sandra Harding puts it: 'one cannot afford to "just say no" to objectivity' (1991: 160).[4] In working in cultural studies, or any other discipline, each of us makes a commitment to objectivity in the sense that we commit to our statements about the world being accountable to others on terms that we do not ourselves set.

It is important to make this our starting point, if only to be clear where we stand against the attacks on the idea of any 'universal' foundation for thought from many thinkers influenced by post-structuralism. I find very helpful here the writings of the political philosopher Seyla Benhabib (1992a), not least because they connect issues of objectivity (and the construction of communities of knowledge) with community in the political and ethical sense. Benhabib works within the general set of problems – about morality, community, democracy, and rationality – staked out by the last major representative of the Frankfurt School, Jurgen Habermas. To that extent, Benhabib stands by Habermas's defence of rationality and consensus against post-structuralist attack. As we saw in Chapter 6, she is also an eloquent defender of a notion of the self as active, reflexive and complex (formed through *inter*subjective processes of exchange and dialogue).[5] At the same time, like other feminist critics of Habermas, Benhabib is critical of his pursuit of a transcendental ground for morality which abstracts from the realities of conflict and difference.

When Benhabib, therefore, argues for a *universalism* as the basis for both rationality and community, she does not mean an abstract universal principle which erases difference or the conflicts of value that reflect difference. Instead, she offers 'universality' as 'a *regulative ideal* . . . that can yield a point of view acceptable to all': 'Universality is not the ideal consensus of fictitiously defined selves, but the concrete process in politics and morals of the struggle [for consensus] of concrete, embodied selves, striving for autonomy' (Benhabib, 1992a: 153). How is such consensus reached? By a process of open-ended dialogue that offers a very useful model for cultural studies. Benhabib calls this 'interactive universalism' (ibid.: 165): a dialogue not with some abstract, 'generalized' other (stripped of all her individual history) but with what she calls 'the concrete other':

> The standpoint of the concrete other . . . requires us to view each and every rational being as an individual with a concrete history, identity and affective-emotional constitution. In assuming this standpoint, *we abstract from what constitutes our commonality, and focus on individuality*. We seek to comprehend the needs of the other, his or her motivations, what she searches for, and what s/he desires. Our relation to the other is governed by the norms of equity and complementary reciprocity: each is entitled to expect and to assume from the other forms of behavior through which the other feels recognized and confirmed as a concrete, individual being with specific needs, talents and capacities. Our differences . . . complement rather than exclude one another. (1992a: 159, emphasis altered)

Any rational consensus reached should take account both of difference and our individual reflexivity in all its emotional resonances. Benhabib envisages in effect an ethics of care,[6] working alongside the principles of rationality and universality: care based not only on common 'humanity', but also on respect for 'human individuality' (ibid.).

This seems to me an excellent general statement of the vision of dialogue and community that we need both for a democratic politics and for a discipline of cultural studies that can truly 'explore the character of the space between [us]' (Geertz, 1994: 463). At a general level, it is much more productive than philosophical positions which reject the very notion of 'community' on the grounds that it is universalist (Young, 1990, discussed by

Benhabib, 1992a: 197–8) or which affirm a radical particularism in various guises (Agamben, 1993; Braidotti, 1994).

There remain dangers, of course, with general statements of 'universalism', even statements as carefully nuanced as Benhabib's. First, specific claims of the 'universal' may disguise particular (and powerful) interests: the continuing history of universalist claims (to history, technology, and so on) in the name of 'the West' is an obvious case (Butler, 1992: 7–8). It was precisely on those types of ground that Benhabib, and other feminist critics of Habermas' early account (1989 [1962]) of the democratic public sphere, depended.[7] More troubling, how effective can any universalist vision such as Benhabib's be unless it confronts the forces within each of us which *are* particular, which *cannot* easily accept the difference of others, precisely because it was on the basis of *excluding* those differences that our own identity was formed? This is what the psychoanalyst and social theorist Jessica Benjamin means when she says that every self, however much it strives for the universal, lives 'in the shadow of the other' – the other we have excluded:

> Merely by living in this world, we are exposed to others and subjected to unconscious, unwilling identification with others (on television, if not begging on the streets). Whether we will or no, the world exposes us to the *different* others who, not only in their mere existence as separate beings reflect our lack of control, but who also threaten to evoke in us what we have repudiated in order to protect the self: weakness, vulnerability, decay, or perhaps sexual otherness, transgression, instability – the excluded abject in either Kristeva's [or] Butler's sense. It is not truly in our power not to identify; what we cannot bear to own, we can only repudiate. (Benjamin 1998: 95, original emphasis)

A similar idea – of the play of inclusion and exclusion in the formation of the self – has been developed in anthropological or sociological terms (Douglas, 1984 [1966]; Sibley, 1995). The only way out of the self's tensions before the excluded other may be for the self to relax its boundaries: to try to integrate the resulting uncertainty through a *mutual* process of recognizing uncertainty and incompleteness, shared with the other. To live with the difference of others we need, as Kristeva (1991) has famously argued, to become 'strangers to ourselves'. Benjamin, more cautiously, puts it in terms of a question: 'What kind of self can sustain multiplicity, indeed, the opposition to identity that the relation with the different other brings?' (1998: 104).

All this suggests we should imagine community as a community of *incomplete, uncertain* selves, working through dialogue to transform one another – a community without closure.[8]

If we accept the value of this vision, we are left with two final questions: can cultural studies be a space for such a dialogue? If so, within what institutional setting, and what wider political context?

## The future space of cultural studies

As was argued in Chapter 1, academic practices are not already 'political', without anything else having to be in place. The actual links between, say, cultural studies and what most would define as politics have been limited (McGuigan, 1996: 12) although exceptions can be argued, such as Stuart Hall's sustained intervention into the 'racial' politics of Britain in the 1980s and 1990s. The importance of Henry Giroux's work lies in his refusal to evade such a challenge. Along with bell hooks and a few others, and following the early example of Raymond Williams, he has asked: how does cultural studies *in the classroom* actually need to change if it is to have any significant impact on the wider culture? Although Giroux began writing as an educational theorist, it is clear that his insights stretch well beyond the classroom; or rather, they point to debates about the place of 'teaching culture' within wider politics.

There is space for only a few brief comments here. First, the relationship of cultural studies (as theory and as taught subject) to the culture around it must be one of tension. Why? Because, to put it crudely, contemporary cultures are *not* democratic, they do *not* satisfy the values for which cultural studies stands: the speech of many is curtailed, the practice of listening to others is limited, the resources of cultural production are emphatically not shared, and all this derives in part from the material bases of contemporary culture, its industrialized form. If the values of cultural studies are to mean anything, they must include the idea of working towards a time (however distant) when the space of culture *does* satisfy more adequately the ideal of discursive community we have been discussing.[9] Giroux's 'critical pedagogy' – with its emphasis on encouraging students to develop critical voices and 'remapping knowledge' (1992a: 30) so that increasing numbers feel able to speak with confidence on cultural matters – is fundamental here.

As Giroux brings out in the context of the USA's multi-ethnic classrooms, Williams' original concept of a 'common culture' must be drastically modified if it is to help us forge spaces where difference can be acknowledged and explored in cultural work in the classroom (cf. Chapter 2). Giroux develops the strategic notion of 'borderlands' as the site for such explorations:

> The pedagogical borderlands where blacks, whites, latinos, and others meet demonstrate the importance of a multicentric perspective that allows teachers, cultural workers, and students to not only recognize the multilayered and contradictory ideologies that construct their own identities but to also analyze how the differences within and between various groups can expand the potential of human life and democratic possibilities. (Giroux, 1992a: 175)

The debate about 'common culture' cannot any longer mean, literally, the achievement of a fully shared culture or unified community. As the American philosopher and social critic Michael Walzer has argued: 'people experience solidarity separately and differently. This is not a paradox, but a simple fact about modern life' (1998: 51). Any vision of 'common culture' must therefore be pluralistic in practice. This is all the more true on a global scale. In an age of global media and commodities, a unified global culture is more threat than promise (Herman and McChesney, 1997); luckily it is a threat that is not being realized in any simple terms (see Chapter 5).

By common culture, then, we now mean the attempt to build a common *space* where cultural differences can be mutually negotiated, explored, reflected upon – a space of speaking and listening between 'concrete others' (in Benhabib's term). But this is far from easily achieved. If Williams' common culture sometimes seemed to be set in an irrecoverable past, ours can only be imagined in an uncertain future.

How can we approach this future, and what role can cultural studies play in it? We need to recognize, first, that we cannot pursue dialogue on any scale (local, national or global) or at any level (classroom, research conference, book) unless we have *the tools* for dialogue. At the very least, that means having a common framework within which we can recognize that we are in dialogue. This framework, I would argue, is necessarily methodological. Respecting the complexity of culture (having the right tools to analyse it) both helps us understand what is 'out there' and motivates us to listen to the particular accounts of others. Without sharing a set of methodological concerns and a precise language for exploring their outcome in different contexts, what stable, consistent basis do we have for talking to each other across cultural divides?

Indeed, in a recent essay Ien Ang (1998) has concluded that the possibilities for cultural studies to be such a space of intercultural exchange have been exaggerated, but in my view she underplays drastically the importance of methodological debate. As the opening quote from the philosopher Donald Davidson suggests, dialogue across difference depends not just on the will to translate – a matter of politics – but also on having the means to translate. We need to *share* many things if we are to appreciate our differences, and one of those things is a commitment to objectivity and dialogue about method.

With this in place we have at least the basis for a truly *comparative* global discipline of cultural studies, something we have lacked until now, and which we badly need if Ang's despair is not to prove justified. Needless to say, such debates will proceed from many perspectives with and without being routed through the West (Nandy, 1998: 144). They must be multi-centred, which means that they do not need legislators from anywhere. At the same time, such debate cannot even properly begin without some shared sense of what is at stake in understanding our respective positions within culture, and it is this that, from an inevitably partial perspective, I have tried to capture.

In the end, however, method is only a tool for understanding and exchange, and we need to be clear about the wider ends which motivate us. They can be summed up best, perhaps, in the single word 'citizenship' (Murdock, 1997: 83 [1989]). It is not, ultimately, as atomized individuals or even as interactive consumers that we need to understand culture, it is *as citizens*. Citizens, not necessarily in the sense of members of one of the particular set of nation-based states that happen to exist at present – since we must allow for disputes about the constitution of particular states and desires for new forms of community that transcend state borders – but 'citizens' in the sense of members of a *potential* common space of cultural exchange where we are committed to listening to each other.

As citizens in this broad and deliberately loose sense, it matters to us that we can hear each other speak; and it therefore matters when (as is almost always the case) the conditions for everyone speaking and being heard are not met. We need to understand why this is so. Understanding how culture works (a question of methodology) is inseparable from understanding who it currently works for (a question about the constitution of citizenship and cultural participation). It is because the links between culture and power threaten to undermine a fully participatory culture that analysing those links matters. It is surely some broad notion of citizenship – a sense that we are obliged to *listen* to each others' cultural experiences – that underlies the various perspectives on cultural studies discussed in this book: Raymond Williams, Stuart Hall, Donna Haraway, Cornel West, Carolyn Steedman, Ulf Hannerz. Paul Gilroy, Elspeth Probyn, and others.

It is from this starting point that cultural studies, wherever it is practised, can consider how it may intervene pragmatically in the arenas of cultural policy and politics; an example in late 1990s Britain would be government-led debates about the constitution of an impoverished, information-starved, unrepresented 'underclass' – a debate which as far as I know has yet to take into account the perspectives of cultural studies. As a rigorous investigation into the material conditions of cultural life on all scales, cultural studies can make, in the form of arguments that are inevitably beyond the scope of this book, a wider series of connections with practical political debate.

There are other models for thinking about culture, of course, but I believe it is only cultural studies that has sufficiently engaged with what is at stake in thinking about culture today. It is cultural studies which has grasped best how analysis and values, methodology and politics, are intertwined. It is, therefore, cultural studies which is best placed to act in relation to the field of culture as what Hannah Arendt (in an essay appropriately entitled 'Crisis in culture') called 'an enlarged way of thinking':

> [an] enlarged way of thinking, which, as judgment knows how to transcend its individual limitations, cannot function in strict isolation or solitude; it needs the presence of others 'in whose place' it must think, whose perspective it must take into consideration, and without whom it never has the opportunity to operate at all. (Arendt, 1961: 221, quoted in Benhabib, 1992a: 133)

It is cultural studies which holds the greatest promise of still guiding us, when (if ever) the 'long dominative mode' of thinking about culture has gone.

## Notes

1  For a clear overview of current debates in this area, see Hesmondhalgh (1999).
2  Bearing in mind well-known feminist critiques, I mean 'political' to cover public debate about all our relations to each other, whether personal or conventionally 'political'. See also Chapter 1 on the highly qualified sense in which I regard intellectual work such as cultural studies as potentially 'political'.
3  Derrida's more recent work has clarified this against the reading of deconstruction as undermining the ideal of truth: see Norris (1991) and for discussion within cultural studies Morley (1998). As Paul de Man puts it (1989: xiii, quoted in Norris, 1991: 154) in relation to deconstructive readings of literature: 'reading is an argument . . . this does not mean that there can be a true reading, but that no reading is conceivable in which the question of its truth and falsehood is not primarily involved'.
4  Cf. Nancy Hartsock (1998: 240): 'we will not have the confidence to act if we believe that we cannot know the world'.
5  Habermas' latest work seems to reflect these critiques (see 1998: 208).
6  Underlying this is an important tradition of feminist work on the ethics of care, starting with Gilligan (1982). For helpful recent discussion within the context of cultural studies, see Stevenson (1997).
7  See Benhabib (1992b), Fraser (1992), and Mouffe (1996).
8  Compare the vision of Elspeth Probyn (1993: 169) discussed in Chapter 6 and the visions of other writers (Haraway, 1991a; Nancy, 1991: 26–7; Butler, 1993: 242; Honneth, 1995: 271).
9  Tony Bennett (as discussed briefly in Chapter 5) has argued strongly against the idea of cultural studies as cultural critique (1993: 83 [1992]) and instead for cultural studies as the means of training 'cultural technicians' who can alter how culture is 'governmentally deployed'. Whether this represents a fundamental shift in values, or an issue of tactics, I'm unclear; either way, I disagree. For a discussion of Bennett's position, see McGuigan (1996: 12–21).

# References

Note to reader: to make it easier to track down material, reprintings in major cultural studies collections are listed, even if they are not the main source of the reference in the text. Where original articles are most conveniently obtained in a later collection, that is the reference used, with the original date of publication noted.

Abercrombie, Nicholas and Longhurst, Brian (1998) *Audiences: a Sociological Theory of Performance and Imagination*. London: Sage.

Abu-Lughod, Lila (1991) 'Writing against culture', in R. Fox (ed.), *Recapturing Anthropology: Writing in the Present*. Santa Fe: School of American Research Press.

Adorno, Theodor (1973) [1966] *Negative Dialectics*. London: Routledge & Kegan Paul.

Agamben, Giorgio (1993) *The Coming Community*. Minneapolis, MN: University of Minnesota Press.

Alvarez, Robert (1995) 'The Mexican–US border: the making of an anthropology of borderlands', *Annual Review of Anthropology*, 24: 447–70.

Ang, Ien (1992) 'Dismantling "cultural studies"', *Cultural Studies*, 10 (3): 311–21.

Ang, Ien (1994) 'On not speaking Chinese', *New Formations*, 24: 1–18.

Ang, Ien (1996) *Living Room Wars: Rethinking Media Audiences for a Postmodern World*. London: Routledge.

Ang, Ien (1998) 'Doing cultural studies at the crossroads', *European Journal of Cultural Studies*, 1 (1): 13–32.

Ang, Ien and Stratton, Jon (1997) 'The Singapore way of multiculturalism: Western concepts/Asian culture', *New Formations*, 31: 51–66.

Appadurai, Arjun (1990) 'Disjuncture and difference in the global cultural economy', in M. Featherstone (ed.), *Global Culture*. London: Sage.

Appadurai, Arjun (1995) 'The production of locality', in R. Fardon (ed.), *Counterworks: Managing the Diversity of Knowledge*. London: Routledge.

Appadurai, Arjun (1996) *Modernity at Large: Cultural Dimensions of Globalization*. Minneapolis, MN: University of Minnesota Press.

Appiah, Anthony (1986) 'The uncompleted argument: du Bois and the illusion of race', in H.L. Gates (ed.), *'Race', Culture and Difference*. Chicago, IL: University of Chicago Press.

Appleby, J., Hunt, L. and Jacob, M. (1994) *Telling the Truth About History*. New York: Norton.

Archer, Margaret (1995) *Realist Social Theory: The Morphogenetic Approach*. Cambridge: Cambridge University Press.

Arendt, Hannah (1958) *The Human Condition*. Chicago, IL: University of Chicago Press.

Arendt, Hannah (1961) 'Crisis in culture', in *Between Past and Future: Six Exercises in Political Thought*. New York: Meridian.

Arnold, Matthew (1970) 'The function of criticism at the present time', in *Selected Prose*. Harmondsworth: Penguin.

Auge, Marc (1995) *Non-Places: an Introduction to an Anthropology of Supermodernity*. London: Verso.

Back, Les (1996) *New Ethnicities and Urban Culture: Racisms and Multiculture in Young Lives*. London: UCL Press.

Back, Les (forthcoming) '"Guess who's Coming to Dinner": the political morality of investigating in the grey zone', in V. Ware and L. Back, *Inside the Whale: Essays on Race and Culture*. Chicago, IL: University of Chicago Press.

Bakhtin, Mikhail (1981) *The Dialogic Imagination*. Austin: University of Texas Press.

Baldick, Chris (1983) *The Social Mission of English Criticism 1848–1932*. Oxford: The Clarendon Press.

Barker, Martin (1989) *Comics: Ideology, Power and its Critics*. Manchester: Manchester University Press.

Barker, Martin and Beezer, Anne (1992) *Reading into Cultural Studies*. London: Routledge.

Barker, Martin and Brooks, Kate (1998) *Knowing Audiences: Judge Dredd: Its Friends, Fans and Foes*. Luton: University of Luton Press.

Bar On, Bat-Ami (1993) 'Marginality and epistemic privilege', in L. Alcoff and E. Potter (eds), *Feminist Epistemologies*. New York, Routledge.

Barthes, Roland (1973) [1957] *Mythologies*. London: Paladin.

Barthes, Roland (1977) *Image-Music-Text*. London: Fontana.

Barthes, Roland (1983) [1954] *The Fashion System*. New York: Hill & Wang.

Barthes, Roland (1990) [1973] *The Pleasure of the Text*. Oxford: Basil Blackwell.

Baumann, Gerd (1996) *Contesting Culture: Discourses of Identity in Multi-ethnic London*. Cambridge: Cambridge University Press

Benhabib, Seyla (1992a) *Situating the Self: Gender, Community and Postmodernism in Contemporary Ethics*. Cambridge: Polity.

Benhabib, Seyla (1992b) 'Models of public space: Hannah Arendt, the liberal tradition and Jurgen Habermas', in C. Calhoun (ed.), *Habermas and the Public Sphere*. Cambridge, MA: MIT Press.

Benjamin, Jessica (1998) *The Shadow of the Other: Intersubjectivity and Gender in Psychoanalysis*. New York: Routledge.

Benjamin, Walter (1968) 'The work of art in the age of mechanical reproduction', in *Illuminations*. New York: Schocken.

Bennett, Tony (1992) 'Putting policy into cultural studies', in L. Grossberg, C. Nelson and P. Treichler (eds), *Cultural Studies*. New York: Routledge [reprinted in Storey (1996)].

Bennett, Tony (1993) [1992] 'Useful culture', in V. Blundell, J. Shepherd and I. Taylor (eds), *Relocating Cultural Studies: Developments in Theory and Research*. London: Routledge.

Bennett, Tony (1995) *The Birth of the Museum: History, Theory, Politics*. London: Routledge.

Bennett, Tony (1997) 'Towards a pragmatics for cultural studies', in J. McGuigan (ed.), *Cultural Methodologies*. London: Sage.

Bennett, Tony (1998a) *Culture: a Reformer's Science*. London: Sage.

Bennett, Tony (1998b) 'Cultural studies: a reluctant discipline', *Cultural Studies*, 12 (4): 528–45.

Bennett, Tony and Woollacott, Janet (1987) *Bond and Beyond: the Political Career of a Popular Hero*. Basingstoke: Macmillan.

Best, Steven and Kellner, Douglas (1991) *Postmodern Theory: Critical Interrogations*. London: Macmillan.

Bhabha, Homi (1994) 'DissemiNation: time, narrative and the margins of the modern nation', in *The Location of Culture*. London: Routledge.

Bharucha, Rustom (1999) 'Interculturalism and its discriminations: shifting the agendas of the national, the multicultural and the global', *Third Text*, 46: 3–23.

Billig, Michael (1992) *Talking of the Royal Family*. London: Routledge.

Billig, Michael (1995) *Banal Nationalism*. London: Routledge.

Blackman, Lisa (forthcoming) 'Ethics, embodiment and the voice-hearing experience', *Theory, Culture and Society*.

Blair, Tony (1999) Text of speech given to the International Convention on Sikhism, Birmingham, 2 May.

Bohman, James (1991) *New Philosophy of Social Science*. Oxford: Blackwell.

Born, Georgina (1991) 'Music, modernism and signification', in A. Benjamin and P. Osborne (eds), *Thinking Art: Beyond Traditional Aesthetics*. London: ICA.

Bourdieu, Pierre (1977) [1972] *Outline of a Theory of Practice*. Cambridge: Cambridge University Press.

Bourdieu, Pierre (1984) *Distinction: a Sociological Critique of the Judgment of Taste*. London: Routledge.

Bourdieu, Pierre (1990) *In Other Words: Essays Towards a Reflexive Sociology*. Cambridge: Polity.

Bourdieu, Pierre (1993) *La Misère du Monde*. Paris: Seuil.

Bourdieu, Pierre (1996) 'Understanding', *Theory, Culture and Society*, 13 (2): 17–37 [Translation of Bourdieu (1993: 903–24)].

Bourdieu, Pierre and Wacquant, Loic (1992) *An Invitation to Reflexive Sociology*. Cambridge: Polity.

Bourdieu, Pierre and Wacquant, Loic (1999) 'On the cunning of imperialist reason', *Theory, Culture and Society*, 16 (1): 41–58.

Bowie, Andrew (1997) 'Confessions of a "new aesthete": response to the "new Philistines"', *New Left Review*, 225: 105–26.

Boyarin, Jonathan and Boyarin, Daniel (eds) (1997) *Jews and other Differences: The New Jewish Cultural Studies*. Minneapolis, MN: University of Minnesota Press.

Brah, Avtar (1996) *Cartographies of Identity: Contesting Identities*. London: Routledge.

Braidotti, Rosa (1994) *Nomadic Subjects: Embodiment and Sexual Difference in Contemporary Feminist Theory*. New York: Columbia University Press.

Brunsdon, Charlotte (1981) '*Crossroads*: notes on soap opera', *Screen*, 22 (4), 32–7.

Brunsdon, Charlotte and Morley, David (1978) *Everyday Television: Nationwide*. London: BFI.

Burston, Jonathan (1999) 'Spectacle, synergy and megamusicals: the global-industrialization of the live entertainment economy', in J. Curran (ed.), *Media Organizations in Society*. London: Arnold.

Butler, Judith (1990) *Gender Trouble*. London: Routledge.

Butler, Judith (1992) 'Contingent foundations: feminism and the question of "post-modernism"', in J. Butler and J. Scott (eds), *Feminists Theorize the Political*. New York: Routledge.

Butler, Judith (1993) *Bodies That Matter*. London and New York: Routledge.

Centre for Contemporary Cultural Studies (1982) *The Empire Strikes Back*. London: Hutchinson.

Chabram-Dernersesian, Angie (1999) 'Introduction: Chicana/o Latina/o cultural studies: transnational and transdisciplinary movements', *Cultural Studies*, 13 (2): 173–94.

Chambers, Iain (1986) *Popular Culture: The Metropolitan Experience*. London: Methuen.

Chaney, David (1994) *The Cultural Turn: Scene-Setting Essays in Contemporary Cultural History*. London: Routledge.

Chen, Kuan-Hsing (1998) 'Introduction: the decolonization question', in K-S. Chen (ed.), *Trajectories: Inter-Asia Cultural Studies*. London: Routledge.

Chow, Rey (1993) *Writing Diaspora: Tactics of Intervention in Contemporary Culture*. Bloomington, IN: Indiana University Press.

Chua, Beng-Huat (1998) 'Culture, multiracialism and national identity in Singapore', in K-S. Chen (ed.), *Trajectories: Inter-Asia Cultural Studies*. London: Routledge.

Clifford, James (1988) *The Predicament of Culture: Twentieth Century Ethnography, Literature and Art*. Harvard, MA: Harvard University Press.

Clifford, James (1997) *Routes: Travel and Translation in the Late Twentieth Century*. Harvard, MA: Harvard University Press.

Clifford, James and Marcus, George (eds) (1986) *Writing Culture*. Berkeley, CA: University of California Press.

Cohen, Anthony (1994) *Self-consciousness: an Alternative Anthropology of Identity*. London: Routledge.

Cohen, Phil (1997a) [1972] 'Subcultural conflict and working-class community', in A. Gray and J. McGuigan (eds), *Studying Culture*. London: Arnold.

Cohen, Phil (1997b) 'Who needs an island?', *New Formations*, 31: 11–37.

Cook, Nicholas (1990) *Music, Imagination and Culture*. Oxford: The Clarendon Press.

Cornell, Drucilla (1992) *The Philosophy of the Limit*. New York and London: Routledge.

Corner, John (1986) 'Codes and cultural analysis', in R. Collins, J. Curran, N. Garnham, P. Scannell, P. Schlesinger and C. Sparks (eds), *Media Culture and Society: A Reader*. London: Sage.

Couldry, Nick (1995) 'Speaking up in a public place: the strange case of Rachel Whiteread's *House*', *New Formations*, 5: 96–113.

Couldry, Nick (1996) 'Speaking of others and speaking personally: reflections after Elspeth Probyn's *Sexing the Self*', *Cultural Studies*, 10 (2): 315–33.

Couldry, Nick (1999) 'Remembering Diana: the geography of celebrity and the politics of lack', *New Formations*, 36: 77–91.

Couldry, Nick (2000) *The Place of Media Power: Pilgrims and Witnesses of the Media Age*. London: Routledge.

Craib, Ian (1998) *Experiencing Identity*. London: Sage.

Cunningham, Stuart (1991) 'A policy calculus for media studies', paper presented to the Fourth International Television Studies Conference, London.

Davey, Kevin (1999) *English Imaginaries: Six Studies in Anglo-British Modernity.* London: Lawrence & Wishart.

Davidson, Donald (1984) 'On the very idea of a conceptual scheme', in D. Davidson, *Inquiries into Truth and Interpretation.* Oxford: Oxford University Press.

Dawkins, Richard (1976) *The Selfish Gene.* Oxford: Oxford University Press.

de Certeau, Michel (1984) *The Practice of Everyday Life.* Berkeley, CA: University of California Press.

de Certeau, Michel (1993) [1974] *La Culture au pluriel,* 3rd edition. Paris: Seuil.

de Landa, Manuel (1994) 'Virtual environments and the emergence of synthetic reason', in M. Dery (ed.), *Flame Wars: the Discourse of Cyberculture.* Durham and London: Duke University Press.

Deleuze, Gilles (1988) *Foucault.* London: The Athlone Press.

Deleuze, Gilles, and Guattari, Felix (1988) *A Thousand Plateaus.* London: The Athlone Press.

DeLillo, Don (1985) *White Noise.* London: Picador.

de Man, Paul (1989) 'Preface', in C. Jacobs (ed.), *Uncontainable Romanticism: Shelley, Bronte, Kleist.* Baltimore, MD and London: The Johns Hopkins Press.

Derrida, Jacques (1976) *Of Grammatology.* Baltimore, MD: The Johns Hopkins Press.

Derrida, Jacques (1978) 'Force and signification', in *Writing and Difference.* London: Routledge & Kegan Paul.

Dews, Peter (1987) *Logics of Deconstruction.* London: Verso.

Dirks, Nicholas (1998) 'Preface', in N. Dirks (ed.), *In Near Ruins: Cultural Theory at the End of the Twentieth Century.* Minneapolis, MN: University of Minnesota Press.

Douglas, Mary (1984) [1966] *Purity and Danger: an Analysis of Concepts of Pollution and Taboo.* London: Ark.

du Bois, W. E. (1989) [1903] *The Souls of Black Folk.* New York: Bantam.

du Gay, Paul (1997) 'Organizing identity at work: making up people at work', in P. du Gay (ed.), *Production of Culture/Cultures of Production.* London: Sage.

du Gay, Paul, Hall, Stuart, James, Linda, Mackay, Hugh and Negus, Keith (1996) *Doing Cultural Studies: the Story of the Sony Walkman.* London: Sage.

Durant, Alan (1997) review of Dan Sperber, *Explaining Culture, New Formations,* 31: 202–5.

Easthope, Anthony (1990) *Literary into Cultural Studies.* London: Routledge.

Eco, Umberto (1981) 'Narrative structures in Fleming', in *The Role of the Reader: Explorations in the Semiotics of Texts.* London: Hutchinson.

Edelman, Gerald (1992) *Bright Air, Brilliant Fire: On the Matter of the Mind.* London: Allen Lane.

Eskola, Katarina and Vainikkala, Erkki (1994) 'Introduction', in *Cultural Studies,* 8 (2): 191–7 [special edition on Nordic cultural studies].

Fanon, Frantz (1986) *Black Skin, White Masks.* London: Pluto.

Featherstone, Mike and Wernick, Andrew (eds) (1995) *Images of Aging: Cultural Representations of Later Life.* London: Routledge.

Ferguson, Marjorie and Golding, Peter (1997) 'Cultural studies and changing times: an introduction', in M. Ferguson and P. Golding (eds), *Cultural Studies in Question.* London: Sage.

Fish, Stanley (1980) *Is There a Text in this Class? The Authority of Interpretative Communities.* Cambridge, MA: Harvard University Press.

Fiske, John (1987) *Understanding Popular Culture*. Boston, MA: Unwin Hyman.

Foucault, Michel (1977a) 'What is an author?' in *Language, Counter-Memory, Practice*. Ithaca, NY: Cornell University Press.

Foucault, Michel (1977b) 'Nietzsche, genealogy, history', in *Language, Counter-Memory, Practice*. Ithaca, NY: Cornell University Press.

Foucault, Michel (1979) *The History of Sexuality, Volume 1: Introduction*. Harmondsworth: Penguin.

Foucault, Michel (1987) *The History of Sexuality, Volume 2: The Uses of Pleasure*. Harmondsworth, Penguin.

Foucault, Michel (1988a) *The History of Sexuality, Volume 3: The Care of the Self*. Harmondsworth, Penguin.

Foucault, Michel (1988b) 'Technologies of the self', in L. Martin, H. Gutman and P. Hutton (eds), *Technologies of the Self*, Amherst, MA: University of Massachusetts Press.

Frankenberg, Ruth (1993) *White Women, Race Matters: the Social Construction of Whiteness*. New York: Routledge.

Frankenberg, Ruth (1997) 'Introduction', in R. Frankenberg (ed.), *Displacing Whiteness: Essays in Social and Cultural Criticism*. Durham and London: Duke University Press.

Fraser, Nancy (1992) 'Rethinking the public sphere: a contribution to the critique of actually existing democracy', in Craig Calhoun (ed.), *Habermas and the Public Sphere*. Cambridge, MA: MIT Press.

Freire, Paulo (1985) *The Politics of Education: Culture, Power and Liberation*. New York: Bergin & Garvey.

Frith, Simon (1986) 'Hearing sweet harmonies', in C. McCabe (ed.), *High Theory/Low Culture*. Manchester: Manchester University Press.

Frith, Simon (1996) 'Music and identity', in S. Hall and P. du Gay (eds), *Questions of Cultural Identity*. London: Sage.

Frith, Simon (1997) *Performing Rites*. London: Arnold.

Frow, John (1995) *Cultural Studies and Cultural Value*. Oxford: The Clarendon Press.

Frow, John and Morris, Meaghan (eds) (1993) *Australian Cultural Studies: a Reader*. Sydney: Allen & Unwin.

Frow, John and Morris, Meaghan (1996) 'Australian cultural studies', in John Storey (ed.), *What is Cultural Studies?* London: Arnold ['Introduction' to Frow and Morris (1993)].

Fuss, Diana (1989) *Essentially Speaking: Feminism, Nature and Difference*. New York and London: Routledge.

Gadamer, Hans-Georg (1975) *Truth and Method*. 2nd edition. London: Sheed & Ward.

Garcia Canclini, Nestor (1995) *Hybrid Cultures*. Minneapolis, MN: University of Minnesota Press.

Garnham, Nicholas (1990) *Capitalism and Communication*. London: Sage.

Garrod, Andrew, Ward, Janie Victoria, Robinson, Tracy and Kilkenny, Robert (eds) (1999) *Souls Looking Back: Life Stories of Growing up Black*. New York: Routledge.

Gates, Henry Louis (1986) 'Introduction: writing "race" and the difference it makes', in H.L. Gates (ed.), *Writing, 'Race' and Difference*. Chicago, IL: University of Chicago Press.

Geertz, Clifford (1994) 'The uses of diversity', in R. Borofsky (ed.), *Assessing Cultural Anthropology*. New York: McGraw Hill.

Geertz, Clifford (1998) 'Deep hanging out', *New York Review of Books*, 12 October, 69–72.

Geraghty, Christine (1996) 'Reflections on history in teaching cultural studies', *Cultural Studies*, 10 (2): 345–53.

Geuss, Raymond (1981) *The Idea of a Critical Theory*. Cambridge: Cambridge University Press.

Giddens, Anthony (1984) *The Constitution of Society*. Cambridge: Polity.

Gillespie, Marie (1995) *Television, Ethnicity and Cultural Change*. London: Routledge.

Gilligan, Carol (1982) *In a Different Voice*. Harvard, MA: Harvard University Press.

Gilroy, Paul (1987) *There Ain't No Black in the Union Jack: The Cultural Politics of Race and Nation*. London: Routledge.

Gilroy, Paul (1992) *The Black Atlantic*. London: Verso.

Gilroy, Paul (1993) *Small Acts*. London: Serpent's Tail.

Gilroy, Paul (1996) 'British cultural studies and the pitfalls of identity', in H. Baker, M. Diawara, and R. Lindeborg (eds), *Black British Cultural Studies*. Chicago, IL: University of Chicago Press.

Giroux, Henry (1992a) *Border Crossings: Cultural Studies and the Politics of Education*. New York: Routledge.

Giroux, Henry (1992b) 'Resisting difference: cultural studies and the discourse of critical pedagogy', in L. Grossberg, C. Nelson and P. Treichler (eds), *Cultural Studies*. New York: Routledge.

Giroux, Henry (1994) *Disturbing Pleasures*. New York: Routledge.

Giroux, Henry (1996) 'Is there a place for cultural studies in colleges of education?', in H. Giroux, C. Lankshear, P. McLaren and M. Peters, *Counternarratives: Cultural Studies and Critical Pedagogies in Postmodern Spaces*. New York and London: Routledge.

Gitlin, Todd (1995) *The Twilight of Common Dreams: Why America is Wracked by Culture Wars*. New York: Henry Holt.

Glazer, Nathan (1997) *We are All Multiculturalists Now*. Harvard, MA: Harvard University Press.

Gleick, James (1988) *Chaos: Making a New Science*. London: Heinemann.

Golding, Peter (1990) 'Political communication and citizenship: the media and democracy in an inegalitarian social order', in M. Ferguson (ed.), *Public Communications: The New Imperatives*. London: Sage.

Golding, Peter and Murdock, Graham (1991) 'Culture, commodification, and political economy', in J. Curran and M. Gurevitch (eds), *Mass Media and Society*. London: Arnold.

Goldman, Lawrence (1995) *Dons and Workers: Oxford and Adult Education Since 1850*. Oxford: The Clarendon Press.

Goodwin, Andrew and Wolff, Janet (1997) 'Conserving cultural studies', in E. Long (ed.), *From Sociology to Cultural Studies: New Perspectives*. Malden, MA: Blackwell.

Gramsci, Antonio (1971) *Selections from the Prison Notebooks*. London: Lawrence & Wishart.

Gray, Ann (1997) 'Learning from experience: cultural studies and feminism', in J. McGuigan (ed.), *Cultural Methodologies*. London: Sage.

Gray, Ann and McGuigan, Jim (eds) (1997) *Studying Culture: an Introductory Reader*, 2nd ed. London: Arnold.

Grossberg, Lawrence (1987) 'The in/difference of television', *Screen* 28 (2): 28–46.

Grossberg, Lawrence (1992) *We Gotta Get out of This Place: Popular Conservatism and Postmodern Culture*. New York and London: Routledge.

Grossberg, Lawrence (1997a) [1989] 'The circulation of cultural studies', in L. Grossberg, *Bringing It All Back Home*. Durham and London: Duke University Press.

Grossberg, Lawrence (1997b) [1995] 'Cultural studies: what's in a name? (one more time)', in L. Grossberg, *Bringing It All Back Home*. Durham and London: Duke University Press.

Grossberg, Lawrence (1997c) [1994] 'Bringing it all back home: pedagogy and cultural studies', in L. Grossberg, *Bringing It All Back Home*. Durham and London: Duke University Press.

Grossberg, Lawrence (1997d) 'Cultural studies, modern logics, and theories of globalization', in A. McRobbie (ed.), *Back to Reality? Social Experience and Cultural Studies*. Manchester: Manchester University Press.

Grosz, Elizabeth (1994) *Volatile Bodies: Toward a Corporeal Feminism*. Bloomington, IN: Indiana University Press.

Gupta, Akhil and Ferguson, James (1992) 'Beyond culture: space, identity, and the politics of difference', *Cultural Anthropology*, 7: 6–23.

Habermas, Jurgen (1989) [1962] *The Structural Transformation of the Public Sphere*. Cambridge: Polity.

Habermas, Jurgen (1998) *The Inclusion of the Other*. Cambridge, MA: MIT Press.

Hall, Catherine (1992) 'Missionary stories: gender and ethnicity in England in the 1830s and 1840s', in L. Grossberg, C. Nelson and P. Treichler (eds), *Cultural Studies*. New York: Routledge.

Hall, Stuart (1981a) 'Cultural studies: two paradigms', in T. Bennett, P. Martin, C. Mercer, and J. Woollacott (eds), *Culture, Ideology and Social Process*. Open University Press [reprinted in Storey (1996)].

Hall, Stuart (1981b) 'Notes on deconstructing "the popular"', in R. Samuel (ed.), *People's History and Socialist Theory*. London: Routledge & Kegan Paul.

Hall, Stuart (1981c) 'The Determination of News Photographs', in S. Cohen and J. Young (eds), *The Manufacture of News*, 2nd edition. London: Constable.

Hall, Stuart (1992a) 'What is this "black" in black popular culture?', in G. Dent (ed.), *Black Popular Culture*. Seattle, WA: Bay Press.

Hall, Stuart (1992b) 'Cultural studies and its theoretical legacies', in L. Grossberg, C. Nelson and P. Treichler (eds), *Cultural Studies*. New York: Routledge [reprinted in Morley and Chen (1996)].

Hall, Stuart (1996a) 'Introduction: who needs identity?', in S. Hall and P. du Gay (eds), *Questions of Identity*. London: Sage.

Hall, Stuart (1996b) 'Cultural studies and the politics of internationalization: an interview with Stuart Hall by Kuan-Hsing Chen', in D. Morley and K-H. Chen (eds), *Stuart Hall: Critical Dialogues in Cultural Studies*. London: Routledge.

Hall, Stuart (1997) [1987] 'Minimal selves', in A. Gray and J. McGuigan (eds), *Studying Culture : an Introductory Reader*. London: Arnold.

Hall, Stuart and Jefferson, Tony (eds) (1976) *Resistance through Rituals: Youth Subcultures in Post War Britain*. London: Hutchinson.

Hannerz, Ulf (1980) *Exploring the City*. New York: Columbia University Press.

Hannerz, Ulf (1992) *Cultural Complexity: Studies in the Social Organization of Meaning*. New York: Columbia University Press.

Hannerz, Ulf (1996) 'Notes on the global ecumene', in A. Sreberny-Mohammadi, D. Winseck, J. McKenna and O. Boyd-Barrett (eds), *Media in Global Context*. London: Arnold.

Haraway, Donna (1991a) 'A manifesto for cyborgs', in D. Haraway, *Simians, Cyborgs and Women*. London: The Free Press.

Haraway, Donna (1991b) 'Situated knowledges: the science question in feminism and the principle of partial perspective', in D. Haraway, *Simians, Cyborgs and Women*. London: The Free Press.

Haraway, Donna (1997) *Modest_Witness@Second_Millennium.FemaleMan©_Meets_OncoMouse™: Feminism and Technoscience*. New York: Routledge.

Harding, Sandra (1986) *The Science Question in Feminism*. Milton Keynes: Open University Press.

Harding, Sandra (1991) *Whose Science? Whose Knowledge? Thinking from Women's Lives*. Ithaca, NY: Cornell University Press.

Harding, Sandra (1993) 'Rethinking standpoint epistemology: what is "strong objectivity"?', in L. Alcoff and E. Potter (eds), *Feminist Epistemologies*. New York: Routledge.

Harre, Rom (1998) *The Singular Self: an Introduction to the Psychology of Personhood*. London: Sage.

Harris, David (1992) *From Class Struggle to the Politics of Pleasure: The Effects of Gramscianism on Cultural Studies*. London: Routledge.

Harris, Roxy (1996) 'Openings, absences, and omissions: aspects of the treatment of "race", culture and ethnicity in British cultural studies', *Cultural Studies*, 10 (2): 334–44.

Hartley, John (1987) 'Invisible fictions', *Textual Practice*, 2: 121–38.

Hartley, John (1996) *Popular Reality: Journalism, Modernity, Popular Culture*. London: Arnold.

Hartsock, Nancy (1998) 'The feminist standpoint revisited', in *The Feminist Standpoint Revisited and Other Essays*. Boulder, CO: Westview Press.

Hazan, Hakim (1994) *Old Age: Deconstructions and Constructions*. Cambridge: Cambridge University Press.

Hebdige, Dick (1979) *Subculture: the Meaning of Style*. London: Methuen.

Hechter, Michael (1975) *Internal Colonialism: the Celtic Fringe in British National Development 1536–1966*. London: Routledge & Kegan Paul.

Herman, Edward and McChesney, Robert (1997) *The Global Media: The New Missionaries of Corporate Capitalism*. London: Cassell.

Hermes, Joke (1993) 'Media, meaning and everyday life', *Cultural Studies*, 7 (3): 493–508.

Hermes, Joke (1995) *Reading Women's Magazines: an Analysis of Everyday Media Use*. Cambridge: Polity.

Hesmondhalgh, David (1998) 'The British dance music industry: a case study of independent cultural production', *British Journal of Sociology*, 49 (2): 234–51.

Hesmondhalgh, David (1999) 'Alternative media, alternative texts? Rethinking democracy in the cultural industries', in J. Curran (ed.), *Media Organizations in Society*. London: Arnold.

Hobsbawm, Eric and Ranger, Terence (eds) (1983) *The Invention of Tradition*. Cambridge: Cambridge University Press.

Hoggart, Richard (1958) *The Uses of Literacy*. Harmondsworth: Penguin.

Honneth, Axel (1995) *The Fragmented World of the Social: Essays in Social and Political Philosophy*. New York: SUNY.

hooks, bell (1991) *Yearning: Race, Gender and Cultural Politics*. Boston, MA: Turnaround.

hooks, bell (1992) 'Representing whiteness in the Black imagination' in L. Grossberg, C. Nelson and P. Treichler (eds), *Cultural Studies*. New York: Routledge.

hooks, bell (1994) *Teaching to Transgress: Education as the Practice of Freedom*. New York: Routledge.

Huntington, Samuel (1997) *The Clash of Civilizations and the Remaking of the World Order*. New York: Simon & Schuster.

Husserl, Edmund (1970) *The Crisis of European Sciences and Transcendental Phenomenology*. Evanston, IL: Northwestern University Press.

Hutnyk, John (1998) 'Clifford's ethnographica', *Critique of Anthropology*, 18 (4): 339–78.

Jackson, Leonard (1993) *The Poverty of Structuralism*. Harlow: Longman.

Johnson, Richard (1996) [1986–87] 'What is cultural studies anyway?', in John Storey (ed.), *What is Cultural Studies?* London: Arnold.

Johnson, Richard (1997) 'Reinventing cultural studies: remembering for the best version', in Elizabeth Long (ed.), *From Sociology to Cultural Studies*. Malden, MA: Blackwell.

Judd, Dennis (1995) 'The rise of the new walled cities', in H. Liggett and D. Perry (eds), *Spatial Practices: Critical Explorations in Social/Spatial Theory*. London: Sage.

Kaliman, Ricardo (1998) 'What is "interesting" in Latin American cultural studies?', *Journal of Latin American Cultural Studies*, 17 (2): 261–72.

Kant, Immanuel (1929) [1781] *Critique of Pure Reason*. London: Macmillan.

Kaur, Raminder and Hutnyk, John (1999) 'Introduction', in R. Kaur and J. Hutnyk (eds), *Travel Worlds: Journeys in Contemporary Cultural Politics*. London and New York: Zed Books.

Kearney, Michael (1995) 'The local and the global: the anthropology of globalization and transnationalism', *Annual Review of Anthropology*, 24: 547–65.

Kember, Sarah (1998) *Virtual Anxiety: Photography, New Technology and Subjectivity*. Manchester: Manchester University Press.

Kline, Stephen (1993) *Out of the Garden: Toys, TV, and Children's Culture in the Age of Marketing*. London: Verso.

Kristeva, Julia (1991) *Strangers to Ourselves*. New York: Columbia University Press.

Kuhn, Annette (1984) 'Womens' genres', *Screen*, 25 (1): 18–29.

Lamont, Michelle (1992) *Money, Morals, and Manners: the Culture of the French and American Upper Middle Class*. Chicago, IL: Chicago University Press.

Levin, David Michael (1989) *The Listening Self: Personal Growth, Social Change and the Closure of Metaphysics*. London: Routledge.

Lewis, Justin (1991) *The Ideological Octopus: an Exploration of Television and its Audience*. London: Routledge.

Lindlof, Thomas (ed.) (1987) *Natural Audiences: Qualitative Research of Media Uses and Effects*. Norwood, NJ: Ablex.

Livingstone, Sonia (1990) *Making Sense of Television: the Psychology of Audience Interpretation*. Oxford: Pergamon.

Lloyd, Geoffrey (1990) *Demystifying Mentalities*. Cambridge: Cambridge University Press.

Lodziak, Konrad (1987) *The Power of Television*. London: Frances Pinter.

Long, Elizabeth (ed.) (1997) *From Sociology to Cultural Studies*. Malden, MA: Blackwell.

Lotman, Yuri (1990) *The Universe of the Mind: a Semiotic Theory of Culture*. Bloomington, IN: Indiana University Press.

Lovelock, James (1979) *Gaia: a New Look at Life on Earth*. Oxford: Oxford University Press.

Lull, James (1995) *Media, Communication and Culture: a Global Approach*. Cambridge: Polity.

Lynch, Kevin (1960) *The Image of the City*. Cambridge, MA: MIT Press.

MacIntyre, Alisdair (1981) *After Virtue: a Study in Moral Theory*. London: Duckworth.

Maffesoli, Michel (1996) *The Time of the Tribes*. London: Sage.

Mann, Michael (1970) 'The social cohesion of liberal democracy', *American Sociological Review*, 35 (3): 423–39.

Marcus, George (1995) 'Ethnography in/of the world system: the emergence of multi-sited ethnography', *Annual Review of Anthropology*, 24: 95–117.

Martin, Emily (1993) [1987] *The Woman in the Body: a Cultural Analysis of Reproduction*. Milton Keynes: Open University Press.

Martin-Barbero, Jesus (1993) *Communication, Culture and Hegemony*. London: Sage.

Marx, Karl (1977a) 'The German ideology' [extract], in D. McLennan (ed.), *Karl Marx – Selected Writings*. Oxford: Oxford University Press.

Marx, Karl (1977b) 'Grundrisse' [extract], in D. McLennan (ed.), *Karl Marx – Selected Writings*. Oxford: Oxford University Press.

Marx, Karl (1977c) 'Theses on Feuerbach', in D. McLennan (ed.), *Karl Marx – Selected Writings*. Oxford: Oxford University Press.

Massey, Doreen (1994) *Space, Place and Gender*. Cambridge: Polity.

Massey, Doreen (1997) [1991] 'A global sense of place', in A. Gray and J. McGuigan (eds), *Studying Culture: an Introductory Reader*. London: Arnold.

McGuigan, Jim (1992) *Cultural Populism*. London: Routledge.

McGuigan, Jim (1996) *Culture and the Public Sphere*. London: Routledge.

McGuigan, Jim (forthcoming) 'British identity and "the people's princess"', *Sociological Review*.

McIlroy, John (1993) 'The unknown Raymond Williams', in J. McIlroy and S. Westwood (eds), *Border Country: Raymond Williams in Adult Education*. Leicester: National Institute of Adult Continuing Education.

McKenzie, Ewan (1994) *Privatopia: Homeowner Associations and the Rise of Residential Private Government*. Yale, CT: Yale University Press.

McRobbie, Angela (1991a) 'Introduction', in A. McRobbie, *Feminism and Youth Culture: From 'Jackie' to 'Just Seventeen'*. London: Routledge.

McRobbie, Angela (1991b) [1982] 'Settling accounts with subcultures', in A. McRobbie, *Feminism and Youth Culture: From 'Jackie' to 'Just Seventeen'*. London: Routledge.

McRobbie, Angela (1991c) '*Jackie* and *Just Seventeen*: girls' comics and magazines in the 1980s', in A. McRobbie, *Feminism and Youth Culture: From 'Jackie' to 'Just Seventeen'*. London: Routledge.

McRobbie, Angela (1992) 'Postscript', in L. Grossberg, C. Nelson and P. Treichler (eds), *Cultural Studies*. New York: Routledge.

McRobbie, Angela (1997) 'The e's and the anti-e's: new questions for feminism and cultural studies', in M. Ferguson and P. Golding (eds), *Cultural Studies in Question*. London: Sage.

McRobbie, Angela (1998) *British Fashion Design*. London: Routledge.

Mead, George Herbert (1967) [1934] *Mind, Self and Society*. Chicago, IL: University of Chicago Press.

Mercer, Kobena (1994) *Welcome to the Jungle*. London: Routledge.

Miege, Bernard (1989) *The Capitalization of Cultural Production*. New York: International General.

Miller, Daniel (ed.) (1995) *Worlds Apart*. London: Routledge.

Miller, Toby (1998) *Technologies of Truth: Cultural Citizenship and the Popular Media*. Minneapolis, MN: University of Minnesota Press.

Miller, Toby and McHoul, Alex (1998) *Popular Culture and Everyday Life*. London: Sage.

Mills, C. Wright (1970) [1959] *The Sociological Imagination*. Harmondsworth: Penguin.

Mintz, Sidney (1998) 'The localisation of anthropological practice: from area studies to transnationalism', *Critique of Anthropology*, 18 (2): 117–33.

Mitsui, Toru and Shuhei Hosokawa (eds) (1998) *Karaoke around the World: Global Technology, Local Singing*. London: Routledge.

Moore-Gilbert, Bart (1997) *Postcolonial Theory: Contexts, Practices, Politics*. London: Verso.

Moore-Gilbert, Bart, Stanton, Gareth and Maley, Willy (eds) (1997) *Postcolonial Criticism*, London: Arnold.

Moran, Joe (1998) 'Cultural studies and academic stardom', *International Journal of Cultural Studies*, 1 (1): 67–82.

Morley, David (1986) *Family Television*. London: Comedia.

Morley, David (1998) 'So-called cultural studies: dead ends and reinvented wheels', *Cultural Studies*, 12 (4): 476–97.

Morley, David and Chen, Kuan-Hsing (eds) (1996) *Stuart Hall: Critical Dialogues in Cultural Studies*. London: Routledge.

Morris, Meaghan (1990) 'Banality in cultural studies', in P. Mellencamp (ed.), *Logics of Television*. Minneapolis, MN: University of Minnesota Press.

Morris, Meaghan (1992) 'On the beach', in L. Grossberg, C. Nelson and P. Treichler (eds), *Cultural Studies*. New York: Routledge [reprinted in Morris, 1998].

Morris, Meaghan (1998) *Too Soon Too Late*. Bloomington, IN: Indiana University Press.

Morrison, Toni (1989) [1978] *The Song of Solomon*. London: Picador.

Morrison, Toni (1997) 'Hope', in W. Lubiano (ed.), *The House that Race Built: Black Americans, US Terrain*. New York: Pantheon.

Morse, Margaret (1990) 'An ontology of everyday distraction: the freeway, the mall and the television', in P. Mellencamp (ed.), *Logics of Television*. Bloomington, IN: Indiana University Press [reprinted in Morse, 1998].

Morse, Margaret (1998) *Virtualities: TV, Media Art and Cyberculture*. Bloomington, IN: Indiana University Press.

Mouffe, Chantal (1996) 'Democracy, power and the '"political"', in S. Benhabib (ed.), *Democracy and Difference: Contesting the Boundaries of the Political*. Princeton, NJ: Princeton University Press.

Mulvey, Laura (1975) 'Visual pleasure and narrative cinema', *Screen*, 16 (3): 16–28.

Murdock, Graham (1995) 'Across the great divide: cultural analysis and the condition of democracy', *Critical Studies in Mass Communication*, 12 (1): 89–94.

Murdock, Graham (1997) [1989] 'Cultural studies at the crossroads', in A. Gray and J. McGuigan (eds), *Studying Culture: an Introductory Reader*. London: Arnold.

Murphy, Patrick (1997) 'Contrasting perspectives: cultural studies in Latin America and the United States: a conversation with Nestor Garcia Canclini', *Cultural Studies*, 11 (1): 78–88.

Nancy, Jean-Luc (1991) *The Inoperative Community*. Minneapolis, MN: University of Minnesota Press.

Nandy, Ashis (1998) 'A new cosmopolitanism', in K-S. Chen (ed.), *Trajectories: Inter-Asia Cultural Studies*. London: Routledge.

Negus, Keith (1992) *Producing Pop*. London: Edward Arnold.

Negus, Keith (1999) *Music Genres and Corporate Cultures*. London: Routledge.

Nelson, Cary (1996) 'Always already cultural studies: academic conferences and a manifesto', in J. Storey, *What is Cultural Studies?* London: Arnold.

Nelson, Cary, Treichler, Paula and Grossberg, Lawrence (1992) 'Introduction', in L. Grossberg, C. Nelson and P. Treichler (eds), *Cultural Studies*. New York: Routledge.

Ngugi wa Thiong'o (1986) *Decolonising the Mind*. London: James Currey.

Norris, Christopher (1991) *Deconstruction: Theory and Practice*. revised edn. London: Routledge.

Nowell-Smith, Geoffrey (1987) 'Popular Culture', *New Formations*, 2: 79–90.

Oakley, Ann (1974) *The Sociology of Housework*. Oxford: Blackwell.

O'Shea, Alan (1998) 'A special relationship? Cultural studies, academia, and pedagogy', *Cultural Studies*, 12 (4): 513–27.

O'Shea, Alan and Schwarz, Bill (1987) 'Reconsidering popular culture', *Screen*, 28 (3): 104–9.

Parker, David (1995) *Through Different Eyes: the Cultural Identities of Young Chinese People in Britain*. Aldershot: Avebury.

Penley, Constance and Ross, Andrew (eds) (1991) *Technoculture*. Minneapolis, MN: University of Minnesota Press.

Philo, Greg (1990) *Seeing is Believing: the Influence of Television*. London: Routledge.

Philo, Greg and Miller, David (1997) 'Cultural compliance: dead ends of media/cultural studies and social science', *Glasgow Media Group*, University of Glasgow.

Pickering, Michael (1997) *History, Experience and Cultural Studies*. London: Macmillan.

Plant, Sadie (1996) 'The virtual complexity of culture', in G. Robertson, M. Mash, L. Tickner, J. Bird, B. Curtis and T. Putnam (eds), *FutureNatural: Nature/Science/ Politics*. London: Routledge.

Polanyi, Michael (1958) *Personal Knowledge: Towards a Post-Critical Philosophy*. London: Routledge & Kegan Paul.

Potter, Jonathan and Wetherall, Margaret (1987) *Discourse and Social Psychology: Beyond Attitudes and Behavior*. London: Sage.

Pribram, Dierdre (ed.) (1988) *Female Spectators: Looking at Film and Television*. London: Verso.

Priest, Patricia (1995) *Public Intimacies*. Creskill, NJ: The Hampton Press.

Probyn, Elspeth (1993) *Sexing the Self*. London: Routledge.

Probyn, Elspeth (1996) *Outside Belongings*. New York: Routledge.

Rabinow, Paul (1987) *Reflections on Fieldwork in Morocco*. Chicago, IL: University of Chicago Press.

Radway, Janice (1988) 'Reception study: ethnography and the problem of dispersed audiences and nomadic subjects', *Cultural Studies*, 2 (3): 359–76.

Richards, I.A. (1956) [1929] *Practical Criticism: A Study of Literary Judgment*. New York: Harcourt Brace & World, Inc.

Robertson, Roland (1990) 'Mapping the global condition: globalization as a central concept', in M. Featherstone (ed.), *Global Culture*. London: Sage.

Robins, Kevin (1997) 'What in the world's going on?', in P. du Gay (ed.), *Production of Culture/Cultures of Production*. London: Sage.

Rosaldo, Renato (1993) *Culture and Truth: the Remaking of Social Analysis*. Boston, MA: Beacon Press.

Rose, Nikolas (1996) *Inventing Our Selves*. Cambridge: Cambridge University Press.

Ross, Andrew (1989) *No Respect: Intellectuals and Popular Culture*. London: Verso.

Rowe, William and Schelling, Vivian (1990) *Memory and Modernity: Popular Culture in Latin America*. London: Verso.

Rubin, Lilian (1976) *Worlds of Pain*. New York: Basic Books.

Said, Edward (1978) *Orientalism*. Harmondsworth: Penguin.

Said, Edward (1990) 'Narrative, geography and interpretation', *New Left Review*, 180: 81–100.

Scannell, Paddy (1996) *Radio Television and Modern Life*. Oxford: Blackwell.

Schatz, Thomas (1993) 'The new Hollywood', in J. Collins (ed.), *Film Theory Goes to the Movies*. New York: Routledge.

Schudson, Michael (1994) 'Culture and the integration of national societies', in D. Crane (ed.), *The Sociology of Culture*. Oxford: Blackwell.

Schudson, Michael and Mukerji, Chandra (eds) (1990), *Rethinking Popular Culture*. New York: Routledge.

Schwarz, Bill (1989) 'Popular culture: the long march', *Cultural Studies*, 3 (2): 250–5.

Schwarz, Bill (1994) 'Where is cultural studies?', *Cultural Studies*, 8 (3): 377–93.

Scott, Joan (1992) '"Experience"', in J. Butler and J. Scott (eds), *Feminists Theorize the Political*. New York: Routledge.

Sennett, Richard and Cobb, Jonathan (1972) *The Hidden Injuries of Class*. New York: Norton.

Sharma, Sanjay (1998) 'Noisy Asian or "Asian Noise"', in S. Sharma, J. Hutnyk and A. Sharma (eds), *Dis-Orienting Rhythms*. London: Zed Books.

Sharma, Sanjay, Hutnyk, John and Sharma, Ashwani (eds) (1998) *Dis-Orienting Rhythms*. London: Zed Books.

Shils, Edward (1961) 'Mass society and its culture', in N. Jacobs (ed.), *Culture for the Millions?* Princeton, NJ: Van Nostrand.

Shotter, John (1993) *Conversational Realities*. Thousand Oaks, CA: Sage.

Sibley, David (1995) *Geographies of Exclusion*. London: Routledge.

Silverstone, Roger (1994) *Television and Everyday Life*. London: Routledge.

Skeggs, Beverley (1995) 'Introduction', in B. Skeggs (ed.), *Feminist Cultural Theory: Process and Production*. Manchester: Manchester University Press.

Skeggs, Beverley (1997) *Formations of Class and Gender: Becoming Respectable*. London: Sage.

Smith, Anthony (1990) 'Towards a global culture?', in M. Feathersone (ed.), *Global Culture*. London: Sage.

Smith, David Lionel (1997) 'What is black culture?', in W. Lubiano (ed.), *The House that Race Built: Black Americans, US Terrain*. New York: Pantheon.

Smith, Dorothy (1987) *The Everyday World as Problematic: a Feminist Sociology*. Boston, MA: NorthEastern University Press.

Smith, Mark (1998) *Social Science in Question*. London: Sage.

Smith, Philip (1998a) *The New American Cultural Sociology*. Cambridge: Cambridge University Press.

Smith, Philip (1998b) 'Introduction', in *The New American Cultural Sociology*. Cambridge: Cambridge University Press.

Soja, Ed (1992) 'Inside exopolis: scenes from Orange County', in M. Sorkin (ed.), *Variations on a Theme Park: the New American City and the End of Public Space*. New York: Hill & Wang.

Spence, Jo (1995) *Cultural Sniping: the Art of Transgression*. London: Routledge.

Sperber, Dan (1985) *On Anthropological Knowledge: Three Essays*. Cambridge: Cambridge University Press.

Sperber, Dan (1996) *Explaining Culture: a Naturalistic Approach*. Oxford: Blackwell.

Spivak, Gayatri (1990) *The Postcolonial Critic: Interviews, Strategies, Dialogues*. New York: Routledge.

Staiger, Janet (1992) *Interpreting Films: Studies in the Historical Reception of American Cinema*. Princeton, NJ: Princeton University Press.

Steedman, Carolyn (1986) *Landscape for a Good Woman*. London: Virago.

Steedman, Carolyn (1992) 'Culture, cultural studies and the historians', in L. Grossberg, C. Nelson and P. Treichler (eds), *Cultural Studies*. New York: Routledge.

Stevenson, Nick (1997) 'Media, ethics and morality', in J. McGuigan (ed.), *Cultural Methodologies*. London: Sage.

Stewart, Kathleen (1996) *A Space on the Side of the Road: Cultural Poetics in an 'Other' America*. Princeton, NJ: Princeton University Press.

Storey, John (ed.) (1996) *What is Cultural Studies?* London: Arnold.

Stratton, Jon and Ang, Ien (1996) 'On the impossibility of a global cultural studies: 'British' cultural studies in an 'international' frame', in D. Morley and K.-H. Chen (eds), *Stuart Hall: Critical Dialogues in Cultural Studies*. London: Routledge.

Strinati, Dominic (1993) *An Introduction to Theories of Popular Culture*. London: Routledge.

Tallis, Raymond (1988) *Not Saussure: a Critique of Post-Saussurean Literary Theory*. London: Macmillan.

Taylor, Charles (1985) 'Foucault on freedom and truth', in *Philosophy and the Human Sciences – Philosophical Papers, Vol. 2*. Cambridge: Cambridge University Press.

Taylor, Jill, Gilligan, Carol and Sullivan, Amy (1995) *Between Voice and Silence: Race and Gender, Girls and Relationships*. Harvard, MA: Harvard University Press.

Thompson, E.P. (1961a) *The Making of the English Working Class*. Harmondsworth: Penguin.

Thompson, E.P. (1961b) 'Review of R. Williams, *The Long Revolution*', *New Left Review*, 9: 17–33.

Thornton, Sarah (1995) *Club Cultures: Music, Media and Subcultural Capital*. London: Faber.

Tsing, Anna Lowenhaupt (1993) *In the Realm of the Diamond Queen*. Princeton, NJ: Princeton University Press.

Tudor, Andrew (1995) 'Culture, mass communication and social agency', *Theory, Culture and Society*, 12 (1): 81–107.

Tudor, Andrew (1999) *Decoding Culture: Theory and Method in Cultural Studies*. London: Sage.

Tulloch, John (1990) *Television Drama*. London: Routledge.

Tulloch, John (1991) 'Approaching the audience: the elderly', in E. Seiter, H. Borches, G. Kreutzner and E.-M. Warth (eds), *Remote Control: Television, Audiences and Cultural Power*. London: Routledge.

Turkle, Sherry (1984) *The Second Self: Computers and the Human Spirit*. New York: Simon & Schuster.

Turkle, Sherry (1996) *Life on the Screen: Identity in the Age of the Internet*. London: Weidenfeld & Nicolson.

Turner, Graham (1990) *British Cultural Studies: an Introduction*. Boston, MA: Unwin Hyman.

Virilio, Paul (1995) 'Red alert in cyberspace', *Radical Philosophy*, 74: 2–4.

Viswanathan, Gauri (1990) *Masks of Conquest: Literary Study and British Rule in India*. London: Faber.

Visweswaran, Kamal (1994) *Fictions of Feminist Ethnography*. Minneapolis, MN: University of Minnesota Press.

Volosinov, V. N. (1986) [1929] *Marxism and the Philosophy of Language*. Harvard, MA: Harvard University Press.

Walkerdine, Valerie (1997) *Daddy's Girl: Young Girls and Popular Culture*. London: Macmillan.

Walzer, Michael (1998) 'Pluralism and social democracy', *Dissent*, Winter: 48–53.

Watson, James (ed.) (1997) *Golden Arches East: McDonald's in East Asia*. Stanford, CA: Stanford University Press.

Weber, Max (1991) [1921] 'Science as a vocation', in H. Gerth and C. Wright Mills (eds), *From Max Weber: Essays in Sociology*. London: Routledge.

Webster, Duncan (1996) [1990] 'Pessimism, optimism, pleasure: the future of cultural studies', in J. Storey (ed.), *What is Cultural Studies?* London: Arnold.

Welsch, Wolfgang (1999) 'Transculturality: the puzzling form of cultures today', in M. Featherstone and S. Lash (eds), *Spaces of Culture: City – Nation – World*. London: Sage.

West, Cornel (1992) 'Nihilism in black America', in G. Dent (ed.), *Black Popular Culture*. Seattle, WA: Bay Press [reprinted in Gray and McGuigan (1997)].

West, Cornel (1993) *Keeping Faith: Philosophy and Race in America*. New York: Routledge.

Wilk, Richard (1995) 'The local and the global in the political economy of beauty: from Miss Belize to Miss World', *Review of International Political Economy*, 2 (1): 117–34.

Williams, Raymond (1958) *Culture and Society*. Harmondsworth: Penguin.

Williams, Raymond (1961) *The Long Revolution*. Harmondsworth: Penguin.

Williams, Raymond (1968) *Communications*. 2nd edn. Harmondsworth: Penguin.

Williams, Raymond (1977) *Marxism and Literature*. Oxford: Oxford University Press.

Williams, Raymond (1979) *Politics and Letters*. London: New Left Books.

Williams, Raymond (1981) *Culture*. London: Fontana.

Williams, Raymond (1983) *Towards 2000*. London: Chatto & Windus.

Williams, Raymond (1989a) 'The future of cultural studies', in *The Politics of*

*Modernism: Against the New Conformists.* London: Verso.

Williams, Raymond (1989b) [1958] 'Culture is ordinary', in *Resources of Hope: Culture, Democracy, Socialism.* London: Verso [reprinted in Gray and McGuigan (1997)].

Williams, Raymond (1989c) 'The uses of cultural theory', in *The Politics of Modernism: Against the New Conformists.* London: Verso [reprinted in Storey (1996)].

Williams, Raymond (1990) *Television: Technology and Cultural Form.* London: Routledge.

Williams, Raymond (1993a) [1961] 'Open letter to WEA Tutors', in J. McIlroy and S. Westwood (eds), *Border Country: Raymond Williams in Adult Education.* Leicester: National Institute of Adult Continuing Education.

Williams, Raymond (1993b) [1959] 'The press and popular education', in J. McIlroy and S. Westwood (eds), *Border Country: Raymond Williams in Adult Education.* Leicester: National Institute of Adult Continuing Education.

Willis, Paul (1990) *Common Culture: Symbolic Work and Play in the Everyday Cultures of the Young.* Milton Keynes: Open University Press.

Wittig, Monique (1992) *The Straight Mind and Other Essays.* Boston, MA: Beacon Press.

Woodward, Kathryn (ed.) (1997) *Identity and Difference.* London: Sage.

Wray, Matt and Nevitz, Karin (eds) (1997) *White Trash: Race and Class in America.* New York: Routledge.

Wright, Handel (1998) 'Dare we decentre Birmingham? Troubling the "origin" and trajectories of cultural studies', *European Journal of Cultural Studies*, 1 (1): 33–56.

Wrong, Dennis (1961) 'The oversocialised conception of man', *American Sociological Review*, 26 (2): 183–93.

Yan, Yunxiang (1997) 'McDonald's in Beijing: the localization of Americana', in J. J. Watson (ed.), *Golden Arches East: McDonald's in East Asia.* Stanford, CA: Stanford University Press.

Young, Iris Marion (1990) 'The ideal of community and the politics of difference', in L. Nicholson (ed.), *Feminism/Postmodernism.* New York: Routledge.

Zizek, Slavoj (1990) 'Eastern Europe's empires of Gilead', *New Left Review*, 183: 50–62

Zizek, Slavoj (1997) 'Multiculturalism, or the cultural logic of multinational capitalism', *New Left Review*, 225: 28–51.

# Index